Backs to the Wall

D. PETER MacLEOD

THE BATTLE *of* SAINTE-FOY
and the CONQUEST OF CANADA

BACKS TO THE WALL

Douglas & McIntyre

Douglas and McIntyre (2013) Ltd.

PO Box 219, Madeira Park, BC, VON2HO

www.douglas-mcintyre.com

Edited by Arlene Prunkl

Typesetting by Shed Simas

Printed and bound in Canada

Douglas and McIntyre (2013) Ltd. acknowledges the support of the Canada Council for the Arts, which last year

invested $157 million to bring the arts to Canadians throughout the country. We also gratefully acknowledge

financial support from the Government of Canada through the Canada Book Fund and from the Province of British

Columbia through the BC Arts Council and the Book Publishing Tax Credit.

Library and Archives Canada Cataloguing in Publication

MacLeod, D. Peter, 1955-, author
    Backs to the wall : the Battle of Sainte-Foy and the conquest of Canada / D. Peter MacLeod.

Includes bibliographical references and index.
Issued in print and electronic formats.
ISBN 978-1-77162-127-4 (hardback).--ISBN 978-1-77162-128-1 (html)

    1. Sainte-Foy, Battle of, Québec, Québec, 1760.
I. Title. II. Title: Battle of Sainte-Foy and the conquest of Canada.

FC384.M22 2016   971.4'471014   C2016-903670-7
                                    C2016-903671-5

Dedicated to
Scott, Rory, Joy, Ian, Catherine, and David

CONTENTS

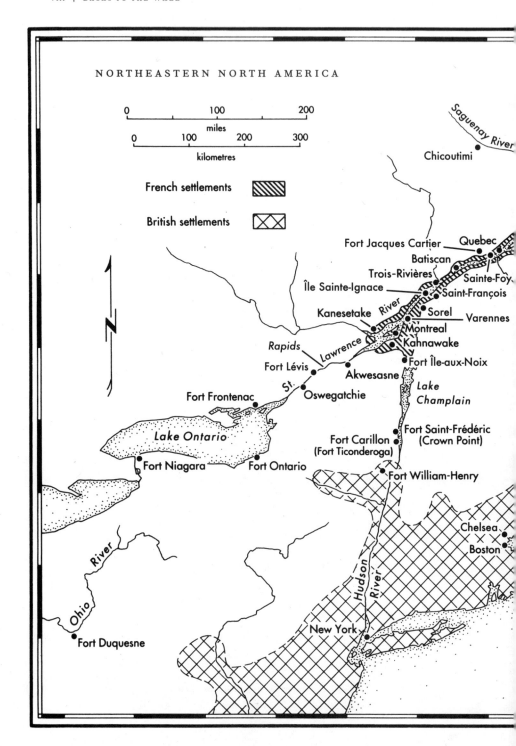

NORTHEASTERN NORTH AMERICA

French settlements

British settlements

Chicoutimi

Saguenay River

Fort Jacques Cartier
Quebec
Batiscan
Sainte-Foy
Trois-Rivières
Île Sainte-Ignace
Saint-François
Kanesetake
River
Sorel
Varennes
Montreal
Kahnawake
Rapids
Lawrence
Fort Lévis
Fort Île-aux-Noix
St.
Akwesasne
Lake Champlain
Fort Frontenac
Oswegatchie
Lake Ontario
Fort Saint-Frédéric (Crown Point)
Fort Carillon (Fort Ticonderoga)
Fort Niagara
Fort Ontario
Fort William-Henry
Chelsea
Boston
River
Ohio
Hudson River
New York
Fort Duquesne

Map | *ix*

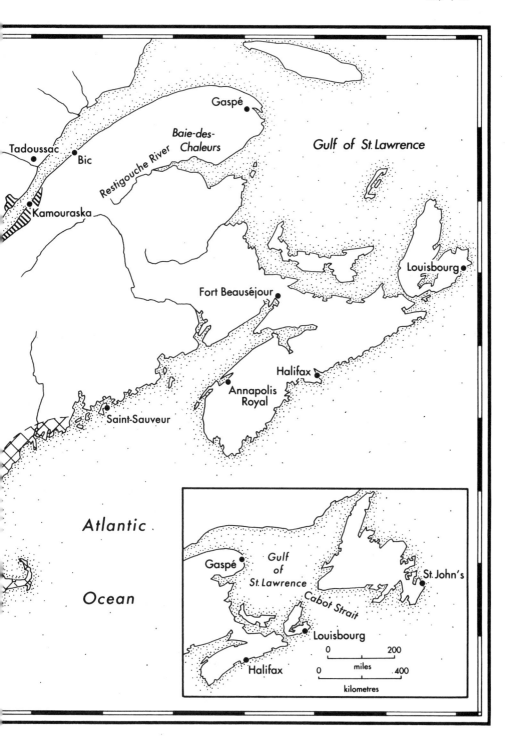

Tadoussac

Bic

Kamouraska

Restigouche River

Baie-des-Chaleurs

Gaspé

Gulf of St. Lawrence

Louisbourg

Fort Beauséjour

Halifax

Annapolis Royal

Saint-Sauveur

Atlantic

Ocean

Gaspé

Gulf of St. Lawrence

St. John's

Cabot Strait

Louisbourg

Halifax

0   200

miles

0   400

kilometres

THE PEOPLE OF 1760

AGNEW, James—major, 58th Regiment

ALBERGATI-VEZZA, François-Marie Balthazara—ensign, troupes de la marine; last commandant of Fort Jacques Cartier

ALQUIER DE SERRIAN, Jean d'—lieutenant colonel, Béarn regiment; commander of the La Sarre brigade at the Battle of Sainte-Foy

AMHERST, Jeffery—major general, British army; commander-in-chief of the British army in North America

ANGEAC, François-Gabriel d'—captain, troupes de la marine; commander of the troupes de la marine at Restigouche in 1760

ANSON, George—admiral, Royal Navy; First Lord of the Admiralty

ARNOUX, André—surgeon major, troupes de terre, cared for the wounded after the Battle of Sainte-Foy

ATIATONHARONGWEN—a celebrated African-Abenaki who became a war chief at Kahnawake; led a contingent of warriors at the Battle of Sainte-Foy

AUGHNEETA—a chief of the Mohawks of Kanesetake; spoke at a conference with the British in 1787

BABY, François—officer, Canadian militia

BARBUTT, James—captain, 15th Regiment; managed spies for James Murray

BARRAUTE, Jean-Pierre Bachoué de—captain, Béarn regiment

BELLECOMBE, Guillaume Léonard de—captain, Royal Roussillon regiment

BENNET, John—private, 35th Regiment

BERNIER, Benoît-François—captain, troupes de terre; commissaire ordonnateur des guerres (financial commissary of wars, or quartermaster
general)

BERRYER, Nicolas René—minister of marine and colonies

BERTET DE LA CLUE SABRAN, Jean-François—chef d'escadre (rear
admiral), French navy

BIGOT, François—intendant (civil administrator) of New France

BIGOT DE MOROGUES, Sebastien François—captain, French navy; captain of the *Magnifique* at the Battle of Quiberon Bay

BOISHÉBERT, Charles Deschamps de—captain, troupes de la marine

BONNE, Louis de Missègle de—captain, troupes de la marine

BONNEAU, Louis de Preissac de—captain, Guyenne regiment

BOUCHETTE, Joseph—Surveyor General of Lower Canada

BOUGAINVILLE, Louis-Antoine de—colonel, troupes de terre; commandant of Fort Île-aux-Noix

BOURLAMAQUE, François-Charles de—brigadier, troupes de terre; second
in command of the troupes de terre in Canada

BRIAND, Jean-Olivier—Vicar General of Quebec

BURTON, Ralph—brigadier, British army; commanded the north wing of
the British army at the Battle of Sainte-Foy

CADET, Joseph-Michel—munitionnaire général (purveyor general)
of Canada; responsible for supplying the French armed forces with
provisions

CASGRAIN, Henri-Raymond—nineteenth-century historian of the Seven
Years' War, author of *Wolfe and Montcalm* and *Montcalm et Lévis*

COLVILL, Alexander—commodore, Royal Navy, commander-in-chief of
the Royal Navy in North America

CONFLANS, Hubert de Brienne de—admiral, French navy

CRAMAHÉ, Hector Theophilus—captain, 15th Regiment; James Murray's
secretary; managed spies for James Murray

DEANE, Joseph—captain, Royal Navy, commander of HMS *Lowestoft*,
the first British ship to reach Quebec in the spring of 1760, and of the

flotilla of ships and boats carrying and escorting James Murray's army from Quebec to Montreal

DESANDROUINS, Jean-Nicolas—captain, Corps royal du génie (Royal Corps of Engineers)

DÉSBRUYÈRES, John—ensign, 35th Regiment

DESCLAUX, Pierre—Joseph Cadet's business partner in Bordeaux

DOMBOURG, Jean-François Bourdon de—lieutenant, troupes de la marine

DOUCET, Pierre—captain, Acadian militia company

DOUGLAS, D'Ailleboust de—acting lieutenant of grenadiers, troupes de la marine

DUMAS, Jean-Daniel—captain and adjutant general of the troupes de la marine; commandant of Fort Jacques Cartier

DUMONT, Jean-Baptiste—owner of a house and windmill on the Sainte-Foy battlefield

DURELL, Philip—rear admiral, Royal Navy

ÉPERVANCHE, Charles-François de l'—second ensign, troupes de la marine

EQUIANO, Olaudah—veteran of the 1758 siege of Louisbourg and the Battle of Lagos, author of *The Interesting Narrative of the Life of Olaudah Equiano, Or Gustavus Vassa, the African*

FONDA, Jelles—captain, Northern Indian Department

FRASER, Alexander—captain, 78th Regiment

FRASER, Malcolm—lieutenant, 78th Regiment; author of *Extract from a Manuscript Journal, Relating to the Siege of Quebec*

FRASER, Simon—lieutenant colonel, 78th Regiment; chief of Clan Fraser

GASPÉ, Philippe, Aubert de—nineteenth-century novelist; author of *Les anciens Canadiens* and *Mémoires*

GASPÉ, Philippe-Ignace, Aubert de—captain, troupes de la marine

GIRAUDAIS, François-Pierre Chenard de la—lieutenant de frégate (sub-lieutenant), French navy; captain of the *Machault* in 1760

GRANT, John—lieutenant, 42nd Regiment (The Black Watch); author of "Journal, 1741–1763"

HAMILTON, Henry— lieutenant, 35th Regiment; author of "Reminiscences"

HAVILAND, William—brigadier, British army; commander of an invasion of Canada by way of Lake Champlain

HAWKE, Edward—admiral, Royal Navy

HAZEN, Moses—captain of a company of American rangers

HOLLAND, Samuel—lieutenant, 60th Regiment

HOWE, Jemima—settler from Hinsdale, New Hampshire; captured in 1755 and held as a prisoner of war in Canada

HUMPHREYS, Richard—private, light infantry; author of *Rich Humphreys, His Journal, Commencing Cork May 1757 with Its Continuation*

INCE, Charles—captain, 35th Regiment

IRVING, Paulus Aemilius—major, 15th Regiment

JAMES, Malachi—mate of the American schooner *Success* and author of "Malachi James Diary, 1759–1761"

JENKS, Samuel—captain, Massachusetts provincials; author of *Diary of Captain Samuel Jenks during the French and Indian War, 1760*

JOHNSON, John—quartermaster sergeant, 58th Regiment; author of *Memoirs of the Siege of Quebec and Total Reduction of Canada in 1759 and 1760*

JOHNSON, Sir William—Superintendent of Northern Indians

JOHNSTONE, James—lieutenant, troupes de la marine; author of *Mémoires de James Johnstone dit le chevalier de Johnstone*

KALM, Pehr—Swedish botanist; author of *Peter Kalm's Travels in North America*

KANON, Jacques—lieutenant, French navy; captain of the *Machault* frigate in 1759

KISENSIK—a chief of the Nipissings of Lac des Deux Montagnes; led a contingent of warriors at the French siege of Quebec

KNOX, John—captain, 43rd Regiment; author of *An Historical Journal of the Campaigns in North America for the Years 1757, 1758, 1759, and 1760*

LAAS DE GESTÈDE, Dominique-Nicolas de—captain, La Reine regiment; commander of the Canadian militia attached to the La Reine brigade at the Battle of Sainte-Foy

LA CORNE, Luc de—captain, troupes de la marine

LAPAUSE DE MARGON, Jean-Guillaume Plantavit de—captain, Guyenne regiment; author of *Mémoire et observations sur mon voyage en Canada*

LA RONDE, Pierre-François Paul Denys de—captain, troupes de la marine

LA VISITATION, Soeur de (Marie-Joseph Legardeur de Repentigny)— nun of the Hôpital Général; author of *Relation de ce qui s'est passé au siège de Québec, et de la prise du Canada*

LEGRIS—officer, Canadian militia

LE MERCIER, François-Marc-Antoine—captain, Compagnie des Cannon-iers Bombardiers (colonial artillery)

LEPAGE, Molé—captain, Canadian militia

LÉVIS, François-Gaston de—maréchal de camp (major general), troupes de terre; commander of the French forces at the Battle of Sainte-Foy

MACDONALD, Donald—captain, 78th Regiment

MACKELLAR, Patrick—major, Royal Engineers, author of "Plan of the Battle Fought on the 28th of April 1760 upon the Height of Abraham near Quebec"

MACPHERSON, Robert—chaplain, 78th Regiment

MALARTIC, Anne-Joseph-Hippolyte Maurès de—captain, Béarn regiment;

MARTIN, Barthélemy—Quebec merchant; British spy

MARTIN, Topez—Quebec merchant; British spy

MAXWELL, John—private, 35th Regiment

M'CARTNY—captain of the *Racehorse*

MILLER, James—private, 15th Regiment; author of *Memoirs of an Invalid*

MILLS, Thomas—lieutenant, 47th Regiment; aide-de-camp to James Murray

MONTBEILLARD, Fiacre-François Potot de—captain, Corps Royal d'Artillerie (Royal Corps of Artillery)

MONTCALM, Louis-Joseph de—lieutenant général des armées (lieutenant general), troupes de terre; commander of the French forces at the Battle of the Plains of Abraham

MONTREUIL, Pierre-André Gohin de—lieutenant colonel, troupes de terre; Lévis' adjutant general

MORRIS, Rodger—major, 35th Regiment

MUNRO, Hector—soldier, 78th Regiment

MURRAY, George—brother of James Murray

MURRAY, James—brigadier, British army; commander of the British forces at the Battle of Sainte-Foy

NADEAU, Joseph—captain, parish of Saint-Charles company of militia

"NAVAL OFFICER"—author of *Diary of a Naval Officer at the Time of the Quebec Campaign*

NAYLOR, Francis—private, 35th Regiment

"OFFICER OF THE 35TH REGIMENT"—anonymous diarist of the 1759 and 1760 campaigns

ORMSBY, Eubule—lieutenant, 35th Regiment

OUIHARALIHTE ("Petit Etienne")—Huron-Wendat teenager, present during the journey of the Huron-Wendat of Lorette from Lorette (Wendake) to Montreal in 1760

POUCHOT, Pierre—captain, Béarn regiment; commandant of Fort Lévis

RÉCHER, Jean-Félix—parish priest of Notre Dame des Victoires; author of *Journal de siège de Québec en 1759*

ROCHEBEAUCOURT—captain, troupes de terre; commander of the Canadian militia cavalry

ROLLO, Andrew—brigadier, British army; commander of British reinforcements from the Louisbourg garrison in 1760

SAINTE-GABRIEL, Sister—nun of the Hôtel-Dieu

SAOTEN—Seven Nations emissary to the Haudenosaunee in 1760

SARREBOURCE DE PONTLEROY, Nicolas—captain, Corps royal du génie (Royal Corps of Engineers); chief engineer of New France

SAUNDERS, Charles—vice admiral, Royal Navy; commander of the British naval forces at the siege of Quebec in 1759

Schomberg, Alexander—captain, Royal Navy; commander of
    HMS *Diana*

Scott, Joseph—private, 35th Regiment

Stone, John—private, 35th Regiment

Swanton, Robert—commodore, Royal Navy

Tarieu de La Naudière, Charles-Louis—officer, La Sarre regiment

Thompson, James—sergeant, 78th Regiment

Thomson, William—author of *A Tour in England and Scotland, in 1785.
    By an English Gentleman*

Townshend, George—brigadier, British army; succeeded James Wolfe in
    command of the British forces at Quebec in 1759

Vassal de Monviel, Germain—captain, Béarn regiment

Vaudreuil, Pierre de Rigaud de—governor general of New France and
    commander-in-chief of the French armed forces in North America

Vauquelin, Jean—capitaine de brûlot (lieutenant), French navy; com-
    mander of *l'Atalante*

Vézon, Joseph Fournerie de—lieutenant; author of "Évènements de la
    guerre au Canada"

Wallis, Samuel—captain, Royal Navy; commander of HMS *Prince of
    Orange*

Walsh, John—private, 35th Regiment

Weld—lieutenant of grenadiers, 35th Regiment

Wilson, John—sergeant, 78th Regiment

Wolfe, James—major general, British army; commander of the British
    forces at the Battle of the Plains of Abraham

PREFACE

BACKS TO THE WALL: The Battle of Sainte-Foy and the Conquest of Canada is the story of the French attempt to reverse the verdict of the Battle of the Plains of Abraham and take back Quebec.

The Battle of the Plains of Abraham was the most dramatic, decisive, and influential military event in Canadian history. Without that confrontation between a French army led by Louis-Joseph de Montcalm and a British army led by James Wolfe, Canada as we know it today might not exist.

But Wolfe's victory on the Plains of Abraham and the subsequent capitulation of Quebec was not the end of the French-British struggle for northeastern North America. Montcalm may have lost the battle, but Governor General Pierre de Rigaud de Vaudreuil had no intention of losing the war. Faced with a choice between waiting at Montreal for the British to attack or striking first to eliminate a deadly threat to Canada, Vaudreuil chose the bolder course.

In the spring of 1760, he sent Montcalm's successor, François-Gaston de Lévis, to recapture Quebec. With him went every combatant—French regulars, Canadian militia, and First Peoples warriors—every cannon, and every bale of provisions the colony could provide. Two hundred and twenty-eight days after the Battle of the Plains of Abraham, the French were back on the plains and ready for a rematch.

The ensuing Battle of Sainte-Foy was less a battle for territory than a struggle for survival between two equally desperate adversaries.

If the French lost the battle, they would very likely lose Canada. Without the resources expended in the campaign, militia and provisions from the Quebec area and reinforcements and supplies that could arrive from France through the port of Quebec, the defeat of Canada in the summer of 1760 would be almost a foregone conclusion.

Brigadier James Murray, commander of Britain's Quebec garrison, was in an equally difficult situation. After a hard winter, during which his troops had suffered and died from cold, malnutrition, and scurvy, he commanded an army of skeletal invalids, isolated from the outside world, outnumbered, and trapped in hostile territory. Believing that the fortifications of Quebec were too weak to resist a siege, Murray planned to confront French attackers outside the walls. Failure in that confrontation could mean the loss of his army and the loss of Quebec.

The result was the Battle of Sainte-Foy, an engagement between two desperate adversaries attacking each other because they each believed that holding back would lead to inevitable defeat. In this battle, first one side then the other had the advantage; victory and defeat remained in the balance until the very end; and both the French and the British had their backs to the wall.

Backs to the Wall and Northern Armageddon: The Battle of the Plains of Abraham

Backs to the Wall is both a sequel and a companion volume to *Northern Armageddon: The Battle of the Plains of Abraham*.

Northern Armageddon tells the story of the 1759 campaign, the Battle of the Plains of Abraham, and the capitulation of Quebec. It then places these events in the context of the European occupation of the Amerindian homelands of North America, French-British imperial rivalry, the independence of the United States, and the post-conquest history of Canada.

Repeating this material, even in an abbreviated form, in *Backs to the Wall* seemed superfluous and unwieldy. *Backs to the Wall* is thus wholly concerned with the Battle of Sainte-Foy the following year, a much more complex engagement than the Plains of Abraham, and with the last months of the Seven Years' War in North America.

Readers interested in understanding the broader context of the Battle of Sainte-Foy are invited to consult the earlier book.

Sources and spelling

Backs to the Wall is based almost entirely upon the letters and journals of participants and allows them, as far as possible, to speak for themselves. For those seeking further information, most of these authors are identified in the endnotes. The anonymous authors of *Diary of a Naval Officer at the Time of the Quebec Campaign* and *Journal of the Proceedings of the 35th Regiment of Foot* appear in the text as "the Naval Officer" and "the officer of the 35th."

Some writers had the annoying (to twenty-first-century readers) habit of writing in the third person, which sometimes makes quotations sound a bit odd.

The spelling in English quotations has been modernized, except where this would distort the meaning or reduce the charm of the original expressions. All quotations from French documents were translated by the author. Place names are rendered in French or English depending on common usage and readability.

PEOPLES, SOLDIERS, MONEY, AND MEASUREMENTS

Participants in the Seven Years' War in North America described a conflict between the French and the English. The realities behind these labels were a little more complicated and best expressed by a wider range of national or descriptive terms.

In this book, "British" refers to subjects of the British Crown wherever they might be. They might have regional identities as Scots, English, Virginians, Pennsylvanians, or New Englanders, but here they are collectively referred to as the British. "Americans" are British subjects from Britain's North American colonies, including Nova Scotia. "Britons" are British subjects from Great Britain.

Depending upon the context, "French" refers either to all French subjects, whether North American or European, or to French subjects from metropolitan France. "Canadians" are permanent French residents of Canada. Reflecting contemporary practice, "Canadians" are specifically Canadian with regard to the French, and "French" with regard to the British. This is less confusing than it sounds.

So is the geography of French North America. "New France" is the French empire in North America, consisting of Canada, Louisiana, Île Royale, and French-controlled parts of Acadia in what are now New Brunswick and Prince Edward Island. "Nova Scotia" is the British colony occupying the mainland of what is now the province of the same name. "Canada" refers only to French settlements in the St. Lawrence valley. Canada itself was divided into administrative districts, known as governments, named for the city and towns that served as their capitals—Quebec, Trois-Rivières, and Montreal.

European maps often showed a huge French empire in North America, consisting of a giant triangle of territory between Louisbourg, Louisiana, and the Canadian Prairies. While claimed by France, most of this territory was in fact owned and controlled by Amerindian nations.

During the 1760 campaign, two types of French regular troops served in Canada. The troupes de terre were battalions of the regular army of France, under the authority of the minister of war, which had been sent to Canada as a special measure during the Seven Years' War. The troupes de la marine formed a second French army, controlled by the Ministry of Marine and Colonies. Organized in independent companies, they formed Canada's regular garrison. Soldiers for this garrison came from France, their officers from the Canadian elite.

The British land forces in the 1760 campaign consisted of regulars, many of whom had been recruited in North America, marines—soldiers employed by the Royal Navy and serving aboard British warships or ashore—and provincials. Provincials were civilians in uniform, raised by colonial governments and subsidized by the Crown, who would support the regulars during a campaign, then return to their homes.

Backs to the Wall uses the metric system for most linear measurements, but employs nautical miles for distances on the St. Lawrence River to emphasize the maritime character of the campaign.

French monetary values at the time were measured in *livres*, *sols*, and *deniers*. These were units of account, not actual coins. There were twenty sols in a livre and twelve deniers in a sol. One livre had the purchasing power of about twenty-five 2016 Canadian dollars.[1]

PART I

PREPARATIONS

CHAPTER I

WAR AND GEOGRAPHY IN THE 1760 CAMPAIGN

SEVENTEEN FIFTY-NINE HAD NOT been a good year for the French in North America.

From the outbreak of the Seven Years' War in the Ohio valley in 1754 to the Battle of Carillon in 1758, the French had won a whole series of striking victories over the British. Yet paradoxically, each of these victories had made British America stronger and New France relatively weaker. Instead of giving up, the British had responded to defeat and humiliation by sending more troops, more ships, and more money to North America. Furthermore, they had shifted their objective from securing their colonies by occupying disputed boundary areas to eliminating the French threat through the conquest of Canada.

Finally, in June of 1759, a British fleet and army commanded by Vice Admiral Charles Saunders and Major General James Wolfe arrived outside Quebec. Following the Battle of the Plains of Abraham three months later on 13 September, Quebec was occupied by an aggressive British army supported by a powerful fleet of warships and transports that could have carried it all the way to Montreal to complete the conquest of Canada.

South of Montreal, an even larger British force had taken Fort Carillon and Fort St. Frédéric at the south end of Lake Champlain, built a vast new fortress at Crown Point next to the site of Fort St. Frédéric, and remained capable of advancing to Montreal and crushing the French through sheer mass. Further west, British forces had captured the French outpost at Niagara, built Fort Ontario on the south shore of Lake Ontario, and seized control of the lake. All other things being equal, there was nothing to stop the British from rolling up France's northeastern North American empire.

But all other things were not quite equal. Canada's geography gave Canada's defenders a second chance.

Faced with the impending onset of winter and the closure of Canada's waterways by ice—the product of the colony's high latitude and continental location—the British backed off. British armies on Lake Champlain and Lake Ontario turned south and prepared to sit out the winter in New York and New England. Royal Navy warships and British and American merchant ships abandoned Quebec and made their way back down the St. Lawrence, leaving behind a land-bound British garrison.

When winter came, falling temperatures locked Canada inside a barricade of ice that closed the waterways leading into the colony. This made large-scale military and naval movement impossible and created a sealed operational environment, isolated from the rest of the world. Within this environment, the French could spend the winter recovering from their crushing defeat on the Plains of Abraham and preparing for the next campaign.

Once the ice broke on the rivers leading to and through Canada in the spring of 1760, internal lines of communication along the St. Lawrence would allow the French to concentrate their entire force against the British garrison of Quebec. If successful, this would allow them to eliminate one threat before dealing with other British forces coming down Lake Ontario and Lake Champlain.

The struggle for Canada was a long way from over.

Chapter 2

THE BATTLE OF LAGOS AND THE DEFENCE OF CANADA

NORTHEASTERN NORTH AMERICA MIGHT have been a long way from anywhere, as far as Europeans were concerned, but campaigns in Canada frequently turned on events and decisions on the far side of the Atlantic. The events of 18 August 1759 were a case in point. No one in Canada knew it at the time, but even as the British besieged Quebec, the first shots of the 1760 campaign to recapture the city were fired five thousand kilometres away off the southwest tip of Portugal.

During the mid-eighteenth century, France maintained two principal fleets—a Mediterranean fleet based at Toulon and an Atlantic fleet at Brest. As James Wolfe embarked upon his own campaign to take Quebec in May of 1759, the Toulon fleet had caused him more than a little anxiety. "If they [the French] can collect a sufficient force, they are sure to find us in the River St. Lawrence any time between this and the month of October, and may fight if they choose. The prize seems to be worth the risk of a battle. If their Mediterranean squadron gets out, I conclude we shall see them."[1]

Wolfe was half right. Three months later, on 5 August, Chef d'Escadre (Rear Admiral) Jean-François Bertet de la Clue Sabran took ten ships of the line out of Toulon. The British blockading squadron was gone, withdrawn to Gibraltar to refit and resupply. Unobserved and unopposed, La Clue set sail for the Straits of Gibraltar.

But La Clue wasn't sailing for Canada. In 1759, the British were on the offensive and the French were under attack all around the world. In Europe, a second great war was underway between Austrian-French-Russian and British-Prussian alliances. On 1 August, British and Prussian troops overcame a French army at the Battle of Minden. In Africa, the British captured the French slave-trading stations at Fort Louis and Saint-Michel in what is now Senegal. In India, the French abandoned the siege of the British emporium at Madras (now Chennai) and lost three outposts to British attacks. By the end of the year, the British had expelled the French from southwest India. In the Caribbean, a British expedition attacked Martinique and captured Guadeloupe.

The British threat in the Caribbean was of particular concern to France. Here, Britain, France, and Spain had created a gulag archipelago of nightmarish but hugely profitable island colonies where enslaved Africans produced crops of sugar and coffee for European overlords. With a British amphibious force on the loose in the region, La Clue had received orders to take the Mediterranean fleet across the Atlantic to shore up the French position in the West Indies.[2]

La Clue's ships remained undetected until British frigates sighted them as they passed Gibraltar. Pursued by a British fleet, the French, organized in two divisions, fled westward into the Atlantic.

One division put into Cadiz; La Clue's remaining ships engaged the British in a running battle that ended with one ship captured, two escaping to Rochefort and the Canary Islands, and four seeking shelter in the neutral waters of Lagos Bay under the guns of Portuguese shore batteries. Ignoring Portuguese neutrality, the British captured two French ships and drove the others ashore, then burned them to the waterline.

Olaudah Equiano, an enslaved African and veteran of the 1758 siege of Louisbourg, watched the action from HMS *Namur*. He described the fate of the *Océan*, the French flagship. "About midnight I saw the *Ocean* blow up, with a most dreadful explosion. I never beheld a more awful scene. About the space of a minute, the midnight seemed turned into day by the blaze, which was attended with a noise louder and more terrible than thunder that seemed to rend every element around us."[3]

Another British squadron blockaded La Clue's remaining ships in Cadiz. They eventually escaped back to Toulon, but *escaped* is the key word. The Toulon fleet had been reduced from a powerful instrument of war to a handful of fugitive warships.[4]

The destruction of a fleet en route to the Caribbean had no impact whatsoever on the course of events in Canada in 1759. But it reduced the strength of the French navy and thus French capacity to intervene overseas in 1760. No ship from Toulon was going to be sailing for Canada anytime soon.

CHAPTER 3

CANADA AFTER THE
PLAINS OF ABRAHAM

CANADA ON THE ROPES

Twenty-six days after La Clue lost his fleet off the coast of Portugal, major generals Louis-Joseph de Montcalm and James Wolfe led French and British armies into battle on the Plains of Abraham. Wolfe formed his line running partway across the plains, west of Quebec. Montcalm led his army off a strong defensive position in a headlong charge that ended in shattering defeat. His regular battalions broke and fled; Canadian militia and Amerindian warriors covered their retreat. The French field army abandoned Quebec that evening. Five days later, the city surrendered.[1]

With the loss of Quebec, Canada lost its Atlantic port and access to reinforcements, provisions, and munitions from France, without which the colony could not be defended for long. The French furthermore lost the Government of Quebec and with it the militiamen and agricultural produce that the region had previously provided.

Following this catastrophe, it would have been hard to blame the French for succumbing to despair. Jean-Guillaume Plantavit de Lapause de Margon, a captain in the Guyenne regiment, spoke of "the sad situation of the colony at the end of the last campaign, lacking provisions and munitions of any kind, robbed of its frontier territories and the Government of Quebec, having only a small body of troops, [that had been] broken by the disaster of 13 September and other defeats."[2]

Wherever the French looked out along Canada's major communication routes leading to the outside world, they saw a British stronghold or a British army.

To the west, Fort Ontario could serve as a springboard for an attack on Canada by way of Lake Ontario and the upper St. Lawrence. To the south, the British could assemble at Crown Point and advance on Canada by way of Lake Champlain and the Richelieu River. To the east, a British army was already inside the colony, occupying Quebec and poised to launch an offensive up the St. Lawrence River. Come the summer of 1760, the French could expect British attacks along all three axes.

Worse, Canada lacked the capacity to alleviate the situation by recapturing Quebec. Shattered morale could recover; broken battalions could reorganize; soldiers could march on short rations. But a besieging army would need siege artillery to blast down city walls. Unfortunately for the French, almost all of Canada's heavy guns—ten thirty-six-pounders, forty-five twenty-four-pounders, twenty-eight eighteen-pounders, and twenty thirteen-inch mortars[3] —were still mounted on the walls of Quebec or the batteries of Beauport, east of the city. More than just inconveniently unavailable, they were now in the hands of the British.

For as long as the French lacked siege artillery, the British in Quebec were pretty much invulnerable. Whatever success the French might achieve outside the city, the British garrison could simply wait within the walls until the French gave up or the Royal Navy arrived.

PIERRE DE RIGAUD DE VAUDREUIL

Dealing with this situation fell to Pierre de Rigaud de Vaudreuil, governor general of New France and commander-in-chief of all French forces in North America, and Maréchal de Camp (Major General) François-Gaston de Lévis, his senior field commander.

Mentored by his father, a former governor general of New France, Vaudreuil had spent the greater part of his career administering North American colonies. Working his way through French North America, he progressed from Trois-Rivières to Louisiana before moving on to Canada, where he took office in 1756, the same year that Britain and France formally declared war.

Heavily outnumbered by the British and continually afflicted with shortages of provisions, which at times approached famine, Vaudreuil proved to be a resolute, activist wartime governor. Constantly under threat of invasion, he responded by striking first and striking hard.

Under his direction, armies commanded by Montcalm razed Oswego on Lake Ontario (1756) and Fort William Henry (1757) on Lake George, both potential staging points for attacks on Canada, and turned back a major invasion at the Battle of Carillon on Lake Champlain (1758). Robert Eastburn of Philadelphia, then a prisoner in Montreal, watched Canadians celebrate the success of the first of these operations. He wrote, "I saw the English standards [the colours of the 50th and 51st Regiments]... and the French rejoicing... great joy appeared in all their faces, which they expressed by loud shouts, firing of cannon, and returning thanks in their churches."[4]

Governing an embattled colony demanded a degree of ruthlessness, but for Vaudreuil, this ruthlessness was tempered, wherever possible, with humanity. Among his first actions as governor general was to intervene to protect an American prisoner of war from a sexually predatory father and son.

After ransoming Jemima Howe of Hinsdale, New Hampshire, from her Amerindian captors, the two Canadians took advantage of her presence in their home to press their attentions upon her. Alerted by another prisoner, Vaudreuil sent the son away on active service and ordered the father to treat Howe with the greatest respect. A grateful Howe referred to Vaudreuil as a "humane and generous gentleman."[5]

When the collapse of the regular battalions at the Battle of the Plains of Abraham ended a four-year string of French victories, Vaudreuil responded with courage and determination. Taking to the field in person, he placed himself in the path of fleeing soldiers and sent officers of the troupes de la marine to coordinate the groups of Canadians and Amerindians who held off the British while the regular battalions escaped. After the battle, he tried to persuade senior regular officers to hit back at the British, but he had to give up in the face of their unanimous refusal. Compelled to retreat from Quebec on the evening of 13 September, he summoned Lévis from Montreal and ordered him to counterattack and break the British siege.

The city surrendered on 18 September before Lévis could intervene. The army withdrew to winter quarters in French-controlled Canada, but the attempted relief marked the beginning of an effective partnership between the governor and the general directed at recovering the colonial capital and securing Canada for both the French Crown and its Canadian population.[6]

FRANÇOIS-GASTON DE LÉVIS

François-Gaston de Lévis, a capable, hard-charging officer, made an ideal associate for Vaudreuil. While Vaudreuil governed the colony and set overall strategy, Lévis could organize and lead an expedition against Quebec.

Coming from a distinguished noble family with very little money, Lévis had chosen to make his career in the army. Extensive service in Germany and Italy won him a reputation for courage and proficiency, along with the prestigious Croix de Saint-Louis; inability to purchase the command of a regiment prevented him from rising beyond brevet colonel.[7]

Lévis' fortunes changed in 1756 when a posting to serve as second in command of the French regular army (the troupes de terre) in Canada gave him a promotion to brigadier, a one-time payment of 9,000 livres for uniforms and transportation, and a salary and supplement totalling 36,000 livres per year. On campaign, he quickly proved to be even more successful as a brigadier in Canada than as an officer in Europe.

While Montcalm captured Oswego in 1756, Lévis commanded on the Lake Champlain frontier, a task he performed so well that he received a thousand-livre pension. Seconding Montcalm at the siege of Fort William Henry and the Battle of Carillon added to his reputation and won him promotion to maréchal de camp in 1758. Replacing Montcalm after the Battle of the Plains of Abraham gave him the opportunity to make an even greater name for himself as the general who recaptured Quebec.[8]

A PLAN FOR VICTORY

With Quebec in British hands and troops, munitions, provisions, and heavy guns in short supply, it didn't take a great deal of strategic thought for Vaudreuil and Lévis to see that they had only one good option. They would count on assistance from France arriving in time, as it had in 1759, and commit everything they had to taking back Quebec before the breakup of the ice on the St. Lawrence allowed the British to reinforce and resupply the garrison.

When Vaudreuil and Lévis planned the transatlantic element of the campaign, they didn't think small. They requested five or six ships of the

line—the most powerful warships afloat, mounting more than sixty cannon each—together with several frigates—smaller, more manoeuvrable
warships—to escort a convoy carrying four thousand troops and two dozen
twenty-four-pounder cannon to blast through the walls of Quebec.[9]

To be of any use, these vessels and their cargoes would have to reach Canada before their British counterparts. This meant not just arriving early, but
being prepared to sacrifice ships for time if the convoy ran into ice. "Precise
orders," declared a memorandum submitted to the minister of marine and
colonies, "should be given to advance on the ice pack as soon as it appears.
Nothing is rarer than losing a ship in the ice, and the loss of one or two vessels to this misfortune would be preferable to arriving too late."

That wasn't all. Resupplying Canada was all very well, but there was still
the small matter of the Royal Navy. In 1759, the French had simply assumed
that navigational hazards on the St. Lawrence that forced a British fleet to
turn back in 1711 would present a major obstacle to a British invasion. That
proved not to be the case, and in 1760, Vaudreuil and Lévis planned to defend
the river actively.

French warships would take the lead, supported by land-based artillery
and blockships. "The objective of these ships of the line and frigates is not
only to escort the fleet, but to deal with the enemy squadron, if they arrive
soon after us."

Fortified batteries at Île-aux-Coudres would cover a difficult stretch
of river and support French warships in action against the British. Farther
upstream, off the northeast tip of Île d'Orléans, sunken ships would obstruct
the Traverse channel, the most dangerous point of navigation on the entire
St. Lawrence. At Quebec itself, batteries on Point Lévis and Île d'Orléans
would cover the Quebec basin and prevent British ships from sailing upriver
beyond Quebec.[10]

While the French high command strategized, Munitionnaire Général
(Purveyor General) Joseph-Michel Cadet, the contractor responsible for
supplying the army with provisions, wrote to Pierre Desclaux, his business
partner in Bordeaux, with a long list of foodstuffs to purchase and ship to
the colony. These included pork, flour, wine, brandy, vinegar, olive oil, rice,
prunes, peas, beans, and butter, to be transported on fifty merchant ships.[11]

Since these purchases would require the approval of the minister of
marine and colonies, Vaudreuil wrote a strong endorsement for Cadet's

request. "In our present circumstances, we must fear the enemy, but famine poses an even greater threat, whose impact would be catastrophic, regardless of the fate of the colony."[12]

MISSION TO FRANCE

To carry these messages to France, Vaudreuil and Lévis needed a trusted officer who could be relied upon to present the case for resupplying Canada firmly and forcefully. They selected Captain François-Marc-Antoine Le Mercier, commander of the colonial artillery.

Capable and active, Le Mercier had saved the 1756 campaign against Oswego. When Montcalm had been prepared to abandon the attack due to the impossibility of landing the heavy artillery, Le Mercier ran the boats carrying his guns ashore and erected a battery to cover the beach. This did not endear him to Montcalm, but did lead to the capture of a key British outpost.[13]

Le Mercier was furthermore of the opinion that Louis-Antoine de Bougainville, a previous envoy on behalf of Canada, had bungled his assignment and endangered the colony in 1759. "M. Le Mercier," wrote Brigadier François-Charles de Bourlamaque, Lévis' second in command, "told me one day that Bougainville had made our situation look too desperate last year, and that he was thus the reason why we did not receive the assistance that would otherwise undoubtedly have been sent, if he had not spoken like that."[14]

Le Mercier, who evidently thought he could do better, would now have his chance. In late September he sailed for France aboard the *Machault* frigate, a private ship of war owned by Cadet and commanded by privateer captain Jacques Kanon. Their voyage began with a blast of artillery fire. On the night of 25–26 November, wrote Kanon, employing the third person, "At three o'clock in the morning he passed under Quebec, from which about three hundred cannonballs were fired at us." After that, Kanon continued on his way down the St. Lawrence and made an uneventful crossing to Brest, France, "without meeting a single British ship."[15]

CHAPTER 4

THE BATTLE OF
QUIBERON BAY

FIVE DAYS BEFORE KANON and Le Mercier ran past the guns of Quebec, French capacity to intervene in Canada suffered a second devastating blow.

Prior to the siege of Quebec, some Canadians believed a hopeful rumour that the Atlantic fleet was already on the way. On 27 May 1759, a British ship in the St. Lawrence River captured a vessel sailing downstream from Quebec carrying letters indicating "that Monsr. Conflans [Admiral Hubert de Brienne, Count de Conflans] was expected with 20 sail of the line from Brest."[1]

The French Crown, however, had other plans for Conflans. The Brest fleet had been ordered to escort powerful raiding forces to the port of Dover and Scotland's east coast. If all went as planned, these attacks would provoke a crisis of confidence leading to the collapse the British financial system. Rather than attempting to defend its global network of colonies, including Canada, one by one, France would land a single massive blow that might knock Britain out of the war.

Alert to the possibility of a French invasion, the Admiralty sent Edward Hawke to blockade Brest in May of 1759. Admiral Hawke remained on station until 7 November, when severe winds drove his ships back to Britain and pinned them in port until the weather improved. On the day that Hawke left Plymouth to return to Brest, Conflans set sail for Quiberon Bay, off the coast of France, to rendezvous with the transports carrying the French landing force. Conflans had a two-hundred-nautical-mile head start on Hawke, but the same winds that took his ships out of Brest forced them far out into the Atlantic before they could turn south.

This gave Hawke just enough time to catch up with the French on 20 November as they approached Quiberon Bay. Lashed by a wild storm and shrouded in darkness, the British pursued the French into the bay. Conflans' ships met various fates—captured, destroyed by gunfire, run aground, sunk in the storm, or breaking away and fleeing to safety.[2] By sunrise, the French Atlantic fleet had been smashed, along with French hopes for ending the war by raiding Britain.

Sebastien François Bigot de Morogues, captain of the *Magnifique*, escaped from Quiberon Bay and sailed to safety in the port of Rochefort, France. After the engagement, he summed up both the mood of the French navy and the influence of the Battle of Quiberon Bay on French strategy. "I don't know everything, but I know too much. The battle on the twentieth of this month has destroyed the navy and its enterprises."[3]

Following the battles of Lagos and Quiberon Bay, France could no longer attempt to deploy large fleets overseas. But many French warships remained at large, and France retained the ability to undertake transatlantic naval operations, provided the objective was important enough. Whether a Quebec expedition fell into this category remained to be seen.

CHAPTER 5

_____

THE BRITISH IN WINTER

_____

JAMES MURRAY

The British began the winter of 1759–60 on a much higher note than the French. They had, after all, captured Forts Carillon, St. Frédéric, and Niagara on Canada's Lake Champlain and Lake Ontario frontiers. Canada's colonial capital and the Government of Quebec were now British territory, ruled by Brigadier James Murray.

Something of Murray's formidable character is reflected in a story from 1759 related by an anonymous officer of the 35th Regiment. It concerned a conversation on the Plains of Abraham, where Brigadier George Townshend had succeeded James Wolfe in command of the British army at Quebec.

> When the battle was over the French army being totally routed & dispers'd, & we in quiet possession of the field, the rest of the Gen[l] officers, went up to Gen[l] T— congratulating him on the success of the day, & saying that Quebec must very soon be in our hands.
>
> Gen[l] T— after some discourse, said it was an uncommon thing for a victorious army to retreat, yet he did not know but it might be our case: at which Gen[l] Murray roar'd out so as to be heard at a considerable distance, Retreat, Retreat, No, bleach our bones here first. We won it & by G— we'll wear it.

Then Gen¹ T— said, I do not say Gen¹ Murray that it will be so, but such things have happen'd.

Gen¹ M— swore again that it must not happen to us.¹

When the British fleet and senior army officers, including Townshend, sailed from Quebec in the fall of 1759, Murray was left behind in command of the Quebec garrison. In a letter to his brother George, he expressed great enthusiasm for his new post and his new domain. "I have the honour to be appointed Governor of Quebec and the conquer'd country, which is a noble one indeed,—infinitely beyond what any Briton imagin'd it to be, whether for the fertility of its soil, or number of its inhabitants."

Governing Quebec, moreover, represented an opportunity, not just for conquest, but also for justice. Which is to say, justice for James Murray. After twenty years in the British army, Murray strongly believed he had earned the prestige and professional recognition that came with the colonelcy of a regiment in addition to his substantive rank of brigadier. As a result, he raged over what he perceived as the grotesque unfairness that had kept him from this reward during the sieges of Louisbourg and Quebec. "I have now serv'd two campaigns under three officers who were put over my head, and I don't find I have got a regiment yet."²

As of October 1759, however, Murray had his own independent command and things were going to be different. He wrote to his brother:

> I think I cannot miss it [the colonelcy of a regiment] now... I have taken it into my head [that] you will hear good news from me in the spring. I am making provision of snow shoes for a winter expedition, and will not allow the Chevalier de Levi to be quiet in his cantonments. I have an eye to his magazines. I have six thousand as brave troops as ever existed. Business may and shall be done with them, that those who have hitherto deprived me of my preferment may repine at [regret] it.³

The French, he was certain, were not going to stand in his way. In a proclamation to the Canadians of the Government of Quebec, Murray reminded them that resistance was futile. Canada was caught in a trap, with "all communications with the ocean being stopped up, without hope, without resources, with an army of experienced veterans in the heart of your country, another at its gates, almost all your frontier barriers snatched from you, or abandoned."[4]

For James Murray, command at Quebec was just a start. One dramatic victory and he would be on his way to taking his rightful place in the world. The next vacant colonelcy in the British army was going to go to the next hero of the war for Canada.

AN ARMY IN PERIL

Things didn't turn out quite as well as Murray had anticipated. October and November passed productively and uneventfully as the new governor consolidated his position in Quebec and tightened his grip on the surrounding countryside by disarming the Canadians, controlling access to the city, establishing outposts, and taking oaths of allegiance. But in December, James Murray's army began to die.

Winter in Canada, as the British soon discovered, involved more than snow on the ground. Below-freezing temperatures meant that fresh fruit and vegetables and the vitamin C they provided were unavailable. Ice on the St. Lawrence made it impossible to import these commodities. Working to exhaustion to provide themselves with firewood—without which they would freeze to death within hours—weakened their resistance to illness.

The result was scurvy, a horrifying disease caused by a lack of vitamin C, completely absent from the garrison's winter diet of salt meat and ship's biscuit. Symptoms began with fatigue and listlessness, followed by soft and bleeding gums, internal bleeding, wounds failing to heal or reopening after they appeared to heal, intense pain in muscles and joints, loss of teeth, and finally death.[5]

By December, Murray's soldiers had gone long enough without vitamin C for the first fatalities to occur. "The weather," wrote Captain John Knox of the 43rd Regiment, "is now become inconceivably severe, and our soldiers grow numerous in the hospitals; some, who died within these few days, are laid in the snow until the spring, the ground being, at this time, impenetrably bound up with frost."[6]

So while the French passed what was for them a normal Canadian winter, the British endured a ghastly season of cold, exhaustion, and disease. "We had a stove," wrote James Thompson, "but our Highlanders . . . would not suffer the door to be closed, as they thought that if they could not actually *see* the fire, it was impossible that they could *feel* it. . . . Three or four would sit up close to the door of the stove, and when these were a little warm'd, three or four others would relieve them and so on. Some days they were almost frozen to death, or suffocated by the smoke."

Thompson himself slept under six blankets, and found, "every morning, the whole surface of the blankets cover'd with ice from the heat of my breath and body."[7]

James Miller, a private in the 15th Regiment, depicted life in Quebec among troops who had never experienced a Canadian winter.

> We were totally unprepared, for such a climate. . . The troops were crowded inside vacant houses, as well as possible, numbers fell sick, and the scurvy made a dreadful havoc among us. The duty became extremely hard, for after being up all night, on guard, the men, were obliged, to go over six miles, through the snow, to cut wood, and then to drag it home on sledges. . . In short, the fatigues of the winter was so great that the living almost envied the dead.[8]

Facing catastrophe, Murray and his regimental surgeons flung remedy after remedy at scurvy. They did everything right, according to their understanding of disease, but since what they understood was wrong, nothing they did actually worked. That fresh provisions, particularly fruits and vegetables, would eliminate scurvy almost immediately was common knowledge. What do to in their absence was a little more obscure.

Captain Knox recorded their efforts in the pages of his journal. On 18 February, Murray ordered double rations of vinegar for the troops, "as nothing is better for the scurvy, which is the cause of the disorders in this army." Vinegar proved less than effective, so Murray tried ginger. "Ginger being esteemed a most specific corrective in scorbutic cases, a quantity of that spice is issued out to the troops."

On 5 March, Murray ordered his troops to cut back on their salt intake by thoroughly soaking and washing all of the encrusted salt from their salt provisions. "As it is impossible to get fresh provisions for the troops, in our present situation; for the preservation of the soldiers' health it is absolutely necessary to give the utmost attention to freshening and boiling pork."

When that didn't work either, Murray turned to wine. "Doctor Russel having represented that wine is actually necessary for the preservation of the health of the troops," he bought 4,752 gallons for distribution to the garrison.[9]

The troops probably appreciated the wine more than the ginger, vinegar, or sodium-reduced salt pork, but none of these remedies made up for a lack of vitamin C. Finally, at the beginning of April, Murray and his surgeons gave up on British theories and turned to a practical Canadian remedy. This consisted of boiling hemlock spruce (*Tsuga canadensis*) needles in water to produce an herbal tea (as opposed to spruce beer, which the British already knew about), which was issued to the troops. The treatment proved effective. "We have . . ." wrote Knox, "the happiness to see our men on the recovery, though they as yet gain ground very slowly. This is attributed to the virtues of the hemlock spruce, which is a particular species, and an excellent antiscorbutic; it has been recommended and drank in the hospitals for some time past, and was discovered by an old Canadian empiric, for which he was suitably rewarded."[10]

By 10 April, Murray could write that "the spruce drinks having been tried in the several hospitals, and found very beneficial to men in scorbutic habits . . . ordered it to be given to all the men as a preservative against that fatal disease."[11]

This was all very well but just a little late. When the campaigning season opened in the spring, Murray's army was a wreck.

On the twenty-fourth day of every month, Murray's officers mustered their troops and counted the fit, the sick, the wounded, and the dead. Every month, the totals of the sick, wounded, and dead climbed higher, while the number of reasonably fit soldiers declined. Murray began in October with 5,077 infantry and gunners fit for duty. By April, he was down 2,829 effectives fit enough to serve in the field. From October to April, 667 soldiers had died from all causes, mostly disease.[12] In contrast, only seventy-one British soldiers had been killed in action on the Plains of Abraham.[13]

With the British garrison growing weaker by the day, Lévis and Vaudreuil weren't the only ones watching the calendar and waiting for the spring breakup. On 25 January, Murray informed Major General Jeffery Amherst, commander-in-chief of the British army in North America, that "I hope . . . [the navy] will take care to be in the basin of Quebec before the Enemy, nothing can hurt but a French squadron getting the start of him."[14]

JOHN GRANT: LIVING THE GOOD LIFE IN NEW YORK

While Murray and his garrison struggled to survive the Canadian winter, Amherst worked out the details of a massive assault on Canada in 1760. Come summer, squadrons of small warships would sweep along Lake Ontario and Lake Champlain, escorting vast fleets of troop-carrying bateaux to the upper St. Lawrence and Richelieu Rivers. If all went well, the two amphibious armies would capture the forts defending Canada's southern and western approaches and rendezvous with Murray's force at Montreal.

In the meantime, Amherst's soldiers settled into winter quarters in the northern British colonies, close to the Canadian frontier. One of these soldiers was Lieutenant John Grant of the 42nd Highlanders (The Black Watch). Born in the Scottish Highlands, Grant's earliest memory was of British soldiers patrolling the region after the Jacobite Rebellion in 1745, telling a tale of searching for hidden treasure. "The first thing I recollect," he wrote, "coming of troopers. Remember my Mother and servants serving out bread cheese & butter—remember their putting into the haversacks and the pawing of the horses—told it was to find out where treasure was hid."

In 1758, now seventeen years old, he decided upon a military career himself. This meant raising twenty-five recruits to obtain a lieutenant's commission. The war had been under way for four years in North America and two years in Europe; competition for recruits was intense. Grant was up to the challenge. "I first got a good piper and then 4 young men good dancers established myself at an ale house. My sergeant Kite made a flowerly [*sic*] harangue [speech]... then came much dancing... this collected a crowd & drink was not scarce... I soon collected my number."

By 1759, Grant was in the British province of New York with the 42nd Highlanders, under Amherst's command. If James Miller—who had said of the harsh winter at Quebec "that the living almost envied the dead"—had been given the chance to trade places with anyone, he might have picked Grant. While ice locked Murray's troops away from the world, Amherst's armies enjoyed the comforts that came from living in prosperous British colonies, linked to the outside world by ice-free ports. The new lieutenant spent most of the winter in a comfortable billet near Albany, engaged in ensuring that local residents transported firewood for the army.

I established myself at the best looking farm house in the district, but owner was a surly Dutch boor and I left it next day and pitched on another [. . .] most fortunately he was a plain blunt honest fellow a large log house and plenty of good cheer, and abundance of cakes of every denomination at tea. The day I went about to see that the wood was sent in, and at night over a blazing fire read an occasional news paper.[15]

When the time came to go on campaign, soldiers like Grant would be well fed, well rested, and ready to play their role in what the British hoped would be the final campaign against the French in Canada.

CHAPTER 6

A DECISION IN PARIS

ON 23 DECEMBER, KANON brought the *Machault* safely into harbour at Brest. Le Mercier promptly disembarked and set off for Paris. In January, he submitted a report to Nicolas René Berryer, the minister of marine and colonies. After explaining Canada's desperate situation, Le Mercier laid out what would be needed to redress the situation, along with a plan of campaign. The memoir culminated in a declaration that only a powerful convoy arriving in time would give Canada a fighting chance. "If France does not send us enough assistance to conduct the siege, it will be useless to send anything, and the colony will certainly be lost."

On the other hand, he continued, "If the King decides to send us the help we have requested and it arrives before that of the English, Quebec will certainly be recaptured, and, having nothing more to fear by way of the [lower St. Lawrence] river, the entire force of Canada can go to the rapids [of the upper St. Lawrence] or Île-aux-Noix [at the outlet of Lake Champlain], before the enemy can arrive there."

But the French government would have to move fast. "We must besiege and capture Quebec during the month of May."[1]

Unfortunately for Vaudreuil and Lévis, what Canada needed, what France could afford to send, and how the Crown chose to allocate its increasingly scarce military, naval, and financial resources proved to be three very different things.

Although France remained a prosperous country, the Crown lacked the ability to mobilize the nation's wealth for the war effort. As expenditures soared and revenue did not, the government drifted towards bankruptcy. With valuable, revenue-generating colonies at risk in the Caribbean, it was perhaps not the right time to propose a major expedition to Canada, a cold, remote colony that represented a financial burden for France.

Moreover, even if adequate funding had been available, Lagos and Quiberon Bay had wrecked France's principal fleets. Sending a naval force powerful enough to defend the St. Lawrence River against the Royal Navy was out of the question.

Faced with a choice between a major expedition he couldn't afford and abandoning Canada completely, Berryer elected to make a gesture that would at least be better than nothing. France would send a few transports to Canada, carrying token quantities of provisions, munitions, and reinforcements. If the ships couldn't reach Quebec, they would divert to Louisiana.

Yet even this minimal effort proved to be almost too much to achieve. To arrive in time to beat the British to the St. Lawrence, the convoy would have to leave in February or March—the sooner the better. On the ninth of March, a ministry of marine official at Bordeaux reported that preparations had stalled. Berryer summed up the situation when he replied to his subordinate on the twenty-second: "You have sent me a report on cargo for the ships we are sending to Canada, and observed that you have not received the funding that has been allocated for this little operation, and that this is causing you a great deal of trouble and extra work."

Berryer's response was not encouraging. "I find myself with the same problems with regard to... [lack of] money to pay for the expedition. I have been obliged to cut costs by limiting shipments to two thousand barrels."[2]

Here, Canada may have paid the price for excessive optimism on the part of Vaudreuil and Lévis regarding what they could expect from France. Had they made a distinction between supplies that were absolutely necessary— including a dozen heavy guns and appropriate munitions—and those that were merely desirable, Berryer might have had them crammed aboard a single ship and sent on their way. Instead, the Ministry of Marine and Colonies was attempting to organize a shipment of miscellaneous supplies, which, if delivered safely to the colony, would have made a welcome but marginal contribution to its defence but left Lévis' army sitting outside Quebec and unable to blast their way in.

February passed into March and March into April, but the ships remained in port.

CHAPTER 7

THE SEVEN NATIONS
OF CANADA

SHARING THE ST. LAWRENCE VALLEY

The French and British were not the only ones watching over events and pondering their options.

On European maps, the entire St. Lawrence valley was a French province, ruled by the French Crown. On the ground, mid-eighteenth-century Canada was divided between French territory and the Seven Nations of Canada, seven autonomous Amerindian communities, each with its own territory, government, law, foreign policy, and armed forces. In 1755, a Mohawk from Kahnawake referred to these communities when he identified the members of a war party by announcing that "We are the 7 confederate Indian Nations of Canada."[1]

These nations were, from east to west, the residents of Lorette (Huron-Wendat), Saint-François and Bécancour (Abenakis), Kahnawake (Mohawks), Oka/Kanesetake (Algonquins, Mohawks, and Nipissings), Akwesasne (Mohawks), and Oswegatchie (Onondagas).[2]

Unlike the French and Canadians, the Seven Nations could choose whether or not they would take part in a campaign to recover Quebec in 1760. Canada's European population was composed of French subjects, bound to obey the orders and abide by the decisions of the Crown and its representatives. The Seven Nations of Canada were independent powers, free to make their own choices about war and peace.

THE SEVEN NATIONS AND THE SEVEN YEARS' WAR

In the first years of the war, the Seven Nations had been able to participate as independent allies of the French without placing their own communities at risk. The French-Amerindian forces won victory after victory; the British were comfortably far away from the St. Lawrence valley.

Now, the British had occupied Quebec and threatened not just New France but the territories of the Seven Nations of Canada. Following the Battle of the Plains of Abraham, the Huron-Wendat of Lorette, northwest of Quebec, had been forced to abandon their homes and travel to Fort Jacques Cartier, a new French fort on the west side of the mouth of the Jacques Cartier River. On 3 October, a detachment of American rangers led by Major Robert Rogers, a Massachusetts-born army officer who had become Britain's foremost practitioner of forest warfare, had attacked the Abenakis of Saint-François, killing men, women, and children. The survivors sought refuge in Akwesasne.[3] A week later, William Johnson, Britain's Superintendent of Northern Indians, offered the Seven Nations a stark choice between neutrality and destruction. "They have it in their power now," he wrote, "by quitting the French, to become once more a happy people, but if. . . they should act a different part, they must expect no quarter from us."[4]

In February of 1760, a delegation of Haudenosaunee (Iroquois) came to Oswegatchie, the Catholic Onondaga community on the upper St. Lawrence River. Allied to the British but speaking for themselves, they formally requested that the Seven Nations "keep out of the way, when the English army approaches." Speaking on behalf of all the nations allied with the French, a Seven Nations speaker refused outright. Making reference to the shared Catholicism that formed one of the ties that bound the alliance together, he announced that "as the French have persuaded us to stay, and embrace their religion, by which we are to be saved, it would be hard brothers for you to expect we should leave them altogether."[5]

It's worth noting here that the Seven Nations explicitly asserted that neither the French alliance nor Catholicism compromised their independence in any way. In 1757, a delegation of Oswegatchie clan mothers and chiefs reminded Vaudreuil that "in causing ourselves to be reborn in the same baptismal water that washed the Great Onontio [the king of France], we have not renounced our liberty, [or] our rights that we hold from the Master of Life."[6]

Nonetheless, they shared a common commitment to the defence of Canada. In that same year, Kisensek, a prominent Nipissing leader from Oka/Kanesetake, declared that the Seven Nations were fighting to "defend our lands against the English, who want to usurp them. Our cause is just and the Master of Life favours it."[7]

Although their deliberations on the subject were never recorded, the Seven Nations chose to support the French in the spring of 1760 with more than just words. On 15 February, twenty-five Onondaga warriors from Oswegatchie travelled to Montreal. There, they formed part of a force of 270 warriors, including Atiatonharongwen, an African-Abenaki who became a war chief at Kahnawake and who would join the march on Quebec.[8]

CHAPTER 8

FRENCH PREPARATIONS

DECEPTION, ESPIONAGE, SABOTAGE

While they waited for winter to end and for the relief convoy to arrive, Vaudreuil and Lévis prepared to launch a spring offensive against Quebec.

They had first considered a winter strike against the city. Attacking in winter might have caught the British when they were most vulnerable, but would have forced the French to march 250 kilometres overland instead of sailing down the St. Lawrence. This was fine as far as the troops were concerned. They could walk. Then, as now, however, strategy might determine an army's goal, but logistics defines what is possible and what is not. Deciding to attack or defend a given position is as easy as drawing an arrow on a map; arranging for troops and supplies to arrive in the right place at the right time and in sufficient quantities represents one of the most difficult aspects of making war.

In this case, Canada lacked the horses to support a major land campaign. "It would have been impossible," Vaudreuil explained to the minister of marine and colonies, "to find enough horses to haul the army's provision carts, artillery train, munitions, and campaign equipment, let alone the forage needed by these same horses."[1] The French consequently limited themselves to going through the motions—building ladders and practising escalades—in the expectation that reports of these activities would reach the British and keep Quebec's garrison in a state of continuous alarm.

This did not prevent the French from conducting a series of covert operations. "I did everything I could," wrote Vaudreuil, "to obtain exact information on the strength, circumstances, and deployment of the enemy."[2] An account of the British outpost in the parish of Sainte-Foy, just west of Quebec, gives an indication of how detailed this intelligence could be.

> The post... is safe against a coup de main. The church has been surrounded with strong palisades, three or four fathoms from the base of the wall. There are four cannon. The walls have been pierced with two rows of loopholes, and you can also fire from the windows since the enemy has installed a wooden gallery for that purpose... The enemy, understanding the weakness of this post will, at the first sign of a French force, send two thousand troops from Quebec to support it.[3]

Vaudreuil's agents also attempted to take more active measures to shake the British hold on Quebec. "I further employed determined men whose zeal and good will I could count on to burn the enemy's provision and powder magazines. These men managed to infiltrate and spend several days inside the city under a variety of pretexts, and made every effort to fulfil my orders when the opportunity arose, but the alertness of the English made this impossible."[4]

LÉVIS' NEW MODEL ARMY

As Vaudreuil's agents prowled the streets of Quebec, Lévis set to work reorganizing the survivors of defeats and retreats on the Quebec, Lake Ontario, and Lake Champlain frontiers into an army, a weapon that could—in concert with the Canadian militia, Seven Nations, and artillery, munitions, and reinforcements from France—break the British hold on Quebec.

To begin with, he ordered his battalion commanders to tighten up discipline in their units. "The power of the infantry consists of order and discipline... which has unfortunately been neglected among our troops." After the Battle of the Plains of Abraham, an engagement where formations broke apart, troops opened fire independently, and the regular component of the army collapsed, Lévis wanted soldiers who could act like the veteran professionals that they were. In action, he warned, "they must pay attention, remain silent, practice self-control, obey the orders of their commanders, and only open fire in response to orders, even if they see others firing everywhere."

Next, he turned to morale, suggesting that colonels remind their troops "that they must repair the loss of 13 September and remember that these are the same enemies they had fought [and overcome] at Oswego, Fort William Henry, and Carillon."[5]

Lévis never recorded the measures his officers and non-commissioned officers took to implement his commands, but subsequent events suggest that they were very effective.

Just as important, Lévis discarded Montcalm's practice of incorporating militia into regular battalions. At the Plains of Abraham, Canadians serving alongside professional soldiers had stopped to fire and reload, breaking ranks with the regulars who marched on ahead without them. On the other hand, Canadians fighting separately, in their own way, had performed exceptionally well. Skirmishing alongside Amerindian warriors, they maintained heavy pressure on the British flanks throughout the action, forcing James Wolfe to take three battalions from his battle line to hold them off. When the French regulars broke and fled, the militia covered their retreat and forced British troops to withdraw three times before they themselves were finally pushed off the field.[6]

To make the best possible use of the Canadians' proven ability as skirmishers, Lévis formed them into companies, taking care to keep the militia from each parish together. Three of these companies were attached to whichever regular battalion had been billeted in their parish over the winter. This allowed the Canadians to serve alongside soldiers and officers they already knew instead of strangers, thereby strengthening the bonds beyond metropolitans and regulars. Each battalion detached an officer to lead the Canadian militia serving alongside them and three lieutenants to command the companies.

This new organization combined the steadiness of the French regulars with the skirmishing ability of the militia, with each component supporting the other. On the battlefield, the militia companies were to advance ahead of the regulars and "seek out the most advantageous situations to get as close as possible to the enemy and open fire, and pursue [the British] closely if they retreat." If they themselves were forced to retreat, they were to fall back on the regulars and "rally in the intervals . . . keeping level with the troops, and march once more against the enemy with the entire army, redoubling their fire until they were close enough to charge the enemy, which they will do, after placing their knives at the end of the barrels of their muskets."[7]

Vaudreuil, for his part, organized the independent companies of the troupes de la marine into two regular battalions, complete with grenadier companies and colours.[8]

To fill out the ranks of the Quebec army, Vaudreuil and Lévis mustered every potential combatant in unoccupied Canada, leaving only minimal garrisons on the Lake Champlain and Lake Ontario frontiers and enough farmers in the countryside around Montreal and Trois-Rivières to prepare for the spring planting. Recruits for the campaign included Acadian refugees like Pierre Doucet, who "had served with great valor in several actions" in Acadia and was later appointed captain of an Acadian militia company.[9] By the spring of 1760, they had assembled a powerful, balanced force of 3,950 French regulars and 2,750 Canadian militia, accompanied by 270 warriors, ready to march on Quebec.[10]

The artillery train was another matter. With most of Canada's heavy guns now in British hands, the French had no choice but to concentrate their remaining artillery at Quebec, leaving the colony weaker everywhere else. "I was obliged," confessed Vaudreuil, "to take the cannon, the mortars, and most of the munitions from our frontiers."[11]

A thorough inventory had turned up just nine heavy guns—a single twenty-four-pounder, and eight eighteens—available for the expedition. All were in poor condition and incapable of firing for an extended period of time. For field guns, Lévis could take his choice from among nine twelve-pounders and eight six- and eight-pounders.[12]

Bread and brandy

As for provisions, in the first week of January, 1760, François Bigot, Canada's Intendant (civil administrator), contacted Joseph-Michel Cadet, the munitionnaire général (purveyor general), responsible for supplying the French armed forces with provisions. He instructed Cadet to "furnish the regular ration [of hardtack, salt pork or beef, and peas] for forty or fifty days to an army of eight or ten thousand men, officers, soldiers, militia, and Natives, that will besiege Quebec." Cadet's first response was to declare the task impossible.

Bigot confirmed the order, but in the end, the beef, pork, and peas the army needed were simply not available. When Lévis' troops set off for Quebec, they would be marching and fighting on punishment rations of hardtack (a type of biscuit) and water.[13]

Thoroughly displeased, Lévis protested to Vaudreuil, insisting upon "the indispensable necessity of adding a shot of brandy to the daily ration . . . on account of the harshness of the season."[14] Brandy, however, was also in short supply. Of the 280 barrels[15] needed for the army, only forty could be found in the royal stores in Montreal. The situation looked impossible, but Montreal wasn't the only source of brandy in Canada.

Barthélemy Martin, a prominent Quebec merchant, had done business with the British in Quebec for three months after the capitulation. In December, he left occupied Canada and travelled to Montreal, leaving behind one hundred quarts of brandy with his brother, Topez Martin, who could if necessary acquire more. In a letter to Bigot, Barthélemy declared himself to be more than willing to "remove about 250 quarts [220 barrels] of brandy from Quebec to be delivered to the King's stores at Jacques Cartier."

He warned, though, that this wasn't going to be easy. Apart from purchasing most of the brandy, Martin and his brother would "be obliged under present conditions to make additional payments . . . to gain the freedom to take the brandy out of Quebec and to pay for its transport to Jacques Cartier, which must be made in hard cash."[16]

Vaudreuil and Bigot agreed, a contract was signed, and Martin set off for Fort Jacques Cartier, on the border between French- and British-controlled territories. From there, he would contact his brother in Quebec and make the necessary arrangements.

To support these efforts, Vaudreuil sent an order to Captain Jean-Daniel Dumas, in command of the fort. He instructed Dumas to do everything he could to assist Martin.

> You will receive this letter, Sir, by M. Martin . . . whatever he can remove from Quebec will be of the greatest necessity for the needs of the service . . . Mr. Martin will have complete freedom to travel to Pointe-aux-Trembles, St. Augustin, and even to Quebec as he judges necessary, you will give him, moreover, all the facilities that will be necessary for him . . . to transport his goods from Quebec . . . you will provide him with carts from St. Augustin; he will be responsible for taking precautions to ensure that they are not arrested at Quebec. When the goods are at St. Augustin you will provide him with all means and facilities at your disposal to bring them to Jacques Cartier.[17]

Martin proved to be as good as his word. Before long, supplies of brandy, together with salt, another scarce commodity, were flowing from Quebec to the storehouses at Jacques Cartier, where they would await the arrival of Lévis' army.

Lieutenant Joseph Fournerie de Vézon was so impressed with this achievement, and perhaps equally grateful for the brandy, that he included a tribute to Martin in his memoir of the campaign. At a time when the French forces were badly in need of this commodity, wrote Vézon, "M. le Marquis de Vaudreuil engaged Sieur Martin, merchant, to attempt to obtain it, as well as salt, from Quebec. In fulfilling this commission, the Sieur Martin proved himself to be in every way as adept an entrepreneur and as zealous a citizen as the government could desire."[18]

CHAPTER 9

BRITISH PREPARATIONS

ON HIS MAJESTY'S SECRET SERVICE

By the spring of 1760, Murray's garrison had been so reduced by scurvy that he had too few healthy troops to guard the walls and fight a battle at the same time. If a French army came to Quebec, he could expect to be seriously outnumbered.

Under these circumstances, Murray needed an edge. More specifically, he needed information. Without a reliable source of intelligence, he wrote, "their army and every peasant able to bear arms might have been assembled without my knowledge." With it, he could ascertain French strength and anticipate French movements.

Much of the information Murray required was not, in fact, closely guarded. Canadians in the occupied parishes were aware of the movements of, and cooperated with, French detachments. Within French-controlled territory, where troops were billeted in private homes and military movements and preparations took place under the eyes of the population, even secret military dispatches quickly became common knowledge. On one occasion, Vaudreuil complained to Dumas that "I was surprised [to find] that no sooner had your news reached me than it had spread throughout the town."[1]

To tap into this web of information, Murray needed French subjects willing to serve as British agents. They proved to be surprisingly easy to find. Soeur Marie de la Visitation (Marie-Joseph Legardeur de Repentigny), a nun at the Augustinian order that managed Quebec's Hôpital Général, reported that many British officers had told her "that they had never seen a people so attached and so faithful to their prince as the Canadians."[2] But just about every population contains people who place tangible rewards ahead of abstract loyalties, and Canada in 1760 was no exception.

So desperate were conditions in occupied Canada that some Canadians were prepared to spy for the British in exchange for food. "I was obliged," wrote Murray, "to subsist [provide with provisions] such as served us... as spies... as no other consideration could engage them to act for us, with any kind of heart or spirit."[3]

These agents could keep Murray informed about local French actions and intentions. For higher-level information, he needed to find a "method of opening and keeping up intercourse [communications] with their head-quarters." That didn't take long. Murray found his agents "by allowing some of the French merchants to carry spirits, wine and some dry goods to their advanced posts, where at first they were stopt, but afterwards (to my great joy) allowed to pass, I imagine from a persuasion, that the merchants and carriers being French would not betray their country."[4]

As well as permission to travel, potential merchant-spies obtained access to otherwise unobtainable goods, in particular "the brandy found in the cellars of Cadet the French commissary," which they could dispose of for a handsome profit.

Rather than handle these transactions himself, Murray tasked two officers to act as spymasters. "I gave... brandy and passports to dispose of it as they pleased to Captains [James] Barbutt and [Hector Theophilus] Cramahé. They spoke French as well and as fluently as English. I therefore gave them the management of the spies, they were indefatigable and gave proofs of incomparable address."[5]

Barbutt and Cramahé's prize recruit was none other than Barthélemy Martin. Born in Marseille, Martin had immigrated to Canada prior to 1749, and assisted by his brother, Topez Martin, quickly made a place for himself as the head of one of Canada's most prominent import/export firms.[6]

Martin got his start doing business in occupied territory when he obtained a contract to ship the belongings left behind by French officers in the Quebec area upriver to Montreal aboard two schooners. French staff officer

Benoît-François Bernier, then acting as liaison between the French and British authorities, kept a wary eye on Martin. He soon discovered that the enterprising entrepreneur was also transporting commercial goods to Montreal at government expense, where they could be sold at a profit of three to four hundred per cent.[7]

Tricking the Crown into paying him to carry his own cargo, however, was the least of Martin's sins. His legitimate activities at Quebec involved working with British officials, including, it would seem, Captain James Barbutt. "Mr. Barbutt," wrote Murray, "sold. . . brandy to Messrs Tropé [Topez] and Bartholomy [*sic*] Martin for eighty thousand livres, for which they gave bills of exchange for different sums to that amount upon their Banker a Monsr [Jean-Louis] Tourton at Paris."[8]

Martin himself travelled from Quebec to Montreal towards the end of December 1759. Long accustomed to dealing with Canada's most senior officials, he quickly became involved in preparations for the one thing Murray most wanted to learn about, the proposed French offensive against Quebec. Martin's friends in high places just happened to be in the market for a supply of brandy, along with salt. Martin was more than happy to offer to provide both commodities.

By 9 March, Martin was at Fort Jacques Cartier, preparing to open communications with Quebec. The documentary record is obscure, as is often the case with spies and traitors, but no sooner had he arrived than Murray began to receive a series of reports concerning French operations in general and the spring offensive in particular.[9] Summing up Barbutt and Cramahé's achievements, Murray later wrote that "no man ever had better [intelligence], I am sure no army ever wanted it more, and that no nation ever paid less for it."[10]

As for Martin, the purely commercial side of his treason at first appeared to have worked out rather well. After buying the brandy from the British for 80,000 livres in bills of exchange, he turned around and sold it to the French for 544,677 livres 10 sols.[11] Better still, his banker in Paris never redeemed his bills of exchange, saving Martin the trouble of actually paying the British for the brandy. On the other hand—and it is hard not to feel that Martin had it coming—the near-bankrupt French Crown didn't pay him for the brandy either.[12]

WAITING FOR LÉVIS

As early as 28 March, Murray had been informed that the French were preparing their vessels at Sorel for "an early expedition in the spring." Four days later, he received "fresh intelligence . . . of the designs of the French." Finally, on 17 April, "the best intelligence was now procur'd," regarding Lévis' intentions.[13] According to this information, the French planned to open their campaign by "making themselves masters of the embouchure [outlet] of the River Caprouge, the most convenient place for disembarking their artillery & stores, and for securing their retreat," then marching on Quebec.[14]

Murray based his plans for the initial stages of the defence of Quebec upon this information. He would forestall the French by fortifying the plateau now known as the Quebec Promontory, which extended westward from the city to the mouth of the Cap Rouge River. By mid-April, a detachment of light infantry had occupied the western tip of the promontory, overlooking Cap Rouge, and a military engineer was laying out fortifications.[15] These measures were intended not to stop a French attack but to divert it northward, "to hinder the enemy," in Murray's words, "from landing their cannon in the river, and to oblige them to bring it round by land [by way of Ancienne Lorette, about twelve kilometres west of Quebec], which, considering the badness of the road, would in that case delay their operations a considerable time."[16]

At the same time, Murray reinforced his northern defences. "Two large field-pieces," wrote Knox, "with a quantity of ammunition, are ordered to be drawn out to [Ancienne] Lorette: the roads being at this time rendered impassable for horses by the mass of dissolving snow that covers them, the soldiers are under the necessity of performing that service."[17]

Once the French had broken through these outposts, Murray planned to confront them from behind a line of entrenchments on the high ground just west of Quebec known as the Buttes-à-Neveu. This ground was at once strategically vital and eminently defensible. "Everyone knows," Murray declared, that "the place [Quebec] is not tenable against an army in possession of the heights."[18] Once entrenched on the buttes, he had assured Amherst in January that "I flatter myself I can defy them [the French, for] as long as my provisions will hold out."[19]

Unfortunately for Murray, the weather refused to cooperate. Between

23 and 25 April, he sent troops onto the buttes to begin construction. They found the ground "still covered with snow in many places, and every where impregnably bound up by frost."[20]

This was a bitter blow, but Murray could take consolation from the fact that another aspect of Canada's geography was now working in his favour. The spring breakup on the St. Lawrence that would allow a French army to float down from Montreal had also reopened the sea route to the outside world. On 21 April, he had sent a schooner downriver, heading for Halifax and bearing an urgent letter to Commodore Alexander Colvill, commander-in-chief of the Royal Navy in North America. The letter contained a stark, simple message. The French were on their way and Britain's Quebec garrison needed help.[21]

THE HALIFAX SQUADRON

Six hundred kilometres southeast of Quebec, Colvill had enjoyed a rather better winter than Murray. Writing in 1761, the commodore declared that "I have now been three winters at Halifax, and have found by experience, that in general, this season is not so boisterous, as 'tis commonly thought. We have much less blowing weather than in England, and much more sunshine... we have always been very well supplied with frozen beef from Boston, which keeps our Seamen healthy."[22]

Colvill had come to Halifax with orders from his predecessor, Vice Admiral Charles Saunders, to have ships in the St. Lawrence River as soon as possible in the spring. These orders were reinforced in March by a letter from Amherst proclaiming that "nothing is more essential, towards ensuring the success of the ensuing campaign, than to prevent any succours getting to the enemy, as well as any advices from their Mother Country, both of which the French will without doubt attempt."[23]

Colvill's spring campaign, however, got off to a frustrating start. He had planned to depart for Quebec on 14 April, but adverse winds kept him pinned in port. The year before, the same thing had happened to the Halifax squadron, and a French convoy carrying vital supplies arrived safely at Quebec. For a while, it must have seemed to Colvill that history was about to repeat itself.

Finally, on 22 April the wind changed and the squadron sailed.

Progress was slow, conditions unpropitious. Colvill later reported being "much retarded in our passage by frozen fogs, seas of compacted ice, and contrary wind." But the Royal Navy was at sea in Canadian waters and heading for Quebec.[24]

CHAPTER 10

THE FRENCH SET FORTH

THE FRENCH LEAVE MONTREAL

By the first week of April, Lévis and his army were ready. All of their preparations had been made; all they needed was an open river to carry them down to Quebec. Morale was high. Captain Anne-Joseph-Hippolyte Maurès de Malartic of the Béarn regiment observed that "the melting of the ice did not correspond to the impatience of the troops to depart."[1]

Even before the main body of Lévis' army moved downriver, Vaudreuil was taking steps to facilitate a smooth linkup between the siege force and the ships carrying artillery, munitions, provisions, and troops from France. French ocean-going vessels had been sailing up the St. Lawrence to Quebec for well over two centuries, but the governor general wasn't taking any chances.

On 16 April, Vaudreuil sent the Sieur Legris, a Canadian militia officer, to Île de Bic, 250 kilometres below Quebec. Legris established one lookout on the island and ordered Molé Lepage, a captain of militia, to establish a second. When the convoy appeared, Legris and Lepage were to urge the captains to make all possible speed upriver and let them know that pilots were waiting at Île-aux-Oies, just below Île d'Orléans, to guide them past the Traverse channel.

As for the pilots, Vaudreuil sent out another set of orders to captains of militia at key points along the river. "I ask you, Sir, immediately upon receipt of this letter, to gather all of the pilots in your [militia] company and any others in the vicinity, and send them to . . . [Île-aux-Oies]. These pilots will be paid as usual, and, in addition to that, I will grant them a bonus."[2]

On 13 April, Lévis announced that the army would embark in a week.[3] The next day Captain Rochebeaucourt, the French officer who commanded the Canadian militia cavalry, led his troops eastward down the Chemin du Roy, mounted on every horse from the Montreal area that was fit for service.[4]

On the seventeenth, Lévis gave Captain Lapause of the Guyenne regiment a new assignment. He sent the captain on ahead to reconnoitre potential landing sites along the north bank of the St. Lawrence and generally do everything possible to facilitate a quick advance to the Quebec Promontory. Lapause's account of his voyage provides the most detailed description of the conditions that Lévis' troops endured on the river.

> The river still not being entirely free of ice, I was almost crushed at the outlet of Lac Saint-Pierre by the banks that, having blocked passage of the river and stopped those who were descending, formed a mountain of ice over fifty feet high with a horrifying noise. We could neither land nor go back up the river, having been carried along with the ice that blocked the exit of the lake. I was fortunately saved by a small opening that appeared in front of me, and carried me with the ice until I reached Trois Rivières.

Below Trois-Rivières, it didn't get any easier. "I continued downstream to Jacques Cartier where I landed with great difficulty, after passing the night in a boat blocked by a bank of ice that was fixed in place."[5]

On 20 April, a fleet of bateaux carrying Lévis' army and several small sailing vessels laden with supplies set out from Montreal. At Sorel, they would be joined by two frigates, l'Atalante and la Pommone, commanded by Capitaine de Brûlot ("fireship captain," equivalent to lieutenant) Jean Vauquelin, a former merchant captain who had joined the French navy when the Seven Years' War broke out. In 1758, Vauquelin had sailed a frigate past the Royal Navy into Louisbourg, spent the siege using his ship's guns to harass the British, and escaped carrying dispatches. He returned to North America the next year to take part in the defence of Quebec.[6]

The troops travelled during the day and spent the night in farmhouses and outbuildings along the shore. Everything depended on speed and secrecy.

Lévis considered it to be "essential to arrive in front of Quebec before the enemy learned of our march."[7]

A convoy from Bordeaux

As Lévis prepared to advance on Quebec, the French relief expedition to Canada finally got under way. On 10 April, Lieutenant de Frégate (sub-lieutenant) François-Pierre Chenard de la Giraudais, the new commander of the *Machault* frigate, sailed from Bordeaux propelled by a northeast wind and escorting five transports.

Between them, the six vessels carried four hundred soldiers of the troupes de la marine, mostly from the former garrison of Louisbourg, and cargoes of flour, salt pork, lard, shoes, clothing, trade goods for Amerindian allies, gunpowder, powder, musket balls, cannonballs, mortar shells, muskets, and gunflints.

The next day, the convoy came apart. When two British ships appeared, wrote Giraudais, "I signalled my little fleet to make a run for it, which they did." As the transports fled, *Machault* manoeuvred to draw off the British, then escaped under cover of darkness. Two of the merchant ships rejoined *Machault* on the twelfth and seventeenth, two more were captured by the British, and the last sank off the Azores.

After that unpromising beginning, however, it was all clear sailing. "I continued my route with the two [transports]... without encountering anything." If all went well, Giraudais and his three-ship convoy would reach Canada in mid-May.[8]

CHAPTER II

ARMIES ON THE MOVE

LÉVIS—24-25 APRIL

On 24 April, the leading French battalions reached Pointe-aux-Trembles, thirty-seven kilometres from Quebec. Conditions along the St. Lawrence River had not improved. The troops, wrote Malartic, "had a great deal of trouble hauling their bateaux on land as a result of the ice."[1] The rest of the army arrived the next day.

From Pointe-aux-Trembles, Lévis dispatched scouting parties towards Quebec. They returned with word that the British continued to occupy the churches of Sainte-Foy and Ancienne Lorette to the north and northwest of Quebec, had expelled residents of the west end of the Quebec Promontory from their homes, and were constructing entrenchments at Cap Rouge.

This intelligence caused Lévis to suspect that the British had learned that the French were on the march. He responded by deciding to divert his advance northeast to Ancienne Lorette, then turn south towards the parish of Sainte-Foy, which ran from the western end of the Quebec Promontory to the Plains of Abraham.[2]

MURRAY—25 APRIL

While Lévis' scouts were reconnoitring the British outposts, Murray had pulled his troops out of Ancienne Lorette and demolished the bridges over the Cap Rouge River. In Quebec, he expelled the population out into the

countryside "in order to shelter the unfortunate citizens from the evils insep-
arable from war."[3]

The Canadians failed to appreciate this generosity. "The wretched citizens," wrote Captain Knox, "have evacuated the town: it is impossible to
avoid sympathising with them in their distress. The men prudently restrained
their sentiments on this occasion, but the women were not so discreet; they
charged us with a breach of the capitulation; said they had often heard, *que les
Anglois sont des gens sans foi* [that the English are a people without integrity];
and that we have now convinced them of the propriety of that character."[4]

About 150 Canadian families remained within the walls. These were
presumably the families of individuals who, in Murray's words, "served us,
either as spies, pilots, artificers, clerks, or for other indispensable uses." As
such, they received special permits signed by Murray's secretary that allowed
them to remain in the city.[5] Murray also "permitted the religious belonging
to the two nunneries to remain in town, as they were extreamely useful in
taking care of our sick."[6]

LÉVIS—26 APRIL

On 26 April the French flotilla left Pointe-aux-Trembles around 8:00 a.m.
and made a quick run downriver to Saint-Augustin, twenty-two kilometres
from Quebec.[7] At some point Rochebeaucourt and the cavalry, which had
come overland from Montreal, arrived and joined the rest of the army.

While the landing was under way, François-Charles de Bourlamaque,
second in command of the Quebec expedition, led the advanced guard of
warriors, grenadiers, and field guns to the Cap Rouge River. The British had destroyed the two bridges closest to the St. Lawrence, but Bourlamaque's troops seized two other bridges further upstream, damaged, but still
standing.[8]

Some troops set to work repairing the bridges; others occupied houses
on the far bank to cover the crossing; scouts ranged ahead. The scouts sent
word back that the British had abandoned Ancienne Lorette and regrouped
at Sainte-Foy. The thousand-metre wooden roadway over an extensive wet-
land between the two parishes, known as La Suette, remained intact.[9] With
the warriors of the Seven Nations leading the way, Bourlamaque took his
advance guard up to the head of the roadway. They deployed in several

houses along the edge of the marsh and settled down to wait for the main body.[10]

As Bourlamaque forged ahead, the army marched from Saint-Augustin around 3:00 p.m. By nightfall, about a third of the troops had crossed the Cap Rouge River. Some of them had a rough time of it. "The bridges broke," wrote Lévis, "flinging soldiers into the water. The workers barely managed to repair them in the darkness, and could not have managed at all, without the [illumination provided by] constant flashes of lightning."[11]

Lapause, placed in charge of supervising the crossing, provides another account. "There was a terrible storm; the ground was still covered with snow; the cold was terrible; you could only see by flashes of lightning. The troops spent the entire night crossing the river, the flood almost carried away the bridges, by daybreak they were in a miserable state, having been chilled to the bone, without fire, and soaked to the skin."[12]

In the Hôpital Général, Marie de la Visitation saw the storm as an omen. "The night [of] the 27–28th was the most terrible. The sky seemed to fight against us, the thunder and lightning, rare during this season on this country, announced in advance the thunderbolts to which our [friends and relatives] would soon be exposed [on the battlefield].[13]

Around 3:00 a.m., Lapause was able to go to Lévis and report that the last soldier had reached the east bank of the Cap Rouge River.[14] Cold, wet, and miserable, the troops settled into the houses and barns of Ancienne Lorette to wait until morning.

Back at Saint-Augustin, the storm disrupted the landing of the French artillery. When inshore ice caught and overturned a boat carrying three light cannon—half of Lévis' field guns—all but one of the crew died in the river.[15]

The survivor, an artillery sergeant, recounted his experiences a few hours later, explaining how "his bateau overset in the great storm . . . and his companions he supposes are drowned; that he swam and scrambled, alternately, through numberless floats of ice, until he fortunately met with a large one, on which, though with great difficulty, he fixed himself; that he lay on it for several hours."[16]

MURRAY—NIGHT OF 26–27 APRIL

Up to this point, Murray had known that the French were coming, but he had no idea where they actually were. All that changed in the night of

26–27 April. Accounts vary; this one comes from the prolific pen of John Knox.

> About two o'clock this morning the watch on board the Racehorse sloop of war in the dock, hearing a distressful noise on the river, acquainted Captain M'Cartny therewith, who instantly ordered out his boat, which shortly after returned with a man whom they found almost famished on a float of ice; notwithstanding all imaginable care was taken of him, it was above two hours before he was able to give an account of himself; when the terrors of his mind had subsided, and he could speak.

The castaway proved to be a French artillery sergeant, who revealed that after ice crushed his bateaux and he survived by clinging to a floe, he had "passed the town with the tide of ebb, which carried him near St. Lawrence's church on the island of Orleans; and was driving up again with the tide of flood, at the time that our boat came to his relief."[17]

What followed became an intelligence disaster for the French. "The poor man," wrote Marie de la Visitation, "overcome by the dangers he had endured, was in no condition to conceal anything. He frankly declared that he was one of the gunners from the army that was two leagues from Quebec, his foot had slipped while he was loading a cannon [into a boat], the ice had carried him off downriver against his will."[18]

More important, wrote Ensign John Désbruyêres of the 35th Regiment, who was the descendant of a French protestant family that had settled in England in the late seventeenth century, the half-frozen sergeant passed on "certain intelligence that the French were in motion to come by ye way of Lorette & St Foy to cutt off our Cap Rouge posts; their frigates wth all manner of stores &c were come down to St. Augustin & ready to advance as soon as the Cap Rouge affair was decided."[19]

CHAPTER 12

FIGHTING FOR SAINTE-FOY

MURRAY—27 APRIL

Blindsided at the tactical level but now aware of the locations and intentions of the French army, Murray moved quickly to retrieve the situation. He set out for Sainte-Foy with the grenadiers and standby detachments of each battalion and the entire 15th Regiment. Behind them came three more regiments with two six-pounders. Unwilling to rely too much on a single piece of intelligence, he sent the 35th Regiment and the second battalion of Royal Americans to Sillery, where they joined a company of volunteers in guarding against a French landing near Quebec.[1]

The British march to Sainte-Foy proved to be as rugged as the French advance to Ancienne Lorette. Lieutenant Henry Hamilton of the 35th never forgot how "the high road . . . becomes in the spring nearly impracticable for man or beast. We frequently sunk into the soaked snow above the knee."[2] Knox recalled marching in "thick and cold misting rain."[3]

When they reached Sainte-Foy, Murray could confirm that the French sergeant's report had been correct in all respects. Looking down from the promontory and across the Suette Marsh, he could see warriors, militia, and regulars among the trees. He formed his troops in line of battle and opened fire with artillery, hoping the French would attack while he held the advantage of the high ground on the Quebec Promontory.

Murray held this position until a startling intelligence report arrived from

Quebec. "Two French ships were at the Traverse." The French relief convoy had apparently arrived and ascended the St. Lawrence as far as Île d'Orléans.

This news, together with the miserable weather, the arrival of more French troops, and apprehension that part of Lévis' force was moving eastward under cover of the forest to get between the British and Quebec, made Murray decide to call it a day. He ordered his troops to shoot the trunions off two eighteen-pounders that could not be hauled away, blow up a supply of munitions and provisions at the church, and fall back towards Quebec.[4]

The French pursued. Murray's rear guard held them off with field guns while the rangers and light infantry covered the flanks so effectively that the French chose to keep their distance.[5] At the western edge of the Plains of Abraham, the troops of the rear guard, stationed in a house and mill and on two small hills, finally halted the French advance. They remained in place until after dark, then slipped away and joined the main body of the British army inside Quebec.

There, Murray allowed his damp, chilled, and thoroughly uncomfortable troops to demolish several houses in the Saint-Roch suburb. They used the wood thus acquired to make fires to dry their clothes, and received a special issue of rum. The report of French ships in the Traverse channel turned out to be a false alarm.[6]

LÉVIS—27 APRIL

When Murray looked across the Suette Marsh from the Quebec Promontory, Lévis had been looking back at him. Lévis had planned to storm the promontory, which he described as "an elevation lined with homes, part of a cliff that that ended in the heights that dominated the Cap Rouge River at one end and at the other ran all the way to Quebec."[7]

But when appalling road conditions delayed his artillery and British troops lined the edge of the promontory, he decided to wait until the twenty-eighth before making a move. The day passed in occasional exchanges of musket and cannon fire, until, wrote Malartic, "At 2 h. [2:00 p.m.] we saw the church of Sainte-Foy on fire and the roof blowing up."[8]

The French set off in pursuit of the British, with their advanced guard and cavalry in the lead. Malartic described the afternoon's events: "That march was as hard as it was painful. All of the officers went on foot, and suffered alongside their soldiers in the rain and snow, as well as the discomfort of walking in water halfway up their legs."⁹

The chase continued until the British rear guard finally halted and took up defensive positions at the edge of the Plains of Abraham, two-and-a-half kilometres from the walls of Quebec. The cavalry exchanged a few shots with the British, resulting in one officer lost and several troopers wounded. Not inclined to press the point, the French fell back a few hundred metres to the nearest houses and took shelter for the night. Behind them, Lévis billeted his troops in the houses and barns along the Chemin Sainte-Foy.¹⁰

PART 2

BATTLE

CHAPTER 13

THE FRENCH REACH THE
PLAINS OF ABRAHAM

A QUIET MORNING ON THE PLAINS

Overnight, the sky cleared. The low-pressure system that had produced thunderstorms and rain moved on. Jean-Félix Récher, parish priest of Quebec and amateur meteorologist, had been keeping track of the weather and temperature in his parish since December. On the morning of 28 April, he recorded: "3 degrees above freezing [1.7 degrees C]. Fine weather and sunny."[1]

After the hard marching of the previous day, Lévis planned to let his troops spend a quiet morning in their billets. Murray's retreat from Cap Rouge left Lévis convinced that the British "had decided to limit themselves to defending the place [Quebec]." Given that he planned to deploy his army outside Quebec and wait for the convoy from France, allowing his troops a half day to rest, eat, and dry their clothing made more sense than wearing them out further by continuing to advance.

Lévis himself, on the other hand, had business to attend to. He planned to use the day to disembark provisions and field guns at the Anse au Foulon, move his army to the Plains of Abraham, and prepare to occupy the Buttes-à-Neveu the following morning.

While his army rested, he sent a messenger upriver with orders for the ships carrying provisions and additional field guns to proceed as quickly as possible to the Foulon. He then rode to the plains to reconnoitre the area and select campsites for the troops to occupy that afternoon. Accompanied by his staff and followed by Bourlamaque and an advance guard, which included the cavalry and ten companies of grenadiers, Lévis headed east along the Chemin Sainte-Foy, through the open country north of Sillery Wood. After a short ride, he reached the Plains of Abraham.[2]

BATTLEFIELD TERRAIN

During much of the year, the plains could be fairly characterized as idyllic, or at least attractive and productive. Decades later, Surveyor General Joseph Bouchette admired a landscape of "rich pastures and well-cultivated fields."[3] Pehr Kalm, a Swedish botanist, was just as impressed with the pastures near Quebec in 1749. "The ground is covered with white clover, so that one cannot wish for finer meadows than are found here."[4]

None of that applied, however, during the bleak micro-season between the spring breakup of ice on the St. Lawrence and the melting of the snow on land.[5] At that time of the year, wrote nineteenth-century historian Henri-Raymond Casgrain, "the sun's rays fell upon a plain which seemed a virtual desert. Traces of snow and pools of frozen water here and there marked the undulations of the ground. The budless, frost-covered branches sparkled like crystals in the early sunlight. The blades of grass beginning to shoot on the eastern slope of the cliff heralded the return of spring."[6]

The plains made up a rough parallelogram, bounded by Sillery Wood and the fifteen-metre-high Buttes-à-Neveu to the west and east, and the cliffs that formed the sides of the Quebec Promontory to the north and south. The northern escarpment was known as the Coteau Sainte-Geneviève; the southern remains nameless to this day. Midway between the buttes and the forest stood a rise in the ground once known as Wolfe's Hill and today occupied by the Pavilion Baillairgé of the Musée des beaux-arts de Québec. Two more hills lay on the west side of the plains along the Sillery Wood treeline— South Hill, directly opposite Wolfe's Hill, and North Hill, midway across the promontory.

All four of the features bordering the plains had military significance. The cliffs to the north and south channelled movement, limiting the possibilities for flanking manoeuvres and forcing armies to go head to head. Troops on the Buttes-à-Neveu gained the advantage of the high ground, screened by a steep, rugged slope. Sillery Wood could shelter an army by providing cover, limiting the effectiveness of artillery and making it impossible for an opponent to advance in formation.

There were three roads on the plains. The Chemin Sainte-Foy began at Quebec's Porte Saint-Jean and ran north of the Buttes-à-Neveu and along the north side of the plains towards Sainte-Foy. The Grande-Allée left Porte Saint-Louis, crossed the Buttes-à-Neveu, then ran over the plains, passed between North Hill and South Hill, and continued on through Sillery Wood. The two roads united at Cap Rouge. A third road began at the beach at the Anse au Foulon, ran diagonally up the side of the cliff, passed south of South Hill, then joined the Grande-Allée on Wolfe's Hill.

During the British siege of Quebec between 13 and 18 September 1759, Townshend's soldiers had built about twenty small, enclosed earthworks, known as redoubts, on and around the plains to protect their camp. Three were still there on 28 April—a large redoubt on Wolfe's Hill and two smaller redoubts on South Hill, guarding the road to the Anse au Foulon.

The most visible human construct on the plains, however, was the Moulin de Dumont (Dumont's Mill), part of the cluster of farm and industrial buildings on the north side of the Chemin Sainte-Foy that had been occupied and abandoned by the British rear guard the previous evening. To the north of the mill, the ground dropped off sharply before levelling out into a second small plain occupied by Dumont's fields. (Today, the site of Dumont's Mill is marked by a stone circle at the Parc des Braves; down below, his fields form the greater part of the park.) Beyond the fields was the escarpment proper that formed the edge of the battlefield and overlooked the Saint-Charles valley.

Jean-Baptiste Dumont, a Quebec merchant who had emigrated from the south of France, had bought the property in 1741. He paid 4,500 livres to the Jesuits, who had been using it "to serve as a country and vacation residence for new boarders at their college in Quebec."[7] Dumont himself described this property in a notice in *The Quebec Gazette/Le Gazette de Québec* in 1779.

To be sold or rented,

A farm situate[d] on the Height near St. John's suburb on the hill of St. Genevieve in the precinct of Quebec, containing about three arpents [1.26 hectares] in front, beginning from the high-road leading to St. Foy's and running back towards the little river St. Charles to the extent of five

arpents, with a fine garden, and all the buildings thereon; consisting of a
stone wind-mill that turns with every wind, fit for grinding bark for a tannery, the situation being very suitable for one, and the water, which never
fails in the driest seasons, is the best in the province for preparing leather,
there having always been a tannery there; a barn fit to contain the produce
of the farm which produces at present from four to five thousand bundles of
hay, and capable of producing much more. Those inclined to purchase or
rent it, may have it on reasonable terms by applying to Mr. Dumon[t] the
proprietor, Merchant in Quebec.[8]

The stone buildings of Dumont's establishment were ready-made fortifications, particularly the mill. A typical tower mill had solid stone walls, a
roof that could be turned to allow the sails to catch the wind, and windows on
each floor for light and ventilation. They were generally three stories tall—a
high tower allowed for larger sails that generated more power—with milling
machinery on the upper floors and storage space on the lower. The Moulin
de Dumont was 4.67 metres in diameter, with walls 0.94 metres thick and an
interior 2.76 metres across at the base. The single doorway was on the west
side facing Sainte-Foy.[9]

LÉVIS' RECONNAISSANCE

Unlike James Wolfe, whose first look at the plains in 1759 had revealed an
empty landscape, Lévis and his followers were not alone. Atop the Buttes-à-
Neveu, they could see British troops moving about.

Lévis wasn't worried. He assumed that "the English detachment which
had abandoned the Dumont house and the small hills where they halted the
day before, had fallen back on the Buttes-à-Neveu about 250 toises [about
500 metres] from the walls of Quebec, which that butte dominates entirely."[10]

Leaving his opponents on the buttes for another time, Lévis turned to
his own plans. He ordered dismounted cavalry across the plains to occupy
the redoubt on Wolfe's Hill and sent an aide back to the Chemin Sainte-Foy
bearing orders for the army to advance to the plains that afternoon.[11] The
British on the buttes, however, proved to be more aggressive.

They fired, wrote Malartic, "several cannonballs at the grenadiers and
Canadians that the general [Lévis] had posted near the city."[12] As British
artillery fire increased, Lévis recalled the cavalry from Wolfe's Hill.[13]

Apart from this minor setback, everything was going well. By that afternoon, Lévis counted on having his troops comfortably ensconced in their new camp and unloading supplies at the Anse au Foulon.

CHAPTER 14

MURRAY ADVANCES TO THE BUTTES-À-NEVEU

THREE SOLDIERS IN THE MORNING

Concealed from the French by the Buttes-à-Neveu, the British garrison was out of sight but far from idle. Up earlier and moving faster than Lévis, Murray had been rousing his garrison and preparing to march out onto the buttes and entrench his army to keep the French away from the walls of Quebec.

For Sergeant John Wilson of Fraser's Highlanders, 28 April began with a wrenching personal encounter. Following the British occupation of Quebec City, the nuns of the Hôtel-Dieu had returned to the city and reopened their hospital, now devoted to caring for sick and wounded British troops. Wilson, described by fellow Highlander James Thompson as "a fine, likely-looking fellow," had been a patient there since the Battle of the Plains of Abraham.

Wilson's wound was serious, but Sister Sainte-Gabriel, the nun assigned to care for him, proved to be a very good nurse. "He lingered," wrote Thompson, "a long time but gradually grew better, and in the course of the winter he was enabled to go about the alleys and passages on crutches, and at length he was able to throw them aside, and do without. This nun was exceedingly attentive, and it was chiefly to her attentions to him, that he got better of his wounds."

When orders came for the army to prepare to march, Wilson joined hundreds of other invalids and convalescents who refused to remain behind. "Altho' not quite reinstated in his health," Thompson continued, "[Wilson] thought himself bound to go out with his Company, in order to avoid being considered as a skulker, a stain which he would not, on any account, allow to rest upon his character."

Sister Sainte-Gabriel, "a fine, comely-looking, young woman as I'd wish to see," was not at all pleased to see her patient marching off to war. "She became very much distress'd, and was taken with violent fits, which was observ'd by the other nuns of the Convent; but no particular notice was taken of the circumstances, because, as she had had the particular care of him her uneasiness of mind was considered as the natural consequence of his having recover'd through her means." Wilson set off regardless, promising to return in the evening. His nurse "immediately became inconsolable."[1]

Thompson himself had his own concerns that morning. Born in 1733 in Tain, Scotland, his later life suggests that he received training as an engineer before a lack of opportunities at home led him to seek his fortune as a sergeant of Fraser's Highlanders in 1757. Although a cousin serving as a captain in that regiment died at Louisbourg before he could fulfill a promise to get Thompson a commission, Thompson remained a sergeant and lived to become the senior British engineer at Quebec, the last survivor of Wolfe and Murray's army, and a celebrated raconteur. His son, another James Thompson, made a written record of Thompson's anecdotes, thereby preserving a unique account of the Seven Years' War in Canada.[2]

But on the morning of 28 April, Thompson was not thinking of posterity. For him, the day began with a meagre breakfast and a fatalistic conversation. "Before the sortie, I took a biscuit and spread a bit of butter over it, and I set about 'cranching.'"

Between "cranches" he told his friend, Hector Munro, a former carpenter, "You had better do as I am doing, for you cannot know when you may be able to get your next meal."

"I will not touch anything," replied Munro. "I have already taken my last meal, for something tells me that I shall never require another in this world."

"Toot man," said Thompson, "you are talking nonsense, take a biscuit I tell you."

Munro refused again. Very soon, continued Thompson, "the hour came for parading, and we were soon after march'd out of the Garrison." Thompson checked the time. It was "at seven in the morning—and cold and raw enough it was!"[3]

Henry Hamilton, on the other hand, was mostly concerned with missing breakfast. Hamilton, born in Ireland around 1734, had grown up in a non-military family and received a classical education. Nonetheless, when Britain declared war on France in 1755, he had joined the 15th Regiment as an ensign and been promoted to lieutenant in 1756. Sailing with his regiment to North America, he had taken part in the sieges of Louisbourg and Quebec. Yet throughout a military career that lasted until 1775, Hamilton remained a civilian in uniform who never quite became a professional soldier. He wrote his memoirs in 1792 while serving as governor of Bermuda.[4]

On the morning of 28 April, Hamilton appears to have overslept. In his memoirs, he commented at length on the apparent absence of an opportunity to feed his soldiers and, incidentally, himself. "I cannot recollect any order of the preceding day for the troops taking their breakfast repast before they took their arms—yet it will appear that they were designed for action whether under arms or with their entrenching tools... for my own part my preparative was a piece of bread crammed into my pocket which I think I did not touch till 2 p.m."[5]

Following these encounters, the convalescent Wilson, placid Thompson, fatalistic Munro, and hungry Hamilton mustered with the rest of Murray's army on the Place d'Armes (parade square) in front of the Château Saint-Louis. As well as a musket, every soldier carried an entrenching tool, either a spade or a pickaxe.

Around 9:00 a.m., the troops began to march. They intended, recalled Ensign Désbruyêres of the 35th, "to possess the heights of Abraham [the Buttes-à-Neveu] & there to intrench themselves."[6]

JAMES MURRAY'S ARMY

The army that marched off the Place d'Armes that morning was not the same as the one that had taken possession of the city in 1759. Sergeant John Johnson of the 58th Regiment provides an eloquent description of the state to which the troops had been reduced over the winter "through the hardness of their duty, the severity of the weather, and the want of provisions and nourishment."

By the morning of the twenty-eighth, he recounted that "any man, who was the least acquainted with the duty we were going upon, would have shuddered at the sight... [of] such a poor pitiful handful of have [sic] starved, scorbutic skeletons; many of who had laid by their crutches on the occasion;

and would not be prevailed on to stay behind, although many of them were absolutely forbidden, and would not be suffered to fall in the ranks with the men; and who followed us out of the gates in the rear, and fell in when we formed the line of Battel."[7]

Healthy or not—and Thompson remarked that "scarcely a man in the garrison but was afflicted with Colds or Coughs"—as they marched off the parade square, the troops split into two columns.[8] One left the city through the Porte Saint-Louis, the second through the Porte Saint-Jean. An advance guard marched ahead of each column: light infantry on the Chemin Sainte-Foy and American rangers, commanded by Captain Moses Hazen, and a company of volunteers, recruited from the regular infantry battalions of the garrison and led by Captain Donald Macdonell, on the Grande-Allée. Behind them came the main body of each column, in total ten battalions strong, along with two twelve-pounders, sixteen six-pounders, and two howitzers. In all, Murray's force that morning totalled about 4,400 troops, 1,500 of whom had, like Wilson, come straight from Quebec's hospitals.[9]

The presence of so many guns was significant. With much of his army composed of invalids and convalescents, Murray's infantry couldn't face the French alone. So he brought along all the field guns he could muster to even the odds. This limited the mobility of his force, but greatly increased its firepower.

THE BUTTES-À-NEVEU

A few hundred metres down the roads, the two British columns reached the Buttes-à-Neveu, which Thompson described as "the high ground that crosses the Plains of Abraham."[10] The Chemin Sainte-Foy column passed north of the high ground; the Grande-Allée column followed the road up and over the east side of the buttes. At about this time the light infantry opened fire on what they believed to be a party of French scouts down in the Saint-Charles valley in the bush near the Hôpital Général.[11]

The British battalions moved up onto the buttes behind the advance guards without breaking stride. To Richard Humphreys, a light infantry private, it seemed that Murray planned to deploy his battalions there, "forming them on the heights of Abraham in order of battle."[12]

Lieutenant Malcolm Fraser of Fraser's Highlanders approved. Holding this terrain, he wrote, would give Murray: . . . all the advantage he could desire with such an inferior Army and where, if the Enemy ventured to attack him he could use his artillery, on which was his chief dependence, to the best purpose: having a rising ground, whereon he might form his army and plant his cannon, so as to play on the enemy as they advanced for about four hundred or five hundred yards with round shot, and when they came within a proper distance the grape shot must have cut them to pieces.[13]

Moreover, by occupying the high ground between the plains and the city, Murray could keep the French at arm's length, preventing them from establishing batteries to batter the walls of Quebec. If Lévis attempted to dislodge him, the French would be forced to advance uphill over rough terrain to reach the British line.

RESTORING HONOUR; RECOVERING QUEBEC

On the other side of the plains, Lévis and his party had reached the North and South Hills. "Crossing over the hills," wrote Lévis in the third person, "he noticed a large column of the enemy coming out of the city."[14]

Lévis hadn't planned to fight that day, but if the British chose to offer battle, he was more than willing to oblige. Almost every soldier in his army would likely have agreed with him. This wasn't a battle the French had come to fight, but it was a battle they desperately wanted—and wanted to win.

The Battle of the Plains of Abraham had been a savage humiliation for the French regular battalions. They had fled in panic, lost their general, been saved by the Canadian militia and Amerindian warriors, and ultimately abandoned Quebec. Malartic, who had been on the field that morning with the Béarn regiment, caught the mood exactly when he wrote in a letter that 13 September 1759 was "a day that I'd like to forget for the rest of my life."[15]

Bourlamaque, the recipient of that letter, had made his own feelings clear in a report to Lévis on the feasibility of undertaking a winter offensive against Quebec. A victory at Quebec would "wipe away the shame of a campaign whose memory we must erase, if that's possible."[16]

The Canadians, for their part, very much wanted their colonial capital back and the British expelled from Canada for good. James Johnstone, Montcalm's former aide-de-camp, took note over the winter of how "the Canadians... remained determined to save their country and never lost hope... They did nothing during the winter but make preposterous, impossible plans for taking back the city. No country was ever this childish, ridiculous, and crazy. Everyone got involved, even the Bishop and his priests made their plans, which were as completely lacking in common sense as all the others."[17]

At the Hôpital Général, Marie de la Visitation spoke of how Canadians in the Quebec area continually manifested "the desire to take back this country" and "joined our flying camps whenever they could." As the French army approached Quebec, she added, there were women who not only "painted pictures in their mind of sieges," but imagined themselves as heroes "who, without mortars or cannon, took the city by assault."[18]

Lévis may or may not have shared this enthusiasm, but he didn't waste any time. He sent his adjutant general, Lieutenant Colonel Pierre-André Gohin de Montreuil, to the Chemin Sainte-Foy to speed up the battalions, and he ordered Bourlamaque to hold his ground. "My advanced guard," recalled Bourlamaque, "was placed in the Dumont house and on the hills on this side of the Buttes-à-Neveu with the right [south] occupying a redoubt in the woods."[19] He retained five companies of grenadiers at Dumont's house and mill and sent the remainder to North and South Hill.[20]

Lapause had a special assignment. "He [Lévis] ordered me to form up the army as it arrived, posting the right [south] on the small hills behind the grenadier companies and the left [north] at the [Dumont] house. Our three small field guns were taken to the hills on the right."[21]

MURRAY'S DECISION

"When we were about three quarters of a mile out of Town," wrote Malcolm Fraser, "the General ordered the whole to draw up in line of battle, two deep, and take up as much room as possible."

The marching columns came to a halt at the western edge of the Buttes-à-Neveu and began to deploy into linear formations. The troops were still carrying their entrenching tools, and it appeared for a moment as if they would spend the rest of the day constructing fieldworks and waiting for the French to come to them. Then everything changed.

As the leading soldiers in Murray's columns reached the top of the slope leading down to the plains, they caught their first glimpses of Lévis' army. "We saw," continued Fraser, "the advanced parties of the Enemy nigh the woods, about half a league distant from us."[22]

Murray made a snap decision. "Whilst the line was forming I reconnoitred

the enemy, and perceived they had begun to throw up some redoubts, tho'
the greater part of their army was on the march. I thought this was the lucky
moment."[23]

Rather than waiting on the buttes through hours, days, or even weeks of
sparring before the French made their move, Murray would act decisively
and "attack them before they had formed," smashing each unit of Lévis' army
as it came onto the field. The next battle for Canada would begin on that day
at that hour.[24]

"We received," wrote Ensign John Désbruyêres of the 35th Regiment,
"orders to quitt ye eminence & advance into ye plain."[25]

WINTER VICTORIES

If a burning desire for professional redemption inspired the French regulars, their British counterparts displayed supreme self-confidence. Scurvy
and hardship had broken the bodies of Murray's troops. But their spirits and
fighting abilities remained very much intact. Over the winter, the Quebec
garrison had secured an unbroken string of small but satisfying victories over
detachments of Canadian militia and Seven Nations warriors. They took
immense pride in beating the irregulars at their own game and dominating
the farms and forests of the Government of Quebec.

Referring to the winter engagements, Désbruyêres declared that "Our
constant success & the facility wth which we obtained them naturally wou'd
create in us a contempt for ye enemy & raise our confidence."[26]

Knox shared this opinion, evaluating the British army as "weak in point
of numbers, but powerful in every other respect; and having an enemy to
encounter, who, by frequent experience and repeated trials, were unaccus-
tomed to stand long before us."[27] As for Murray himself, in a letter to Amherst
he spoke of "the superiority these troops had acquired over the enemy ever
since the last campaign."[28] Writing to William Pitt, he assured the prime
minister that "our little army was in the habit of beating the enemy."[29]

Sergeant Johnson, as was frequently the case, said much the same thing
at greater length.

By this time [October] our small reconnoitring detachments began to
appear terrible among the skulking parties of Canadians and Indians; they
would never dare to face them in an open plain; although very often they

would be greatly superior in number; at our approach they would always betake themselves within the skirts of the wood and lye concealed behind the trees and bushes till we were within their reach, and then suddenly fire upon us, and rush out upon us before we would be prepared to receive them; and very often would beset us round about, and do us considerable damage before we were aware of them; till at length, they learned us to be as good hunters as themselves, and very often, a small number of our men, would put to flight a considerable party of those cannibals.[30]

CHAPTER 15

MURRAY'S ADVANCE GUARD

THE LIGHT INFANTRY AT DUMONT'S MILL

As Murray commanded his battalions into motion, his light infantry (troops that had been trained for skirmishing and scouting) lunged ahead towards Dumont's Mill and South Hill, the key terrain features on the north and south sides of the battlefield.

James Johnstone was not present at Sainte-Foy. But he had plenty of friends on the field that day who provided him with enough details to compose a dramatic account of the attack on Dumont's house. He mistakenly declares that the British attackers were entirely composed of Highlanders, but he nonetheless captures something of the desperate quality of the action inside the house. "The battle began with an attack on a house between their right flank and our left, sustained for a long time with ferocity and stubbornness by five companies of grenadiers against as many Scottish highlanders... The grenadiers and highlanders, alternately in possession of that house... [and] each worthy of the other, were no sooner forced out the windows than they returned to the charge and forced their way in through the doors."[1]

Lapause, an eyewitness, provides a more concise account. "The enemy was stopped at the door of the house they were attacking; our grenadiers held out for a long time but were finally compelled to give way in the face of superior numbers."[2]

The death of Pierre de LaRonde

Once they had captured the house and mill, the light infantry charged after the retreating French grenadiers down the Chemin Sainte-Foy. The French fled before them, exposing Lévis' northern flank.

Philippe Aubert de Gaspé, a nineteenth-century Canadian novelist, heard about one incident of this retreat from a participant.

> I was crossing [the Sainte-Foy battlefield, near Dumont's Mill] with my uncle [François] Baby, when he stopped the carriage and said to me:
>
> —You see that stream that flows northward; well, right there, during the battle in 1760, on these plains, lay Monsieur [Captain Pierre-François Paul Denys] de LaRonde [commanding a grenadier company of the troupes de la marine], a brave officer, mortally wounded. We were retreating very quickly, riddled with English grapeshot... when I passed near that officer. He said to me "A drink! My dear young fellow, I beg of you." I pretended not to hear. The enemy was firing a hellish fusillade at us, and if I had stopped to give him a drink, an instant later I would very likely have needed the same service from my friends.

Another uncle, Charles-Louis Tarieu de La Naudière, confirmed Baby's story and added some details. La Naudière, who had graduated from the Séminaire de Québec in 1756 and joined the La Sarre regiment, was just seventeen years old at the time of the battle. "I was repeating," wrote Gaspé, "the story of Monsieur LaRonde to my uncle Lanaudière when he said to me... Indeed, our poor cousin LaRonde was mortally wounded near Dumont's Mill, while repeating, they say, something he often said, even amid the carnage [of battle]. 'Ah! People are insane!' [Ah! Que les hommes sont insensés!] He was a gentle, sensitive man, but very brave on all occasions, and honour alone brought him into battle."[3]

The British take South Hill

While the British light infantry and French grenadiers turned Dumont's quiet establishment into a battleground, off to the south, Hazen's Rangers, a company of American rangers commanded by Captain Moses Hazen, a veteran of Rogers' Rangers, passed between South Hill and the edge of the Quebec

Promontory and took up position on the Foulon Road where it entered Sillery Wood.[4] Macdonell's Volunteers, supported by the grenadiers of the 28th Regiment, stormed the South Hill redoubts.

Macdonell, wrote Thompson, "rush'd forward to the attack of a small Redoubt, which he entered, and from which he drove away the French, many of whom were cut to pieces."[5] Lashed by cannon fire and under assault by elite regulars, the French grenadiers withdrew behind the tree line. The Volunteers raced after them, down the side of South Hill and into Sillery Wood.

In the centre, on North Hill, wrote Knox, the French, "seeing their right and left give way, fled without firing a shot."[6]

CHAPTER 16

LINES AND COLUMNS

ADVANCING IN LINE

The success of Murray's advance turned on seizing a crucial moment of French vulnerability. Everything depended on speed. Murray needed to move from the Buttes-à-Neveu to the west side of the plains faster than Lévis' battalions could arrive on the field and form up. If he won this race, Murray stood a good chance of destroying the French army, raising the siege of Quebec before it began, and effectively ending the war in North America that morning.

There was just one problem. Not only did Murray's troops need to arrive first—they needed to arrive ready to fight.

To make maximum use of the firepower of the flintlock musket, armies needed to deploy in line to form a double or triple row of troops that allowed every soldier in a company or battalion to fire simultaneously. The result would be a deadly cloud of musket balls, slashing across the field. Arriving ready to fight meant more than just being first onto the battlefield; it meant advancing into contact with the enemy with one's own troops formed into a cohesive battle line, ready to fire—a difficult and potentially dangerous operation, especially in the presence of a capable enemy.

When Montcalm performed the same manoeuvre in 1759 and moved down off the buttes to attack Wolfe's army on the plains, the results were catastrophic. "Our troops," a Canadian officer later lamented, "fell recklessly upon the enemy, but their poorly formed ranks broke very soon, partly because of their speed, partly because of the rough ground."[1] "We hadn't gone twenty steps," added Malartic, "before the left was too far behind and the centre too far in front."[2] Montcalm quickly lost control of his troops, who engaged Wolfe's line more as a disorganized crowd than a cohesive, coordinated army, and who were quickly broken by disciplined volley fire from the well-formed British ranks.

To avoid Montcalm's fate, Murray needed to keep his army together, trading speed for coherence. When his army came within musket shot—about thirty metres—of the French, it would be in perfect formation, under control, and ready to fight.

In Murray's account, everything happened at once: "I thought this was the lucky moment, and marched with the utmost order to attack them before they had formed."[3]

On the ground, however, marching "in the utmost order" meant making a slow, methodical advance. Fraser provides the most detailed description. "Soon thereafter, he ordered the men to throw down the intrenching tools, and the whole army to advance slowly, dressing by the right."[4]

From the Buttes-à-Neveu, continued Fraser, "we advanced, about one hundred paces, when the cannonading begun on our side, and we observed the French advanced parties retiring, and their main body forming in order of battle at the edge of the wood, about three hundred paces distant, we continued cannonading and advancing for some time."[5]

Easier said than done. Abandoning the high ground of the Buttes-à-Neveu meant descending a rugged slope to a plain of fields and pastures separated by fences and hedges and largely covered by a layer of snow, slush, water, and ice. "In the course of the action," wrote Knox, "we were insensibly drawn down from our advantageous situation into low swampy ground, where our troops fought almost knee-deep in dissolving wreaths of snow and water, whence it was utterly impracticable to draw off our artillery under those unhappy circumstances."[6]

Under these conditions, any forward movement represented an achievement. To do so while holding formation in a line a thousand metres long, composed of infantry and artillery moving at different speeds, was altogether remarkable and unavoidably slow. Without constant pauses to maintain alignment—Fraser's "dressing by the right"—the troops on higher, drier, firmer patches would have moved faster, while those in wetter, softer, lower spaces would have lagged behind. Artillery caught in the mud and slush would have been out of action for the duration of the engagement. The officer of the 35th recorded that "our cannon were of no service to us, as we could not draw them through the soft ground & gullies of snow, near three feet deep."[7]

All this cost Murray time he couldn't afford. While the British made a slow, measured advance, dragging cannon and halting frequently to adjust their formation, Murray's "lucky minute" slipped away. With it went the chance to defeat the French battalions in detail as they arrived on the field.

MARCHING IN COLUMN

While the British traded speed for cohesion, the French accepted vulnerability in exchange for speed.

The British had a head start—as Murray's soldiers took their first steps down the slopes of the buttes, most of Lévis' forces were still in their overnight billets, from one to eight kilometres away. But Lévis moved fast to set his army into motion, riding back to the Chemin Sainte-Foy to personally hurry the troops.

And if the French started late, they moved more quickly. Compared to advancing in line, marching columns were fast and manoeuvrable, equally suited to heading down a road or moving cross-country. And as the British encountered fences, hedges, and other obstructions, the French marched up a road, muddy and treacherous, but free of obstacles.

As they approached the plains, French troops turned right off the Chemin Sainte-Foy, into Sillery Wood. When they reached the treeline, Bourlamaque and Lapause deployed them across the field. "He [Murray] advanced slowly," wrote Bourlamaque. "I had time to arrange three brigades in line."[8]

But just as advancing in line slowed the British, arriving in column and forming on the field carried a price for the French. To fight most effectively, the French regulars, like their British counterparts, needed to deploy from column into line, even as Murray's cannon and howitzers flung shot and shell across the field. "Our brigades," wrote Malartic, "formed under the fire of this artillery, which did not prevent some of them from forming into line and others remaining in column, waiting until the terrain permitted them to deploy."[9]

The French, however, were not entirely helpless. The regulars needed to

form in line to fight. The Canadians did not. While their professional comrades arranged themselves in linear formation, the militia could take cover
and open fire immediately. Malartic, describing the overall performance
of the militia, declared that "the Canadians... who were in the intervals
between or in front of the brigades fired for a long time and very well. They
inflicted many casualties on the English."[10]

ARTILLERY VS. INFANTRY

The Battle of the Plains of Abraham had been a battle between formations of
infantry. At Sainte-Foy, it was also a battle of French infantry against British artillery.

French infantry, like their British counterparts, carried flintlock muskets.
France's *fusil d'infanterie* fired a slightly smaller ball than Britain's Land Pat-
tern muskets. Other than that, these weapons were virtually identical in construction and performance.

Fired at ranges under about thirty metres, flintlock muskets were deadly,
accurate weapons. Experiments in the 1830s demonstrated that a musket
ball fired at that range, which would have been moving at about 3.5 metres
per second, could penetrate one centimetre of sheet iron. Loading a musket
meant tearing cartridges apart, pouring a pinch of powder into the priming
pan and the rest down the barrel, adding the cartridge paper and musket
ball, using the ramrod to shove everything into place, presenting the weapon,
aiming, firing, then doing it all again. On the drill field, a trained soldier
could load and fire a musket in about twenty seconds. On the battlefield, it
could take well over a minute.[11]

Murray's artillery consisted of cannon and howitzers. Howitzers, like
mortars, fired shells on a high, arcing trajectory. These shells were hollow
iron spheres, packed with gunpowder. When a shell exploded, the force of
the explosion shattered the sphere, converting it into a spray of lethal frag-
ments that could wound or kill people up to fifteen metres away, although the
effective blast radius was much smaller.[12]

In contrast, cannon fired solid shot or tin case-shot on a reasonably flat
trajectory, inflicting damage by converting the chemical energy of gunpowder into the kinetic energy of an iron projectile hurtling through the air
until it landed harmlessly or struck a human target.

Cannonballs from a six-pounder cannon—the most common gun on the

Sainte-Foy battlefield—left the muzzle at a velocity of 475 metres per second and could blow through fifteen centimetres of stone or thirty centimetres of timber at a hundred paces.[13] Any soldier struck by a cannonball could count on being severely wounded or killed.

As an anti-personnel weapon, however, roundshot had its limits. A six-pound shot at any distance from point-blank range up to its effective range of about 640 metres had a killing zone 8.89 centimetres wide, the width of the cannonball itself.[14] Fired into a three-rank battle line, it could at best kill two or three people, if they were standing one behind the other.

Given that it took far less than a cannonball to kill a human, when the range closed to about 275 metres, gunners switched from solid shot to firing larger numbers of smaller projectiles, packed into a tinned metal cylinder that disintegrated as it left the muzzle, releasing the shot in an expanding cone.[15] Combatants at Sainte-Foy generally referred to these munitions as "grape-shot," a generic term for multiple small projectiles that were formally known as tin case-shot, tin case grapeshot, or canister.[16]

Firing almost the same weight of tin case-shot from the same six-pounder gun (the case holding the shot weighed a little over a pound) in the form of fifty-five 1.5-ounce musket balls opened the killing zone into a wide fan, ten metres across at ninety metres' distance. A single blast of tin case-shot from a six-pounder could, in theory, kill twenty-seven people when fired against troops in line.[17]

When Murray formed his battle line, he deployed his guns in a chain stretching almost all the way across the Quebec Promontory, with infantry battalions in the intervals between them.[18] In action, while Murray's artillery poured cannonballs, grapeshot, and shells into Lévis' army, the infantry pinned the French in position and protected the guns.

BRITISH CANNON; FRENCH MUSKETS

So it is not surprising that the vicissitudes of the British half trudging, half wading through snow, water, slush, and mud were not apparent to the French. Instead, they saw before them a red-coated juggernaut composed of ten veteran battalions, twenty guns, and two howitzers that swept across the plains, firing blasts of grapeshot as they went. The result was an encounter between twenty giant shotguns firing grapeshot at ranges as short as thirty metres and thousands of French regulars and Canadian militia armed with muskets.

Flailed by grapeshot, roundshot, and howitzer shells, the French line at times came close to breaking. Captain Benoît-François Bernier, the French commissaire ordonnateur des guerres (quartermaster general) watched as "our troops endured several volleys of grape shot at musket range, which threw them into disorder."[19]

THE BRITISH AND THEIR GUNS

The British were just as aware as the French of the impact of their guns. Malcolm Fraser spoke of Murray's "artillery, on which was his chief dependence." "Our field-pieces," wrote Knox, "were exceedingly well served, and did amazing execution." Sergeant Johnson of the 58th shared this opinion. "All the while we maintained the fire of our artillery, they dared not face us on the open plain; but pressed themselves into the skirts of the wood in their rear." Henry Hamilton, who had a chance to see the wounded of both sides after the battle, noted that "the wounds of the French particularly were serious being chiefly from grape shot."[20]

Yet French, Canadian, and Seven Nations muskets could be just as dangerous as British grapeshot. "When they [the French] first appear'd, out of the cover. . ." noted James Miller of the 15th Regiment, posted just south of the Chemin Sainte-Foy, "every shot of ours told." The French returned fire, but for the 15th, at least, this hardly mattered. "At first we were drawn up in a hollow, with a height in front, on which the enemy's [musket] balls struck, and flew over our heads."

This advantage, however, didn't last. James Miller continued:

When we repulsed the enemy in our front, we unfortunately advanced, which gave them an opportunity of cutting us up, they being up under cover, and taking aim at leisure, while we could only see them, through the intervals of the trees. In short, in half an hour, ten officers, from twenty, were dropped, twelve sergeants, from twenty four, and near two hundred rank and file, from less than four hundred in the field! The corps was broken, and retreated to their former ground ["in a hollow"], happy would it have been, had they never left it.[21]

At the south end of the British line, James Thompson had a more personal encounter with the power of French musketry.

Thompson came to the battle as the covering sergeant (a sergeant serving as a personal bodyguard for his company commander, who stood behind that officer, ready to defend him against attack), a position of particular trust and responsibility. Through no fault of Thompson's, this did not turn out well. Early in the action with the French . . ." he wrote, "[Captain Alexander] Fraser received a shot in the Temple, which fell'd him to the very spot on which he stood at the instant, and, as not an inch of ground was to be lost, I had to move up into line, which I could not have done without my resting one foot upon his body!"

Standing on the body of the officer he had been ordered to defend cannot have been a pleasant experience for Thompson, but he joined his comrades as they continued to fire into the French line.[22] At some point during the day, Thompson's friend Sergeant Wilson was killed in action.[23]

BATTLE LINES

As the firefight reached its peak, roughly 2,000 British regulars and 4,000 French regulars, Canadian militia, and Seven Nations warriors were shooting at one another. The 28th Regiment was on South Hill, Fraser's Highlanders occupied the ground between South Hill and North Hill, the 47th held North Hill, and the 2/60th (the second battalion of the 60th Regiment), 43rd, 15th, and 58th stood between North Hill and Dumont's Mill. The 35th and 3/60th remained in reserve behind the British line. Farther back, one hundred troops occupied the redoubt on Wolfe's Hill, recorded Fraser, "to cover our retreat in case of necessity."[24]

On the other side of the field, the Royal Roussillon brigade (the Royal Roussillon and Guyenne regiments) formed the south end of the French line. Holding the centre were the Berry brigade (the first and second battalions of the Berry regiment) and the Marine brigade (the first and second battalions of the troupes de la marine), together with the five companies of grenadiers that had been pushed off North and South Hills and the Montreal militia battalion. The La Sarre brigade (La Sarre and Béarn regiments) was on the Chemin Sainte-Foy, moving up to occupy the north end of the line. The La Reine brigade (the La Reine and Languedoc regiments) remained behind the army inside the forest, held in reserve with the cavalry.[25] The Seven Nations contingent was towards the south end of the French line, inside Sillery Wood.

JAMES MURRAY IN ACTION

Thompson's misfortune and the ordeal of the 15th notwithstanding, everything seemed to be going well for Murray.

He outlined his actions during the battle by posing and answering a rhetorical question in a letter to his brother George. "Where was the general in this battle?—Betwixt his own line and that of the enemy—everywhere, where the enemy made a push animating his men, by his presence. He had two horses shot under him, and his cloaths riddled by the enemy's musketry."[26]

When the 47th Regiment seized North Hill, Murray was right there with three six-pounders. Immediately the hill was secure, wrote Sergeant Johnson, Murray occupied himself "placing the cannon on the heights, in the centre," directly in front of the infantry.[27]

This must have been a good moment for Murray. Perhaps an hour after he had led the march out through the gates of Quebec, he owned the Plains of Abraham. His advance guard had occupied South Hill, North Hill, and Dumont's house and mill; his battalions held the intervening ground; his soldiers and artillery were hammering their opponents. If Murray had known what Lévis was planning to do next, he might have felt even better.

CHAPTER 17

THE FRENCH HIT BACK

PLANNING TO RETREAT

Partway through the firefight, Lévis realized that he was losing the battle.

The "two leading brigades," the Royal Roussillon and Berry brigades of the French army, he wrote, "were further forward than he had ordered. Under attack by the entire enemy army, they were being cut to pieces. He [Lévis] could not support them with the other brigades which were still on their way."[1]

Farther back, the troops of the La Sarre brigade, marching up the Chemin Sainte-Foy, had their own problems. A map of the battlefield from the Lévis Papers notes that the road was "hammered by enemy artillery as the French advanced against the English army, which was already formed in order of battle."[2]

Anticipating that Murray would overwhelm his leading brigades before La Sarre and Béarn could arrive, Lévis reacted quickly and decisively. "As the enemy continued to advance, I . . . [sent orders to withdraw] back to the border of the wood to give the rest of the army time to [arrive and] form up, and to await the Natives."[3]

This was a supremely rational decision. Instead of standing and fighting with part of an army that had never quite managed to shake itself into order, Lévis would pull back, put some space between his forces and the devastating British artillery, and get everyone in place and everything under control.

Then, once he had done what he could to stack the odds in his favour, he would move against Murray with every combatant in his command.

Murray had marched off one natural fortress, the Buttes-à-Neveu; Lévis took advantage of another, Sillery Wood. Characterized by Bourlamaque as "impenetrable,"[4] the forest was dense enough to pose a barrier to troops advancing in formation and to drastically limit the effectiveness of artillery, but open enough to allow free movement to the French. The Canadians and Seven Nations, moreover, could be employed to maximum advantage among the trees.

If everything had gone reasonably well, this manoeuvre might very well have won Lévis a brilliant victory. But it never happened. "The courage of the troops," he confessed, "didn't give him enough time [to implement his plan]."[5] While Lévis, as commanding general, attempted to impose his will upon events, his subordinates took their own decisions and translated them into actions that dictated the course of the battle.

THE MILITIA AND THE GRENADIERS

The French situation was desperate all along the line, but nowhere more so than on the Chemin Sainte-Foy. Under heavy and continuous attack from four field guns clustered just south of the mill, firing straight down the road,[6] as well as the elite light infantry that had captured Dumont's house and mill, the French north flank hovered on the brink of collapse.

Here, the French found themselves trapped in a narrow stretch of open country between Sillery Wood and the cliff, "unable," wrote Bourlamaque, "to occupy the woods which were covered in snow and a marsh whose water was up to our waists."

Bourlamaque himself had just been seriously wounded. Writing to Bougainville after the battle, he reported that "as I retreated with the grenadiers... I was hit by a cannonball that killed your horse [which Bourlamaque had evidently borrowed] and tore off part of the flesh of my leg."[7] His soldiers carried their fallen brigadier to a field hospital.

No single officer replaced Bourlamaque in command. With the grenadiers retreating, the Béarn and La Sarre battalions advancing, and British fire continuing, the only control over the troops came from their own inclinations and whatever officer or non-commissioned officer happened to be near a group of soldiers who were willing to listen to him. The troops, wrote Lévis, "which were not in formation, wavered under the most murderous artillery and musket fire."[8]

But if the French were in trouble, they were a long way from defeat. As the British light infantry charged down the Chemin Sainte-Foy, the Montreal militia battalion opened fire from south of the road. "The determination and the fusillade" of the Montrealers, wrote Vaudreuil, "slowed down the enemy's close pursuit of our left... and gave it the chance to rally and strike back."[9]

Malartic, then serving as the major of the La Sarre brigade, had not been fond of Canadians. Following the Battle of the Plains of Abraham, he had bitterly criticized the militia that had been incorporated into Béarn for disrupting his regiment's formation. "The Canadians of the second rank... fired without any order," then lay down to reload while the regulars pressed ahead.[10] Now, he sung their praises. "We took particular notice of the Canadians of Montreal... who saved the grenadiers who had been stationed at the Dumont mill."[11]

Marie de la Visitation, reporting from the sidelines, presented a version of this incident as it was understood by Canada's non-combatants. "Most of our army was still a half-league away from the place where the first shots were fired. Our troupes de la marine and militia, more familiar with the roads [than the French] arrived in time to support a regiment that was being cut to pieces rather than retreat."[12]

All in all, the Montreal militia battalion, which had missed the Battle of the Plains of Abraham when Montcalm ordered a charge before they reached the field, performed very well at Sainte-Foy. Vaudreuil wrote of Louis Legardeur de Repentigny, a captain in the troupes de la marine, that:

M. de Repentigny, who led the reserve militia battalion from Montreal... occupied the open ground [north of North Hill] at the centre of the army with just his brigade. They managed to stop the enemy center, which was rapidly advancing, and forced it to pull back to its original position. This brigade also threw back two attempts by troops detached from the [British] right to force them off their ground... Finally, that brigade was the only one that never gave an inch of ground to the enemy.[13]

COUNTERATTACK

As the British faltered, the French regulars, protected by Canadian gunfire, bounced back. "In spite of everything," wrote Malartic, "our army continued to advance. The left [north] wing formed by the La Sarre brigade marched forward without firing, although very badly hurt by the English grape shot."

At this point Lapause arrived on the scene, bearing orders from Lévis to pull off the Chemin Sainte-Foy and fall back. The first officer he met was Malartic, who received this command without any great enthusiasm. "Very distressed by this order, [I] went to the detachment from Béarn that formed the right of the brigade, to command them to make a half-turn to the right."

Malartic gave the order; no one obeyed. Captain Jean-Pierre Bachoué de Barraute of Béarn, who Malartic described as a "distinguished captain," refused outright. "Major," he replied, "if we make a half-turn to the right, the enemy will follow us and they will beat us. Charge them without firing [with fixed bayonets] and we will beat them." Unable to compel the troops to withdraw, Malartic did the next best thing. He "moved fifteen paces out in front so that the brigade could see that they had to advance."[14]

Battles are chaotic events. As Malartic joined the counterattack, he had an encounter, which demonstrated, in his words, "how easy it can be for soldiers to lose track of their commanders during an action."[15] In this case, the officer in question was Lieutenant Colonel Jean d'Alquier de Serrian of Béarn, commanding the La Sarre brigade. Johnstone considered d'Alquier to be "a veteran officer, steady and intrepid."[16] But the lieutenant colonel had detractors as well as admirers, including a captain "who didn't like this commander [and] came to tell me [Malartic] that he [d'Alquier] wasn't at his post."

A moment later, d'Alquier appeared out of nowhere. Ignoring the captain, he addressed Malartic. "Major, I take full responsibility for contradicting the general's order. We should take advantage of the spirit of our troops. Don't fire, fall upon the enemy with the bayonet, and we'll defeat them."[17]

After that, he shouted to the soldiers around him. "When you're twenty steps from the enemy, it's no time to retreat. Fix bayonets and charge the enemy, that's the way to win." Instead of retiring, wrote Johnstone, "he charged the enemy with headlong recklessness."[18]

François Baby saw this episode from another viewpoint. "We reformed our ranks again behind some trees, whose remains you can see, and attacked the position for the third time with the bayonet. We overwhelmed the enemy, and never abandoned the mill again except to pursue the enemy [fleeing in] disorder.[19]

When Lévis made his way to the north flank and met up with d'Alquier, he found the situation under control. A breakdown in command had been averted, and the French forces along the Sainte-Foy road were all working together under d'Alquier's orders, pushing hard against the British. Malartic summarized Lévis' side of the conversation. "By [ignoring orders and] not making a half-turn to the right [into Sillery Wood], you have performed the greatest possible service for the King. Hold on for five minutes and I will give you a victory."[20]

THE LIGHT INFANTRY BREAKS

Taking Dumont's house and mill had been a brutal ordeal for the British light infantry. Many officers, including their commander, were wounded. Their absence, combined with the chaotic confusion of a hard-fought action, led to a total breakdown of discipline. Instead of holding the house and mill and waiting for support, the light infantry had charged up the Sainte-Foy road until the Montreal battalion opened fire.[21]

Henry Hamilton related what happened next, as seen from the 15th Regiment, just south of the Chemin Sainte-Foy. "The attack on our right attracted our attention when the Light Infantry under Dalling acted like Englishmen, & the French grenadiers, with that spirit courage & generous order they have been so often signalized for, did wonders, they attacked [and] were expulsed, [the French] returned to the charge, bayoncts & knives were employed, the windows of the house and mill occupied by the English were stormed, numbers prevailed."[22]

Outnumbered, outfought, and leaderless, the light infantry had endured just about all they could take. They broke and fled, running eastward past the mill towards the British main body. Their flight didn't just lead to the loss of the house and mill to the French. It placed them between the French and the British artillery and infantry of Murray's north wing, four battalions and seven guns commanded by brigadier Ralph Burton.

There, they screened the French from Burton's artillery and got in the way of his battalions. Their obstruction, wrote Murray, "prevented Colonel Burton from taking advantage of the first impression they had made on the enemys left flank." When the light infantry attempted to regroup and recapture the mill, he continued, "they were charged, thrown into confusion, retired to the rear, and could never again be brought up during the action."[23]

PUSHING PAST THE MILL

As the British wavered, the French kept up the pressure. British reinforcements pushed the French back from the mill; the French drove them off in their turn. More British reinforcements appeared; the fighting continued. The combat on the north flank was vicious and prolonged. Both sides suffered heavy casualties.

Ensign D'Ailleboust de Douglas took part in the battle as an acting lieutenant of grenadiers from the troupes de la marine. Reporting on his experiences that day, Douglas wrote that "I returned from that affair with a fifteenth of the company, after being struck by two bullets which did not prevent me from leading the glorious survivors to victory."[24]

Malartic, for his part, endured a deeply unpleasant encounter with British grapeshot.

> I was wounded by a grapeshot that hit me in the chest as I marched forward. The blow threw me down and knocked me out. When I regained consciousness a sergeant and a soldier . . . were trying to pick me up. I begged them to let me die right there. As they lifted me up regardless, I felt something cold slide over my stomach. I opened my vest, which had been torn. The lower part of my left chest was as big as a fist and very black. I found the bloody grapeshot below my stomach. I was placed in the hands of a surgeon who opened the bruise with a dozen cuts from a scalpel.[25]

D'Alquier too was seriously wounded, right at the moment of success. "He . . . captured their artillery," wrote Johnstone, "and at the same time took a bullet that went right through his body, already covered with scars, which did not stop him from continuing to give orders."[26]

The Canadians of the Montreal battalion, the grenadiers of the advanced guard, and the regulars and militia of the La Sarre brigade had saved the French north flank and turned the situation around. "The manoeuvre of the right [north]," wrote Lévis, "forced the English left to bend backwards."[27] Now it was the British who were in trouble.

CHAPTER 18

THE BRITISH FALTER

TROUBLE ON THE NORTH FLANK

"WHERE WAS HE WHEN the right wing falter'd?" asked Murray, posing another rhetorical question to his brother George. "He was placing the cannon on the heights, in the centre, but rode instantly to the right, and there recover'd the confusion."[1]

In his report to Amherst on 30 April, Murray went into more detail. "I no sooner perceived this disorder than I sent to Major [Rodger] Morris who commanded Otway's Regiment [the 35th] in the 2d line, to wheel to the right and support our right [north] flank."[2] He noted in particular that the British north had endured two successive attacks by the French, and that "on these occasions Captain [Charles] Ince with the grenadiers of Otway's were distinguished."[3]

COURT MARTIAL CLOSE-UP

At this point, the records of the British at the Battle of Sainte-Foy become, for a few brief moments, much more intimate. Following the battle, one officer of the 35th accused another, Lieutenant Eubule Ormsby, of hiding behind an ammunition cart when he should have been fighting. The result was a court martial, in which the witnesses spoke of their actions around Dumont's Mill on 28 April. The dry, formal sentences of their testimony provide a unique glimpse into the small details of an eighteenth-century battle, details that were generally ignored by writers of letters and journals.[4]

When Murray noticed British troops retreating on the north flank, he committed one of his reserve battalions to reinforce the threatened sector. "I carried," testified his aide-de-camp, Lieutenant Thomas Mills of the 47th Regiment, "an order from General Murray to the 35th Regiment to march up immediately, and cover the right wing of the army." Charles Ince's grenadier company received a special assignment. They were "to advance, and take possession of a mill in their front."

When Murray himself arrived on the scene, continued Mills,

> I left the Regiment and rid [sic] up to the front of the line, passed between Amherst's [the 15th], and the 48th, and went to Captain Ince, who, by this time, had got very near the Wind Mill, shewed him the Ground, went back, and passed thro' the company, which were crossing a little gully, that had thrown them into some disorder, and were forming as soon as they got over; there I saw Lieutenant Ormsby.[5]

When his turn came to testify, Ormsby described the grenadiers' advance, beginning with their arrival on the British north flank. "The situation our company was in, when we gave our first fire, was in a regular manner, the front rank kneeling, drawn up with the ravine just in our front, and I believe about 50, or 60 yards from the windmill, in which position we continued for a little time."

Next, Ormsby reported the grenadiers' progress towards Dumont's Mill:

> Captain Ince, perceiving that our fire had forced the enemy to withdraw from thence . . . called out loud to follow him, and he immediately crossed the ravine, by a little gap, upon the right, only by one, or at most two men a breast, as the path was very narrow; Therefore as my post was upon the left of the Company, and of course the last person that was to cross over, it is not improbable that Captain Ince, with the Right of the company, might have been at the wind mill, by the time I was crossing, after the left had got over.

Finally, he summarized his last conversation with Ince. "Captain Ince was wounded soon after we got to the wind mill, he immediately called for me, which upon my hearing went from the left, and when he was going off only said, 'My Dear Ormsby, keep what we have got.'"[6]

With Ince wounded, command of the company devolved on Ormsby, who struggled to exert control over an increasingly fragile situation. Even before Captain Ince was struck down, declared Lieutenant Weld, another grenadier officer, "we were a good deal broke."[7] Private John Maxwell agreed. "The Company, was in great confusion, and divided in several small bodies; I was with Lieutenant Ormsby, nigh the Mill."[8]

Private John Bennet also portrayed the company as dispersed in small clusters of troops rather than acting as a single unit. "I was not in Lieutenant Ormsby's platoon; the Company advanced in different bodies to the Mill, and I saw Lieutenant Ormsby there." Ormsby, he continued, "was behind the Wind Mill when I saw him; and the men were firing all around it."[9]

Private John Stone lost track of Ormsby during the advance but encountered him at the mill, directing fire against the French. "He [Ormsby] advanced with the Company to the Mill, pointed out to me, and ordered me to fire where he saw them stand very thick."[10] When Private John Maxwell became overexcited, Ormsby tried to calm him down. "I set up a kind of Indian Hollow [holler], and he ordered me to hold my tongue."[11]

Two other privates gave testimony highlighting the ability of individual soldiers to act independently on the battlefield.

Private Francis Naylor explained his late arrival at the mill. "I fired at the enemy, and lost my ammunition; while I was getting more [from an ammunition cart] the company advanced to the wind mill; I endeavoured to overtake them, and I saw Lieutenant Ormsby a little to one side in a ditch with his face to the enemy, but did not observe his position; this ditch was about one hundred yards of this side of the wind mill."[12] Private John Walsh, in response to a question from Ormsby, replied that "I remembered you ordered them to Fire, you was then [or "there"] before me, for I stopped a little behind to put in a flint."[13]

Private Joseph Scott's testimony portrays relations between officers and soldiers in the eighteenth century as a good deal more informal than one might expect. When he saw Ormsby near the mill, he declared, in response to a question from that officer, "the Engagement had began some time, and I was very much tired, I took out a little bottle to refresh myself, and offered it to you."[14]

With one company of grenadiers trying to hold off five companies of French grenadiers and an entire brigade of French soldiers and Canadian militia, the pressure quickly became too much. Lieutenant Weld, another grenadier officer, told the court that "We [Weld and Ormsby] retreated together with what men we could collect of the company."[15]

"When we were retreating," said Private Stone, "we met a piece of cannon, which Lieutenant Ormsby ordered me and some other men to assist in drawing off."[16] Unfortunately, added Weld, "the enemy pressed so close upon us, we were obliged to abandon it, and make the best of our way to town."[17]

The grenadiers of the 35th lost that particular gun, but Lieutenant Fraser of the 48th, serving with the artillery attached to his regiment, overflowed with praise for their conduct. "I cannot speak, as to any particular officer, but I know it was owing to the singular good behaviour of that company that the howitzer, and ammunition cart, I commanded, were not taken before the line retreated, and I told Lieutenant Ormsby, I should ever esteem them for it; I saw no bad behaviour in any Officer."[18]

As the British line teetered on the verge of collapse, Ince, wounded and helpless, tried to save himself. Lieutenant William Johnson of the Royal Artillery testified that "Captain Ince sent [word] to me twice, to desire he might be put in the ammunition carts, being wounded, and I sent him word he might; Just as this happened the line retreated, and I cannot say, whether he was carried to it, or not, but I have reason to think he was."[19]

Johnson was wrong. Ince had been abandoned. Thomas Wilkins, surgeon of the 35th, stopped for just long enough to examine the fallen officer, then went on his way. Asked if Ince had "received a wound upon a gun carriage," Wilkins replied that "Upon my finding out a contusion upon Captain Ince's leg, he told me he had received it upon a gun carriage, and repeated it several times."[20]

Wilkins' testimony, combined with Johnson's, was good news for Ormsby, since it allowed him to provide a plausible response to the charges against him. "I humbly submit it to the Court, whether it was or not more likely, it was Captain Ince [who] was behind the Carriage, as he was wounded; he had received but one wound before he was carried from me."[21]

The court accepted this explanation and returned an honourable acquittal, together with a sharp reprimand for Ormsby's accuser. "There is not the least foundation for the accusation, and . . . the aspersion upon said Lieutenant Ormsby is scandalous and infamous."[22] No one at the court martial showed any interest in what had happened to Ince, who had been left behind to an uncertain fate as the British north flank collapsed around him.

THE TROUPES DE LA MARINE AND BERRY REGIMENT ADVANCE

The La Sarre brigade's attack on the mill and the British north flank produced a chain reaction along the French north wing. First the Marine brigade, then the Berry brigade, wrote Lévis, "supported, with the greatest courage, the decisive movement of that brigade [La Sarre]." Of the four battalion commanders in the Marine and Berry brigades, only one escaped unwounded.[23]

The fighting there was so severe and waged at such close quarters that the British nearly seized the colours of one battalion of the troupes de la marine. Second Ensign Charles-François de l'Épervance later recounted how "I carried a flag, which led to my being cut twice in the hands."[24]

As the British north flank reeled backwards and their centre came under attack, Lévis turned his attention to the southern side of the battlefield. He "ordered the five companies of grenadiers on the right [which had been deployed at the onset of the battle on North and South Hills] to march against the redoubts that were on the hills the enemy had occupied."[25]

PRESSURE ON THE SOUTH FLANK

Macdonell's charge into Sillery Wood had not ended well for his Volunteers. Pursuing the French across the treeline involved an abrupt transition from a European-style battlefield of open spaces, artillery support, and marching troops to an Amerindian environment of trees, rocks, and bush. Sergeant Johnson described what happened next.

> They engaged the Savage Indians and Canadians who were advanced in the front of the enemy's right flank, and posted under some rocks and bushes, and intirely out of the sight of Captain McDonald [Macdonell], or any of his men, and quite unsuspected by them, and by whom they were put into disorder the very first fire, and not able to recover themselves on a sudden, after such an unexpected surprise; and a regiment of French regulars coming up instantly upon them, Captain Macdonald [Macdonell] and his whole company, officers and men, were cut off, except five or six private men; they were all killed before the Light Infantry [*sic*] to get up to their assistance.[26]

Macdonell himself did not survive. According to James Thompson, "there came upon him a stronger body of French that overpower'd and completely butcher'd his whole party, and he himself was found cut and hack'd to pieces in the most shocking manner! There was an end of him!"[27]

The destruction of the Volunteers just inside Sillery Wood was the first in a series of actions that broke the British south flank. "By this means," wrote Malcolm Fraser, "the left of the 28th Regiment was exposed, and this obliged them to give ground after an obstinate resistance."[28]

Now under attack by five companies of French grenadiers, the British grenadiers of the 28th continued to hold out in the two redoubts on South Hill, but, wrote Patrick Mackellar, "being at length surrounded they were oblig'd to force their way back."[29]

After a rough beginning marked by a string of British successes, hard fighting by French regulars, Canadian militia, and Seven Nations warriors had turned the battle around. The key terrain features on the northern and southern edges of the battlefield were back in French hands.

CHAPTER 19

LÉVIS' CHARGE

LÉVIS' COMMANDS

Ever since he had first caught sight of a British column on the Buttes-à-Neveu, Lévis had been playing catch-up, responding to Murray's moves. Now, with the La Sarre, Marine, and Berry brigades, the grenadiers, and the Montreal battalion pushing hard against the British in the north and centre, it was time for him to seize the initiative and strike back hard.

Throughout the clash between the French and British lines, Lévis had held the La Reine brigade in reserve inside Sillery Wood. Even when British pressure became so great that he had ordered a withdrawal, Lévis kept his last fresh troops out of the fray rather than rushing them forward to shore up the battle line. As Lévis shifted from defence to attack, he planned to use these troops as the hammer that would shatter Murray's army.

While Lévis struck the south end of Murray's line with the Royal Roussillon brigade and five companies of grenadiers, pinning his battalions in place, the La Reine brigade would slip past the fighting at the south end of the battlefield, lunge north, and roll up the British line. If all went as planned, Lévis' troops might be inside the walls of Quebec that afternoon, without needing to conduct a siege and without waiting for help from France.

This decision taken, Lévis sent an officer to Brigadier Jean-Georges Dejean de Roquemaure, who commanded the La Reine brigade. The officer arrived safely and delivered the order. His exact words to Roquemaure and his senior officers were not preserved, but Lapause reported that "he told them [to strike] behind the left."[1] A moment later, a stray shot killed the messenger.[2] This did not prevent the brigade from moving off immediately, ready for action.

Immediately after his courier departed, Lévis rode south. For the first time in the battle, he would take a direct role in combat. "I placed myself on the right [south], gave the signal to charge the enemy, and . . . joined the Royal Roussillon brigade in falling upon the enemy's left [south] flank."[3]

THE CHARGE

Lévis' charge, which should be as well known as Montcalm's charge across the Plains of Abraham in 1759, Isaac Brock's charge at Queenston Heights in 1812, and the Canadian advance on Vimy Ridge during the Battle of Arras in 1917, has passed almost unrecorded.

Lévis contented himself with saying that "After gaining the heights [South Hill], I charged and overwhelmed them [the British] to the point that they withdrew in haste to the place [Quebec]."[4] His orders to his officers prior to the campaign give just a hint of what might have occurred on the field. "When you charge, march with all possible order and, when you are forty or fifty paces from the enemy, move as fast as possible to increase the shock."[5]

Lapause added a few details. "He [Lévis] wheeled to the left and charged the [British] flank. The enemy, having made a quick movement to cover that flank, found themselves thrown into confusion and overpowered by the steady advance of that brigade."[6]

Johnstone was more dramatic. "The enemy," he wrote, "no sooner noticed this movement . . . than they were overcome with panicked terror and fled. The English soldiers ran so fast that their officers could not hold back a single one."[7]

Other details come from observations by French officers of the Canadian militia and Seven Nations warriors. When the troops of the Royal Roussillon brigade advanced, they weren't alone. In recording the events of his assault on the British south flank, Lévis took particular note of Captain Dominique-Nicolas de Laas de Gestède and the 223 Canadians attached to the La Reine regiment. Out of touch with the brigade command and left without orders, they were close enough to the battle line to watch the action. "Seeing the Royal Roussillon brigade advancing, they joined [in the attack] and conducted themselves with great skill and valour."[8]

This was praiseworthy and perhaps to be expected from a veteran French officer and highly motivated militia. What was truly remarkable that day was the decision of some of the Seven Nations warriors to join the charge alongside the Canadians. For generations, Amerindians had served alongside their French allies, but they had refused to become involved in European-style combat. As a Nipissing chief explained to Montcalm in 1756, Amerindians fought "in the forest where they understood war, and where they could find trees for cover."[9]

Yet on 28 April, some of these warriors abandoned the shelter of Sillery Wood and moved out into the open fields and pastures of the Plains of Abraham to take part in a clash between regular battalions. This display of valour and adaptability won them no thanks from Lévis, who focused on the warriors who held to their traditions and remained behind. The Canadians, he wrote, were "supported in that manoeuvre by the Sr. de St. Luc [Luc de La Corne] who could persuade only a small number of Natives to follow him."[10]

MURRAY'S LAST RESERVES

French sources give the impression that the Roussillon brigade, the Canadians of La Reine, and the warriors of the Seven Nations smashed Murray's army with one hard punch. But nothing at the Battle of Sainte-Foy came easily—not for the British, not for the French.

Murray's south flank didn't collapse all at once. His troops held on for as long as they were able to resist. Murray had been attempting to shore up the British position on the north side of the field when he noticed that down in the south, "the left... began to retire, tho they had early made themselves masters of the two redoubts." He pulled the 43rd Regiment from a relatively quiet section of the line and sent that battalion, together with the third battalion of the 60th Regiment, the last of his reserve units, to support the beleaguered 28th Regiment.

John Knox, present with the 43rd, witnessed the result. "The enemy possessed themselves of two redoubts upon our left, which gave them a great advantage; but, by an excellent movement of the forty-third regiment... from the center, to support the third battalion of [Royal] Americans on the left, both these corps made a vigorous effort to recover those works, and succeeded; they maintained them for some time with admirable firmness."[11]

BATTLEFIELD LOGISTICS

Lévis, however, had chosen just the right time to make his move. All along their line, British gunners and infantry were running out of ammunition.

Hours of continuous fire by muskets, cannon, and howitzers meant that sooner or later the troops in the field were going to need to resupply. On 28 April, this involved transporting cartloads of musket cartridges, powder charges for the artillery, cannonballs, howitzer shells, and tin case-shot across the mud and snow of the battlefield.

On the French side, this passed without any incident worth recording. Among the British, things were more difficult. Along the Chemin Sainte-Foy, ammunition carts followed the troops right up to the battle line, allowing soldiers like Private Francis Naylor of the 35th to replenish at will.[12]

Elsewhere on the battlefield, the troops who hand-hauled the carts found themselves engaged in a losing battle with the geography of the Plains of Abraham in spring. Sergeant Johnson, who, as a quartermaster sergeant, was sensitive about these things, observed that "the ammunition waggons were no sooner out of the gates, but they were bogged in deep pits of snow, and therefore intirely unable to come up to us, to our assistance."[13]

James Thompson explained what this meant for Fraser's Highlanders. "We . . . fought as long as our ammunition lasted, which was thirty rounds a man, and the same for our Field pieces, but 'afaith the French were too many for us, and we were oblig'd to retreat."[14]

Johnson said much the same thing about the 58th. "We took with us into the field . . . twenty brass field pieces . . . and so long as we had ammunition to support them we maintained our ground." But the French "no sooner perceived that our artillery slackened their fire but they began to wax more bold, and advanced . . . as soon as they found that our artillery had intirely ceased, and that our musquetry was so very light, that they advanced boldly upon us, which in a little time forced us to give way."[15]

THE LOST BRIGADE

When the Royal Roussillon brigade charged, Lévis was out in front. This was entirely appropriate and, indeed, expected of military leaders in this period. Montcalm had done the same thing at the Battle of the Plains of Abraham. So had Wolfe.

Leading a charge that smashed the flank of a powerful enemy would inevitably become a high point of an eighteenth-century officer's career. A general who led such a charge demonstrated his courage, inspired his troops, and could expect to be rewarded with honours, promotion, and remuneration in the form of a pension. Focused on the task at hand, however, he could neither keep track of what was happening elsewhere on the battlefield nor command the rest of his army.

In this case, Lévis couldn't simultaneously lead a charge and make sure that his orders to La Reine had been obeyed. When Lévis' messenger passed on his orders to get behind the left flank, Roquemaure and his officers appeared to have believed that Lévis meant the French left (on the north side of the battlefield) instead of the British left (on the south side). Considering that the British north flank was in the process of collapsing, this would have made a certain amount of sense. A fresh brigade going into action may have been just what was needed to turn retreat into rout.

So, acting in the belief that he was following the orders of his commander and about to strike a blow for France, Roquemaure led his brigade in precisely the wrong direction, to the north and out of the fight, instead moving south to support Lévis' charge. The messenger died at the worst possible time, after he had delivered the order but before he could correct this mistake. As a result, wrote Lévis, "the La Reine brigade, instead of heading towards the edge of the woods [and joining in the charge], ended up behind the [French] left."[16]

Instead of rampaging across the British rear, striking their opponents from behind, the regulars of La Reine and Languedoc missed the battle altogether. For all the good they did for France that day, they might just as well have spent the campaign in Montreal.

RETREAT IN THE SOUTH

Sending two more regiments to support the 28th couldn't save the British south flank. The French kept coming; the British could not hold.

John Knox was there as the British reeled back from their battle for the two redoubts on South Hill. He wrote:

> ... at length being reduced to a handful, they were compelled to yield to superior numbers... and our communication with the town in danger of being intercepted, we were obliged to give up the contest. The troops being

ordered to fall back, a command they were hitherto unacquainted with, as if sensible of the critical posture of our affairs, they drew a natural conclusion; and, growing impatient, some of them cried out, *Damn it, what is falling back but retreating?*[17]

CHAPTER 20

BREAKING THE LINE

COLLAPSE IN THE CENTRE

Formerly poised on the brink of victory, the British were now in serious trouble. As the three battalions on the south end of the line pulled back, they exposed the south flank of the 78th. The Highlanders, wrote Malcolm Fraser, were "next to them [the 28th] to the right, and being in danger of being surrounded, and at the same time extremely galled by a fire from the bushes in front and back, were under a necessity of falling back instantly."[1]

Their retreat did not go well. James Thompson described his fleeing comrades as "a raw undisciplin'd set, [who] were got into great disorder, and had become more like a mob than regular soldiers."[2] So desperate was their situation that the Highlanders came very close to the ultimate military disgrace of losing their colours. Robert Macpherson, the regimental chaplain, wrote of how "In the battle of the 28th where our whole officers except three or four were kill'd or wounded & very few men indeed at last in the field, he [Ensign Lachlan Macpherson] had the good fortune to carry off both our Colours from out of danger, and not to receive any hurt."[3]

The Scots, however, had a secret weapon. Their piper, who had been in disgrace ever since he had refused to charge with the regiment at the Battle of the Plains of Abraham, "luckily bethought himself," wrote Thompson, "to give them a blast of his pipes." The running Scots stopped dead in their tracks, "and they soon allow'd themselves to be form'd into some sort of order." The retreat continued in a more orderly fashion, and the troops forgave the piper's previous lapse.[4]

In 1785, William Thomson, a Scottish librarian and minister turned professional author, heard another version of this incident while travelling in Scotland.

> At the battle of Quebec, in April 1760, whilst the British troops were retreating in great confusion, the General [Murray] complained to a field-officer of Fraser's regiment, of the bad behaviour of his corps. "Sir," answered he with some warmth, "you did very wrong in forbidding the pipes to play this morning: nothing encourages Highlanders so much in a day of action. Nay, even now they would be of use." "Let them blow like the devil, then," replied the General, "if it will bring back the men." The pipes were ordered to play a favourite martial air. The Highlanders, the moment they heard the music returned, and formed with alacrity in the rear.[5]

Next in line, moving from south to north, the 47th Regiment was still holding out. "They were," observed Malcolm Fraser, "drawn up with a small rising ground [North Hill] in their front, which till then covered them pretty much from the enemy's fire." But with the 78th on the run, "it was absolutely necessary for the 47th to quit that ground, otherwise they must inevitably have been surrounded in a few minutes."[6]

North of the 47th, the 58th had foundered as well. John Johnson described the fate of his battalions after their supporting artillery ran out of ammunition. The French:

> advanced boldly upon us, which in a little time forced us to give way; and which we did gradually for some time, keeping a good front towards them: but through the smallness of our number, and the quantity of ground we had to cover, to secure the flanks of our line, the intervals between the battalions, so excessive large, and the cannon ceased firing, which used to cover those intervals, they advanced and broke in hastily upon us, like a hasty torrent from a lofty precipice and got into our front through those intervals, which obliged us to retire in confusion each one striving to shift for himself, and yet under the fire of the garrison in the best manner he

was able; leaving behind us all our artillery, and about a thousand as brave men as ever faced an enemy, in the field, to the enemy, as a trophy of their victory.[7]

Northern retreat

Things were just as bad along the northern end of Murray's line. "By this time," wrote Private James Miller of the 15th, "the left and centre had given way, and were retreating confusedly towards Quebec, we brought up the rear, as well as possible, but could hardly be kept together, the wounded men were supported by their comrades."

As the troops around Miller fell back, they held together and kept on fighting.

> The commanding officer of the corps [Major Paulus Aemilius Irving], did all that a man could do to keep it in a body, in order to cover the retreat, ordering them to turn round frequently, and fire by platoons, or volleys, in the hurry had like to have lost his wig, he however put it under his arm, with great sang froid, and said "damn the old wig," a name by which he is known to this day, by the old soldiers.[8]

Miller didn't realize it, but the 15th had broken apart. The other half of the story comes from Henry Hamilton, who had a very different experience. Hamilton's account, a minor classic, provides the most vivid account of chaos and collapse on the Sainte Foy battlefield and the abrupt change of status from armed combatant to helpless prisoner that comes with surrender.

For Hamilton, the collapse began with the horrifying moment when he realized just who was needed to retrieve the situation and save Murray's army from defeat—Major General James Wolfe.

Although never quite sure if this actually happened, Hamilton remembered that "our soldiers called out in a sort of desperate enthusiasm 'Oh God! Just give us Wolfe for 1/2 an hour.'" Immediately thereafter, he wondered whether "it was all imagined... and I think it was... but had our late red headed hero appeared for but 5 minutes as our head... confidence would have been ready to have seconded his orders" and turned defeat into victory.

Instead, the French advance continued. "The English, feeble two deep line gave way... The enemy came in a disorderly throng—there was discipline & courage to have ousted them—a head was wanting—we had no Wolfe."

The continued French advance coincided with the sudden realization by Hamilton that he had somehow lost touch with the rest of the British army. "I found myself commanding two companies on the left wing of the 15th Regt. The remainder had melted away—what wonder—There was not a captain in the field. They had either been wounded in the preceding campaign, or were (as the Jockey's term it) out of the course, alas, no where."

Hamilton had nothing but praise for the courage and composure of the troops he commanded, while condemning the French for a lackadaisical pursuit. "When the French miscellany came down, my brave fellows being cool and collected gave a fire but observing that their right had disappeared, thought it high time to join them, however I declare they twice faced about and by word of command fired on the pursuers, who indeed were not formidable, for if we fled like quicksilver, they pursued with the composure & gravity of a cathedral."

Hamilton himself was another matter. Before long, the gallant young officer decided that he, for one, had had enough, and that his brave fellows could manage perfectly well on their own. "I, poor I, at length fagged, disheartened, unbreakfasted, booted, wet and dirty, concluded that I should be arrested by a ball in my back, that there was nothing but vanity in resisting, and vexation of spirit in running away from Frenchmen. So I bravely stood my ground for I was done up, and two [French] soldiers . . . me couchèrent en joue [levelled their muskets at me]."

The following dialogue ensued:

"'Bas les armes [drop your weapons],' cried Monsr le Rouge—done. '. . . le Bayonnette [and the bayonet]'—Done. 'Rendez-vous! [Surrender!]'—Done."

The two "honorable & humane common French soldiers" took Hamilton to an officer of Berry. This officer's first concern was protecting his prisoner from Seven Nations warriors, who were attempting to fulfill their own victory conditions by taking prisoners and scalps. "'Sir,' said he, 'your situation is very dangerous, the savages are at hand, exchange uniforms with me, I will furnish you an escort.'"

Hamilton at first attempted to refuse on the grounds that he was wearing a private's coat, which would not make a fair exchange for a French officer's coat, over a striped flannel vest, which was presumably too disreputable to allow him to pose convincingly as an officer of the troupes de terre. His French counterpart, however, quickly overcame Hamilton's sartorial scruples. "I accepted his coat, turned my waistcoat [inside out], mounted his white cockade, & then thankfully taking my leave of this generous officer, I turned to my escort and with the authority of an officer wearing a French cockade cried, 'Allons mes enfans marchez [Let's go, my children. March!].'"

The two soldiers took Hamilton first to an artillery officer, who passed them along to Captain Charles Deschamps de Boishébert of the troupes de la marine. Boishébert, recalled Hamilton, "treated me with great complacency, directed the party to protect me from the Indians, and to put me under a safeguard at a neighbouring house—On the way the straggling Indians showed a curiosity, but my guardians were watchful, and kept [their] curiosity off by their fixed bayonets."

At the house, Hamilton was taken up a ladder to the second floor, where he met other British captives. He remained there until after the battle, when he was taken to the Hôpital Général.[9]

A CIVILIAN PERSPECTIVE

The only civilian witness who left an account of the battle was Marie de la Visitation. The staff of the Hôpital Général, which was located just under two kilometres from Dumont's Mill, saw very little but heard everything. "The clash took place a few steps from Quebec, on a height [the Quebec Promontory] opposite our house," she wrote. "There was not a cannon or musket shot that did not echo in our ears. Judge from that our situation. The fate of the nation and of our loved ones among the combatants [were at stake]. I cannot describe our anguish."

Jean-Olivier Briand, vicar general of the Government of Quebec and a future bishop of Quebec, was there at the hospital, where he "suffered no less than us." After praying at the foot of the altar, "asking confidently for God in all his mercy to stop the fighting and spare the people entrusted to his care," Briand informed the nuns that "there would not be enough priests to minister to the dying, who he was afraid would be there in great numbers." With him went the chaplain of the hospital, whose only brother was with the army. The two priests arrived late in the action, just in time to have "the consolation of seeing the enemy turn their backs and flee."[10]

THE FRENCH PURSUE

With both flanks in a state of collapse and their centre driven in, the British finally broke. The French pursued but couldn't catch up; the British got away but lost their artillery.

British accounts of the retreat talk about the snow that prevented them from saving their guns. "We were oblig'd," confessed the officer of the 35th, "to leave our cannon sticking in the snow."[11]

French accounts stress the fatigue that slowed them down. Captain Louis de Preissac de Bonneau of Guyenne, who had charged with the Roussillon brigade, related how "We chased them right up to the city gates, had our army not been completely exhausted, we would have gone into the city with the English."[12] Lapause added a whole list of reasons for the British escape, including a reference to Murray's savagely effective field guns. "If our soldiers had not been afflicted with cold, exhaustion, snow, rain, and above all, hunger, and had not so many of them been killed by enemy artillery, we would have made an energetic strike and entered the city with our enemies."[13]

JAMES THOMPSON AND MOSES HAZEN

This fatigue was not at all apparent to James Thompson. As the British army came closer to the safety of the city walls, he portrayed Lévis' pursuit as "a solid column of the French coming on over that high ground [the Buttes-à-Neveu]... and headed by an officer who was some distance in front of the column."

At this point, Thompson "fell in with a Captain Moses Hazen... who commanded a Company of Rangers, and who was so badly wounded, that his Servant who had to carry him away, was obliged to rest him on the ground at every twenty or thirty yards, owing to the great pain he endur'd."

Pain notwithstanding, Hazen took time to stop to take one more shot at the French. This gave Thompson the opportunity to record an eyewitness account of a French officer in action at the head of his troops.

> "Do you see," says Captain Hazen [to his servant], "that rascal there, waving his Sword to encourage those fellows to come forward?"
>
> "Yes," says the Servant, "I do Sir."
>
> "Then," says the Captain again, "just place your back against mine for one moment, 'till I see if I can bring him down."

He accordingly stretch'd himself on the ground and, resting the muzzle
of his fuzee on his toes, he let drive at the French Officer.

The shot struck home, much to Thompson's surprise, although the officer survived. By this time the Scots had put a good deal of distance between
themselves and the French, and Thompson felt free to spend a few moments
praising Hazen's marksmanship. Hazen shrugged off the compliments.
"'Oh,' says Captain Hazen, 'you know that a chance shot will kill the devil
himself.'"[14]

THE BRITISH RETREAT

Hazen's sharpshooting aside, if anything saved the British army, once the
general retreat began, it was the redoubt on Wolfe's Hill. This fortification,
noted Mackellar on his map of the engagement, "was of great service and
kept the enemy at bay for above ten minutes which saved our rear and many
of our wounded from being cut off from the town. This was raised only a few
fascines [bundles of sticks used to construct temporary fortifications] high on
account of the frosts, but there being two pickets left there during the action
it deceived the enemy as a compleat work."[15]

But if the British escaped, they left their guns behind. "Most of the cannon was left," wrote Richard Humphreys, a private in the light infantry, "as
the roughness of the ground, and the wreaths of snow, made it impossible to
bring them off, but what could not be brought off, were nail[ed] [made temporarily unserviceable by driving a spike into the touchhole]."[16]

Malcolm Fraser said much the same thing.

Most of the Regiments attempted to carry off their artillery, but the ground
was so bad with wreaths of snow in the hollows, that they were obliged to
abandon them, after nailing them up, as well as the intrenching tools. Every
Regiment made the best of their way to Town, but retired however in such
a manner that the enemy did not think proper to pursue very briskly, otherwise they might have killed or made prisoners many more than they did.[17]

Henry Hamilton obtained a different perspective on the last phase of the
battle when he took advantage of an opportunity to discuss it with Lévis. "I
asked M. de Lévis one day what sort of retreat the English had made on the

28th. He said they had retreated in very good order. I could have informed him better and indeed it was not surprizing that harassed and ill fed troops should give way having of 3000 men lost 1100 & 120 officers killed, wounded, or prisoners."[18]

The British made one more effort to salvage the day when, recalled John Désbruyêres of the 35th, "some vain efforts were made to rally on the heights of Abraham."[19] The effort failed, and the British kept on running until they reached the city gates. Murray remained outside the walls until the last of his soldiers had entered the city.

CASUALTIES

By the time the gates of Quebec closed behind James Murray, his troops had killed 266 French, Canadian, and Seven Nations combatants and wounded 733. In return, Lévis' force had killed 292 British soldiers, wounded 837, and taken 53 prisoners.[20]

Following the Battle of the Plains of Abraham, the nuns of Quebec's Hôpital Général had managed to care for the wounded of both armies using nothing but their own resources. This time, they were almost overwhelmed. A shaken Marie de la Visitation described the situation.

> It would take another pen than mine to portray the horrors we saw for the twenty-four hours taken up by the arrival of the wounded, the cries of the dying, and the anguish of their relatives... After setting up more than five hundred beds [for the wounded; they still had to find space for another five hundred casualties]... Suffering unfortunates filled our barns and stables. We had hardly enough time to look after them all. There were seventy-two officers in our infirmaries, of whom thirty-three died. We saw nothing but amputated arms and legs.[21]

To support the work of the Hôpital Général, Lévis turned to Surgeon Major André Arnoux. A surgeon turned entrepreneur who had made his fortune buying and selling medication before settling in Quebec in 1751, Arnoux had served with the troops since the beginning of the war. "The hospital nuns finding themselves lacking everything, as a result of the cost of provisions, the Chevalier de Lévis ordered Sieur Arnoux to transport all of the wounded, English and French, to the Quebec Hospital, and provide them with food and medication."[22]

Arnoux accordingly hired stretcher-bearers to carry the wounded from the battlefield to the hospital and assistant surgeons and sick-berth attendants to treat and care for them. He supplied them with provisions and medicine and established field hospitals for those who could not be accommodated in the Hôpital Général. By the end of the campaign, Arnoux had paid for the housing, treatment, and provisioning of about six hundred wounded soldiers.[23] These expenditures left him heavily indebted; his exertions following the battle likely contributed to his own death in July 1760.[24]

The challenges faced by the nuns and Arnoux and his employees did not prevent them providing a high level of care and, at least for the officers, even a degree of comfort. Henry Hamilton, describing his stay at the Hôpital Général, wrote that:

> I was in good hands here, for the Nuns who the year before had received some civilities at my hands, were zealous to requite them with every possible attention. These tender & delicate women were chiefly employed in succouring 700 wounded men English as well as French... We prisoners, petitioned Monsr de Levis to grant us permission to have our servants sent to us out of the town, with some cloathes and money, which was granted.[25]

Some French soldiers found themselves under the care of family members. After La Naudière was wounded, wrote Gaspé:

> his bleeding body had been carried to the General Hospital where a great many wounded, French and English, received the most charitable care. Two elderly nuns, Mother Saint-Alexis, my aunt, and Mother Sainte-Catherine, my cousin, often spoke to me of these events, saying, "That spoiled brat Lanaudière, all by himself gave us more trouble during his convalescence than all of the other wounded in the hospital." My dear uncle, finding himself among family, evidently exploited his privileged position to annoy his nurses.

This story—doubtless softened by time—of La Naudière's comic mischief calls to mind Jules de Haberville, the genial hero of Gaspé's *Les Anciens*

Canadiens. La Naudière himself may have harboured darker memories that, like many combat veterans, he preferred to keep to himself. "I often walked with him," wrote Gaspé, "over the battlefield that witnessed our last victory before the conquest, but strangely, he never said anything to me of the glorious role he had played at the age of sixteen."

The only time La Naudière broke his silence, he spoke of the death of the mild-mannered LaRonde, left behind to die at Dumont's Mill lamenting the murderous folly of humanity.[26]

Inside the walls, the British wounded who returned to Quebec came under the care of the Canadian nuns of the Hôtel-Dieu and Ursulines convents, supported by the wives of British soldiers. "I ordered," wrote Murray, "the wounded to be put in the two convents, the women to . . . attend the sick, in order to save as many hands as we can."[27]

At the Hôtel-Dieu, surrounded by British wounded, Sister Sainte-Gabriel quickly learned of John Wilson's death in action. Upon hearing this news, wrote James Thompson, she "was again taken with fits and convulsions." Upon examination, Sainte-Gabriel proved to be pregnant. The child was adopted by a Canadian family; Sister Sainte-Gabriel made a successful career in the convent.[28]

As for Hector Munro, the carpenter turned soldier, his fears that he would not survive the battle proved correct. When Thompson returned to his billet after the battle, "I there found poor Hector Munro, who, not being able to walk, had been carried in, owing to a wound he had received in the lower part of the belly, thro' which his bowels were coming out! He had his senses about him, and reminded me of our conversation just before the battle. He was taken to the Hotel Dieu, where he died the next morning, in great agony."[29]

VICTORY AND VINDICATION

The French victory at Sainte-Foy had been a remarkable feat of arms, arguably the greatest single military achievement of the Seven Years' War in North America.

Every other major battle in the Seven Years' War in North America had been won by armies whose opponents set themselves up for defeat. At Monongahela in 1755, the British neglected the careful precautions they had taken throughout their march and walked right into the Amerindian-French force that cut them to ribbons. At Carillon in 1758, the British ignored other options such as bombarding the French from a nearby mountain or marching past Montcalm's defences to attack his army from the rear, and made a series of frontal assaults against massive field fortifications. At the Battle of Montmorency in 1759, the British charged uphill against entrenched troops. At the Plains of Abraham, the French abandoned a strong defensive position and charged downhill.

Murray's decision to charge did indeed attract a certain amount of contemporary criticism, not least from some of his own officers, but it didn't hand the French a victory. They seized it themselves, after hours of hard fighting against a skillful, resolute adversary whose murderously effective line of field guns came close to breaking the French army.

Yet Lévis, nominally the victor, had mixed feelings about the battle. It had been a triumph, to be sure, but less than a complete victory. Things could have gone better. "If the La Reine brigade had been at its post, we would have enveloped our enemies by their left, and could very likely have cut off their retreat to Quebec, which would have been decisive."[30]

Nonetheless, the victory had tilted the military balance in favour of the French. "Besieging Quebec," he noted, "which had seemed almost impossible before the battle, given our situation and lack of resources, now, with the enemy locked up inside the city, became reasonable."[31]

More important for many of the French regular officers, they had secured the professional vindication they so deeply desired. All the English officers, wrote Malartic, "freely admit that we took our revenge for 13 September on the 28th."[32]

Better still, they hadn't just beaten the same army that had beaten Montcalm; they had done so in the same place. Indeed, almost every French account refers to the field of Sainte-Foy as being on the same terrain as the Battle of the Plains of Abraham, even though it was actually just to the west of the 1759 battlefield. Minor points of geography, however, didn't matter to these officers. Like Bourlamaque, they rejoiced that "we beat the English on the same ground where they were victorious on 13 September."[33]

Even French officers who did not take part gloried in the news. Louis-Antoine de Bougainville, far away at the foot of Lake Champlain, replied to a letter announcing the victory by writing that "the honour of the troops has been fully restored; nothing could be better than forming three times under fire from 23 cannon."[34]

As for the Canadians, they were, according to French officers speaking with their British counterparts in the Hôpital Général, "elated with the success of their victory." But they still wanted their colonial capital back and were not inclined to wait for help from France. A delegation of Canadians consequently approached Lévis and "besought their general, in the most earnest manner, 'to proceed [to besiege Quebec] with the artillery and ammunition in his possession, assuring him, [that] if he would make a breach or opening in any part of our works [the city walls], they would force their way in, without requiring the least assistance from the regular troops.'"[35]

PART 3

SIEGE

CHAPTER 21

QUEBEC BESIEGED: TRENCHES

The siege begins 28 April–1 May

After the battle, the weather changed again. The afternoon and evening of 28 April were just as miserable for the French, Canadians, and Seven Nations as the day before and the day before that. "The army spent the night in bivouac," wrote Lapause, "despite the most frightful possible weather, rain falling on the troops, and cold without fire."[1]

This did not prevent Lévis from opening the siege. Expecting French sails to appear on the St. Lawrence at any moment, he moved fast to have everything in place when the reinforcements and heavy artillery arrived.

Following the British retreat, French soldiers occupied the Buttes-à-Neveu, overlooking Quebec, and gathered up the picks and shovels that the British had discarded that morning. Captain Fiacre-François Potot de Montbeillard, Canada's ranking artillery officer, and Captain Nicolas Sarrebource de Pontleroy, chief engineer of New France, walked over the buttes and marked out the siegeworks.

When completed, these works would consist of an approach trench, a parallel, and batteries. The approach trench would link the western edge of the buttes, a point safe from British artillery fire, to the parallel. The parallel, as one might expect from the name, would be a second trench facing the city walls on the east side of the buttes. It would link a chain of batteries, housing the heavy guns that would pound the city walls.

While the army prepared for a siege, Vauquelin and the French flotilla dropped down the river with the tide.[2] "I arrived at the Anse au Foulon," he wrote, "just after the battle... We had the satisfaction of seeing our troops in quiet possession of the Heights of Abraham.... Every day we unloaded artillery, munitions and provisions according to the needs of the army."[3]

That night, French soldiers employed Murray's picks and shovels to begin work on the approach and parallel. The buttes were a rock outcropping covered by a thin layer of earth and vegetation. Lapause noted that "There was only a half-foot of soil on the heights."[4]

For the first fifteen centimetres, digging was difficult. "Our workers," observed Malartic, "could hardly remove the soil which was still frozen."[5] After that, French spades hit rock and digging became impossible.

So instead of digging the parallel into the earth, the French brought earth to the parallel. They made hundreds of *gabions*—wicker baskets—placed them in front of the parallel, and filled them with earth carried from hundreds of metres away. As they worked, British projectiles pounded the parallel and soared over the buttes. "Cannonballs [and shells] plunged behind the heights," wrote Lévis. "There were very few safe places, we even had to move the camp."[6]

Descendants of the individuals involved remembered the impact of one mortar shell over a century afterwards. Philippe Aubert de Gaspé told the story. On 29 April, his grandfather,

Captain [Philippe-Ignace Aubert] de Gaspé was peacefully smoking his pipe during the siege of Quebec in 1760, with two brothers in arms, Captains [Germain] Vassal [de Monviel of Béarn] and [Louis de Missègle] de Bonne [of the troupes de la marine], in a hole made the night before by an enemy shell. This retreat sheltered them from a glacial northeast wind, accompanied by torrential rain, and seemed as well to provide shelter from enemy shells and cannonballs.

"It would take the devil himself," said Captain Vassal, laughing, "for another bomb to throw us out of this hole on such a dark night. So we can smoke and chat in peace."

They were there for several minutes... when Captain de Gaspé, thinking he heard someone calling, said, on leaving the shell hole, "Someone seems to think we need some exercise to stretch our legs."

But he had only gone a few steps when a second bomb fell into the refuge he had just left, and killed his two friends.[7]

On 1 May, the besiegers completed their parallel, such as it was. Although the French called it a trench, the result of their labour was more like a line of gabions along a very shallow ditch. Lévis was not impressed. "The parallel being very bad, the troops there are hardly protected."[8]

That notwithstanding, the French had completed the first element of their siegeworks. Next, they would move on to constructing batteries.

THE BRITISH DEFENCE 28 APRIL–1 MAY

The British defence of Quebec got off to a very shaky start.

A tactful Malcolm Fraser confined himself to observing that "for the first two days after the battle there was very little done by us."[9] John Knox was less restrained. "Immense irregularities are hourly committed by the soldiery, in break-open [*sic*] store and dwelling houses to get at liquor: this is seemingly the result of panic and despair, heightened by drunkenness" and their "despondent state of mind."[10]

Murray dealt with this breakdown of discipline by confiscating and disposing of all the hard liquor in private hands and hanging one soldier as an example.[11] By 2 May, troops were back under control and ready to be put to work to defend the city.

"On the 3rd day after the battle," wrote Fraser, "the General set about to strengthen or (I may say) fortify the Town, and the men worked with the greatest alacrity."[12]

Under pressure, Murray's army became a defensive machine. Convalescents who could walk reported to Porte Saint-Louis every morning at seven to make and fill sandbags. Those who could not remained in hospital and made wads—plugs to hold powder charges in place—for the artillery.[13]

As well as assisting the nuns in caring for the wounded, the women of the army began cooking for all of the troops, instead of just their own families, to free up fit soldiers who would otherwise have performed these tasks. Ten women per battalion were assigned—and paid—to assist the walking wounded in making sandbags and wadding.

The troops moved out of billets in city buildings and camped in tents on the open ground between the built-up area and the walls, so as to be at hand to respond to any emergency.

Some soldiers worked on the fortifications, opening new embrasures and constructing gun platforms. Others—including officers—hauled artillery from Lower Town batteries up the Côte de la Montagne (a street connecting Lower Town and Upper Town) to be mounted on the ramparts, until 132 guns and mortars faced the French.[14] "The best thing we could do," wrote Murray, "was to endeavour to knock their works to pieces before they could mount their cannon."[15]

Quartermaster Sergeant Johnson of the 58th, while lamenting the sight of officers working with their hands, inadvertently provides a fine portrayal of the garrison at work.

> None but those who were present on the spot, can imagine the grief of heart the soldiers felt, to see their officers doing the common labour of the soldier, equal with themselves; to see them yoked in the harness dragging up cannon from the Lower Town, the same as themselves:—to see Gentlemen who were set over them by His Majesty, to command and keep them, to their duty, to be at work on the batteries, with the barrow, pickax, and spade, with the same ardour as themselves.[16]

All this came at a price. By 9 May, noted James Miller, "the garrison were almost exhausted, by fatigue."[17] This did not prevent morale from soaring back to pre-battle levels. "Our troops," wrote Knox, "are in great spirits, and work with the utmost diligence."[18]

Yet the British hold on Quebec was still a long way from secure. On 1 May Murray had judged the French threat to be serious enough that he had sent the sloop *Racehorse* down the river to Louisbourg and Halifax with a second request for assistance.[19]

CANADIANS IN THE CITY

The British were not alone inside Quebec. Apart from the staff of the Hôtel-Dieu and the Ursulines convent, the 150 Canadian families Murray had allowed to remain in their homes were still there. On the morning of 1 May, wrote Récher, "M. Murray's aide-de-camp went from house to house to warn the French families . . . that they could leave the city until 4:00 p.m. that day and not return during the siege, but they could also remain in their homes, if they preferred, although the General would not be responsible for any accidents that might arrive from French shells and cannon."

A day later, Murray ordered them to relocate to the two convents or leave the city. The Canadians chose the convents. On 3 May, Récher reported that "not a single French person could be seen anymore on the streets."[20]

CANADIAN REINFORCEMENTS

As the siege began, new recruits flooded in to join Lévis' army.

During the winter, residents of the Government of Quebec had engaged in quiet, careful resistance to the British occupation, dragging their heels at British requests for goods and services, concealing French agents, withholding information about French activities, and helping British soldiers to desert. Now, with a French army outside Quebec, they could once again act openly against the British.

Many Canadians from the Quebec area began to arrive spontaneously the day after the battle.[21] Others responded to formal mobilization orders that Lévis' officers carried into the countryside. These orders were brief and to the point. This one went to the Saint-Charles parish on the south shore of the St. Lawrence: "The Sr. [Joseph] Nadeau, captain of the Saint-Charles company of militia, and the militia of his company fit to bear arms are ordered to join our army upon receipt of this order on pain of death."[22]

With the outcome of the campaign still uncertain, Lévis may have hoped that demanding that the militia report for duty or face execution would shield them against British retaliation. Should the French be defeated, militia captains would have written evidence that they had had no choice but obedience to French commands.

In any event, compulsion was hardly necessary. By 2 May, Malartic could write that "many Canadians have joined us from the parishes below Quebec."[23] The British had confiscated their muskets, but this didn't pose a problem. In a labour-intensive operation like a siege, victory depended as much on moving earth, hauling artillery and munitions, and constructing earthworks as actual combat.

Better still, not all of the Canadians came empty-handed. Following the French army's withdrawal in 1759, Beauport residents had salvaged what they could from the French batteries and fortifications between the Saint-Charles and Montmorency Rivers. All through the winter, they had kept this material hidden away. Everyone kept the secret; the British had not the faintest suspicion that Beauport contained an impressive store of munitions. When the French army arrived, wrote Vaudreuil, "the residents of the parish of Beauport. . . rushed to our depot. . . to deliver one thousand livres of powder and 1,500 to 2,000 cannonballs."[24]

Writing on the other side of the siege lines, the officer of the 35th noted that the new arrivals were joined by "merchants from Montreal crowding to the camp with their goods as they thought, having gain'd the action, they were certain of taking the town in a few days."[25]

AMERINDIAN REINFORCEMENTS

Canadians from the Government of Quebec and merchants from Montreal were not the only ones who joined the siege. Many potential combatants from the Seven Nations and the nations of Acadia had been away in winter hunting camps when the Quebec expedition set out. When they returned, they made their way first to Montreal or Trois-Rivières, where they drew provisions and equipment from French stores, then headed down the St. Lawrence.

Much to Vaudreuil's annoyance, some of these warriors were not alone. "I learned," he wrote, "that, in spite of my orders, they had taken their wives with them. I beg you, sir, to refrain from providing rations for these women . . . you [Lévis] can send them to Trois-Rivières, where M. de Longueuil [the governor] will supply them with provisions according to my directions."[26]

Kisensik, a chief of the Nipissings of Lac des Deux Montagnes, on the other hand, arrived at Quebec with a dozen Nipissing and Mohawk warriors and a personal recommendation from Vaudreuil to Lévis. "I am certain you have known for a long time of the service of this chief" who had taken part in the sieges of Forts Oswego and William Henry in 1756 and 1757 and the defence of the Lake Champlain frontier in 1758 and 1759.[27]

Once at Quebec, Kisensik and his fellows found themselves in a military environment even more alien than a European battlefield. Yet in a confrontation between heavy guns and stone fortifications, the warriors carved out a useful role for themselves that combined their particular military skills and practices with the necessities of siege warfare. Every night, Lévis posted about eighty warriors, accompanied by a French liaison officer and dismounted soldiers of the Canadian cavalry, to screen the siegeworks against sorties from the garrison. "These Natives," wrote Vaudreuil, "performed this service with great diligence."[28]

PROVISIONS

Feeding a steadily growing army might have posed a problem for Joseph Cadet, but with the British pinned inside the walls, the French had free access to the farms of the Government of Quebec. Over the winter, Cadet's clerks, covered by French troops, had signed contracts with farmers on the south shore of the St. Lawrence. As the siege began, the farmers had the livestock and vegetables ready for delivery.

As early as 30 April, Cadet and his employees had improved the provision situation to the extent that the troops could add peas and pork to their rations of hardtack, water, and a daily shot of brandy, along with a small ration of beef for the wounded. By 5 May, wrote Vaudreuil, Cadet "was now able to issue... a quarteron (122.35 grams) of meat every day to each of the soldiers, militia, and Natives of the army, who until that moment had gone without." That evening, Lévis sent a schooner downriver to collect Cadet's provisions. Within a week, four to five hundred cattle were on their way overland from parishes on the south shore to be ferried across the river to Quebec.[29]

OPTIMISM

Everything was going well. Captain Louis de Preissac de Bonneau of Guyenne had lost a brother at Sainte-Foy. This did not prevent him from writing an upbeat account of morale among the besiegers, although his reference to French rations was a little unfair to Cadet and his colleagues.

> I don't know how to tell you how much enthusiasm everyone in Canada brought to this expedition, throughout the siege the troops had nothing but bread, without any other food, and you did not hear one person complain. The hope of seeing a few French ships appear before help arrived for [the British in] the city sustained the greatest fatigues... day and night in the trench during the 19 days the siege lasted.[30]

When the French saw the *Racehorse* sail from Quebec on 1 May, they took this as an indication that the British might be preparing to give up. "We thought," wrote Malartic, "that it carried all of our deserters."[31] (French prisoners and deserters from 1759 who had chosen to serve with Murray's army would face execution if captured by the French after a British capitulation.)

THE BRITISH REACH THE GULF

The French were making rapid progress in the siege, but they were also running out of time. On 1 May, HMS *Diana* and *Vanguard*, sailing from Britain under the command of Commodore Robert Swanton and escorting a convoy of merchant ships, reached the Cabot Strait, the southern entrance of the Gulf of St. Lawrence. Here, noted the *Diana*'s master in the ship's log, they "sailed through a great stream of ice" that held them up for days. Not until 4 May did the squadron break through the ice barrier and proceed towards Quebec.[32]

CHAPTER 22

QUEBEC BESIEGED: BATTERIES

BUILDING BATTERIES, ANTICIPATING SUCCESS

With their parallel complete, if less than satisfactory, the French set to work on three batteries facing the La Glacière and Saint-Louis bastions, the weakest points of Quebec's defences. A fourth lay just to the north. If all went well, these batteries would house the heavy guns that would batter a breach in the city walls. To harass British gun crews on the ramparts, the French built a fifth battery, mounting four guns on the west bank of the Saint-Charles River.[1]

The convoy and siege guns had still not arrived on 8 May when Lévis' troops completed work on the batteries. But Lévis decided that as long as the batteries were there, the French might as well get some use out of them. "If our feeble artillery," he wrote to Vaudreuil, "can open [a breach in] the wall, I assure you that I will be the first [into the city]."[2]

As the siege progressed, back in Montreal a confident François Bigot turned his mind to the question of post-victory accommodations for senior officers and officials in Quebec. "I fully expect," he wrote to Lévis, "that if the English relief force gives you enough time to take Quebec, you will stay in the Intendance [Bigot's headquarters and residence]. In that case, I will bring a small bed with me, and put it in a small room while you take the large one."[3]

This thoughtful missive proved to be magnificently ill-timed. At 11:00 a.m. that same day, the event that everyone in the French and British armies and everyone in Canada had awaited for so long finally happened. Under the eyes of thousands of soldiers, sailors, militia, warriors, and civilians, inside and outside the city, the first ship to reach Quebec hove into sight as it rounded the western tip of Île d'Orléans, propelled by a rising tide and northeast wind.

Malartic tells the story: "Wind still from the northeast. Works, trench guards, and fire from the besieged as usual. At 11:00 someone saw a ship rounding point Lévis. It anchored nearby. We hoped for a moment that it was French. It proved to be English when it replied to signals from the city. It sailed again at 3:00 p.m. and anchored very near the lower town."[4]

BRITISH CHEERS

About six hundred metres away, on the far side of the no-man's land separating the French parallel from the city walls, John Knox was decidedly more enthusiastic.

> The gladness of the troops is not to be expressed: both Officers and soldiers mounted the parapets in the face of the enemy, and huzzaed, with their hats in the air, for almost an hour; the garrison, the enemy's camp, the bay, and circumjacent country for several miles, resounded with our shouts and the thunder of our artillery; for the Gunners were so elated, that they did nothing but fire and load for a considerable time.[5]

James Thompson provides further information.

> There came a Frigate in sight, and she was, for some considerable time, tacking across and across between Pointe Levis and the opposite shore. We were at some loss to know the meaning of all this, when the Commanding Officer of Artillery bethought himself to go and acquaint General Murray (who had taken up his quarters in Saint Louis Street, now the Officer's Barracks) of the circumstance. He found the General sitting before the chimney, his chair somewhat leaning backwards, and one foot resting upon the cheeck of the Chimney, thinking of matters and things that had just taken place; not the most pleasant.
>
> On the Officer acquainting him that there was a Ship-of-War in sight, the General was so electrified that he sprang himself over the back of his

chair, and stumbled on the floor! He instantly got up, and in the greatest fury order'd the Officer to go to the Citadel, and to have the Colors hoisted immediately! Away he went, but devil a bit could they get the halliards [ropes] to go free, until at last, they got hold of a Sailor, who soon scrambled up the flagstaff, and put all to rights in a jiffy.

All this time, the Ship-of-War did not shew her own colors, not knowing whether the Town was in the hands of the French or the English. But as soon as she perceiv'd our flag, she hoisted English Colors, and shaped her course towards the town, and was safe at anchor opposite to the King's wharf... The Frigate proved to be the "Lowestoffe" [commanded by Captain Joseph Deane], which had been detach'd from the main fleet below, with orders to make the best of her time thro' the ice, and take up the earliest intelligence of the approach of the Fleet. Her sides were very much torn by the floating ice.[6]

All the same, the arrival of a single ship, welcome as it was, did not lift the siege. It still left, Knox conceded, "the safety of this garrison depending on the arrival of a British fleet."[7] One frigate could neither hold off a French fleet nor carry the provisions and stores that Murray's garrison so desperately needed.

MERCHANT SHIPS

With the melting of the ice and the opening of the St. Lawrence to navigation, Quebec would change from an isolated outpost, deep in French territory, to a British port, connected by sea to a transatlantic Anglosphere, and a magnet for British and American commerce. There was money to be made supplying the British garrison, and enterprising merchants and seafarers were more than willing to take advantage of the opportunity.

Among these seafarers were Malachi James and Ashley Bowen. In Philadelphia on 8 May, James, a Massachusetts sailor serving as a mate aboard the schooner *Success*, wrote in his journal that "at 2 AM weighed anchor... bound for the City of Quebeck" with a cargo of flour. James' first indication that all might not be well at his intended destination came on the twenty-sixth when "at 2 afternoon spoak with a sloop from Port Roseway [Shelburne, Nova Scotia]—Told us Quebec was besieged by the French & Indians."[8]

"In May 1760," wrote Ashley Bowen of Marblehead, Massachusetts, who had served with the Royal Navy on the St. Lawrence in the 1759 campaign, "I engaged with Mr. Joseph Weare of old York to go in his schooner Swallow [as] master and pilot for the river St. Lawrence."[9] On 22 May, the *Swallow* "Received on board 18 bundle of hay. Ditto 6 shovels, 6 hand pumps, 1 lantern, 6 water pails, 1 pair of ox slings, ditto 7 pounds of deck nail. Ditto receive on board 28 oxen."

Three days later, Bowen took the *Swallow* out to sea and set sail for Quebec.[10]

THE FRENCH OPEN FIRE

One British ship had arrived and more might be on the way, but Lévis had no intention of giving up. On 11 May, the French batteries opened fire at noon. Despite heavy counter-battery fire from the walls, they continued until the evening—loading, firing, and loading again, flinging every shot and every shell as fast as they could against Quebec's defences. The guns continued to fire on the twelfth, but without quite the same exuberance. Lévis' scrapyard artillery was just not up to the job.

"Our batteries are in a bad way," he reported to Vaudreuil on the thirteenth. "Yesterday evening two eighteen-pounders blew up, the twenty-four had already been put out of service by a mortar shell. With so few heavy guns left, and their poor quality, we cannot expect to make a breach."

Despite the loss of his heavy artillery, Lévis kept on firing with twelve-pounders and mortars, limiting their fire to twenty rounds per day to conserve munitions. If he could not make a breach, he could at least make the British keep their heads down until the convoy arrived from France.[11]

If, of course, the convoy ever came. On 14 May, wrote Lapause, "the strong northeast wind that had prevailed for the last few days made us hope for help [from France] and at the same time fear that it would only come to the enemy."[12]

THE BRITISH UNDER FIRE

While the French pondered the wind, Johnson described the French artillery as experienced by those inside the city walls. "The first day and night they kept up a severe fire upon the town both of shot and shells; as also the second, but not so hot as the first, but every day afterwards they slackened their fire considerably; for meeting with a superior fire from the garrison than they expected; they slackened daily after the first day; till at length it was reduced to almost nothing but a blockade."[13]

Still, the bombardment and cannonade did have an effect. Murray himself suffered some inconvenience: "My house with [a] great part of what was in it crushed with three shells."[14] Knox relates how "as four officers of the forty-third regiment were sitting on the ground in a soldier's tent, eating a dish of pease-porridge, a shell pitched within a yard of the door of the tent, and they had barely time to stretch themselves at length, when the shell burst; but, being extended flat on the ground, they happily received no other damage than losing their mess, which was overset in the bustle."[15]

THE BORDEAUX CONVOY IN THE GULF OF ST. LAWRENCE

The French at Quebec didn't know it, but help from France was close at hand.

By 15 May, Lieutenant La Giraudais and the Bordeaux convoy had proceeded through the ice choking the Cabot Strait between Cape Breton Island and Newfoundland and into the Gulf of St. Lawrence. Passing Île-aux-Oiseaux, the northernmost of the Îles de la Madeleine, the French captured a stray British merchant ship from Commodore Swanton's convoy. On the sixteenth, Giraudais took four more prizes, most of the remainder of the convoy.

But along with the prizes, they acquired some very bad news. "I captured," wrote Giraudais, "a British vessel heading for Quebec and learned from letters I found in it that five or six ships of the line and as many frigates had preceded me to that city."

He assembled a council of war, which decided to make for the Baie des Chaleurs in Acadia between the Gaspé Peninsula and what is now New Brunswick. There, they could send their dispatches on to Montreal and await orders from Vaudreuil. On the seventeenth the convoy sailed into the bay; on the nineteenth the ships entered the Restigouche River and dropped anchor.[16]

The French attempt to resupply and reinforce Canada had come to a halt.

CHAPTER 23

QUEBEC BESIEGED: SHIPS

THE LAST NIGHT OF THE SIEGE

Outside Quebec, the warriors of the Seven Nations and Acadia continued to play their part in the siege, mounting a watch on the city during the night to prevent the British from interfering with the siegeworks.

On the evening of 15 May, a dozen British soldiers and an officer slipped out of the city and advanced towards the chain of sentries. Knox recounts how this worked out. The warriors "crept upon them unperceived, and gave them a brisk fire; which our little party spiritedly returned, and then fell back to the blockhouse, lest they should be surrounded."[1] The detachment left behind a prisoner, who provided vital if unwelcome intelligence to the besiegers.

As night fell, French lookouts had spotted two warships rounding Point Lévis but were uncertain as to their national identity. Assuming they were British, since they made no attempt to contact the shore, Lévis ordered his troops to remove the artillery from the batteries and prepare to lift the siege. This assumption was confirmed, he wrote, when "he was informed in the night by a prisoner that had been taken by our Natives, that the two ships that had appeared were English."[2]

This was the end for Lévis. "I very much fear that France has abandoned us... [the wind] has blown northeast for a long time... and nothing has arrived. We have done and are doing what we can. I think that the colony is lost."[3]

Quebec City: Canada could not survive as part of the French empire without Quebec. As the colony's sole Atlantic port, it was the gateway for convoys from France carrying supplies and reinforcements that Canada needed to make war. (LAC C-000355)

François-Gaston de Lévis: Able and ambitious, François-Gaston de Lévis
assumed command of the French regulars in Canada after the death of
Louis-Joseph de Montcalm. Lévis came to Quebec in the spring of 1760 to
recover the city and reverse the verdict of the Battle of the Plains of Abraham.
(STEWART MUSEUM 1984.8)

James Murray: Aggressive and impulsive, James Murray had planned to fight a defensive battle on the high ground just west of Quebec. Instead, he seized what he hoped would be an opportunity to smash Lévis' army and win the war for Canada in a single day. (LAC C-002834)

TOP LEFT The battlefield: This 1838 painting shows the southern half of the Sainte-Foy battlefield, including the treeline of the Sillery Wood where the French and British formed their battle lines. The open ground has become the Playing Field in National Battlefields Park. The hill in the foreground, occupied by lounging soldiers, was known to the British as Wolfe's Hill. It is now the site of the Pavillon Charles-Baillairgé of the Musée national des beaux-arts du Québec. The pillar at the base of the hill is a monument to James Wolfe, on the site of the present Wolfe Monument. (LAC C-045480)

BOTTOM LEFT Dumont's Mill: Joseph Légaré's *La bataille de Sainte-Foy* provides a fine view of the site of Dumont's house and mill and the terrain along the northern edge of the battlefield. Only the foundations of these buildings remained in the 1850s when Légaré painted this work, but the mill has since been excavated by archeologists and is marked by a stone circle in the Parc des Braves. Légaré's attempt to crowd the entire battle into this limited space, however, is more dramatic than historical. (NATIONAL GALLERY OF CANADA, 18489)

ABOVE The St. Lawrence River: Following the lifting of the French siege, Murray took an army up the St. Lawrence River to Montreal in a flotilla of small warships, merchant ships, and flat-bottomed boats. On their way, they passed Cap Santé, 115 nautical miles from Montreal, seen in this engraving. (LAC C-001510)

ABOVE The upper St. Lawrence River: The main British army, commanded by Major General Jeffery Amherst, ran the rapids of the St. Lawrence River, heading east towards Montreal. (LAC C-000577)

TOP RIGHT Montreal: The 1760 campaign ended on 8 September 1760 when the French surrendered at Montreal. In this image, painted two years later, Montreal has become a British port with ocean-going warships and merchant ships anchored offshore. (LAC C-002433)

BOTTOM RIGHT "Capitulation Cottage": According to local tradition, Major General Jeffery Amherst signed the capitulation of Canada in this house, just northwest of the walls of Montreal. Governor General Pierre de Rigaud de Vaudreuil had already signed this document, so Amherst's signature brought the war for Canada to a close. (MCCORD MUSEUM M2000.75.26)

Britannia triumphant: In this benign fantasy of the conquest of Canada, Jeffery Amherst, personifying a just and compassionate British empire, extends a reassuring hand to Britannia's new Canadian subjects. Beside the general, a servant brings a giant basket of bread, ready for distribution to the hungry. On the far right, a redcoat defends frightened civilians against sinister Amerindians. In the final version of this painting, now lost, the pillar bore the inscription "Power Exerted/Conquest Obtained/Mercy Shewn!" (cwm 19940037)

Vanguard and Diana

On 15 May, Commodore Swanton arrived in HMS *Vanguard*, accompanied by two smaller vessels. The schooner Murray sent downriver on 11 May had met Swanton at Île de Bic; a strong northeast wind propelled him up the river in a single day. On the evening of the fifteenth, wrote Knox:

> At night-fall came to an anchor in the bason, to the unspeakable joy of this harassed garrison, the Vanguard ship of war Commodore Swanton, with the Diana frigate, Captain [Alexander] Schomberg, and the armed schooner, which was sent down the river on the 23d ultimo; our gunners immediately gave the enemy a general discharge of all our artillery, three times repeated.[4]

John Désbruyêres had a less heroic but very human response to the same event. "Our frigates are now stationed at Cap Rouge, & every face in the garrison is brightened up to a degree a *peine reconnoisable, entre nous soit dit nous sommes heureux d'avoir été quittés pour la peur* [that they are hardly recognizable. Just between ourselves, I can say that we were very happy to finally shake off our fears]."[5]

Swanton had won the race to Quebec, but Colvill and the Halifax squadron were right behind him. By 14 May, Colvill was off the Gaspé Peninsula; by the sixteenth, he had reached Île de Bic. It had not been an easy journey. Colvill later recalled "a most tedious and troublesome passage, being almost continually impeded, by running among great quantities of loose ice, and confused by thick fogs." Along the way, he had managed to lose his convoy. "Notwithstanding our greatest care all the convoy lost company, more from their own bad conduct, than on account of the ice or weather." Absent the protection of their escorts, the errant merchant ships fell in with the French relief expedition and were snapped up by Giraudais.[6]

At Île de Bic, Colvill found a sloop bearing an urgent message from Murray. "The enemy having collected the whole force of Canada, is at present laying siege to this town, before which they have opened trenches ever since the 29th of last Month. Capt. Deane of the Lowstoff is arrived, but has not strength sufficient to attack the enemy's naval force... I need not use more words to press your arrival in the Bason of Quebec.[7]

MARCHING ORDERS

On 16 May, the French army at Quebec began to disband. With his artillery secured, Lévis ordered the militia home to their parishes and the regulars to withdraw to Fort Jacques Cartier. The most vulnerable members of the army, the militia from the Government of Quebec, were the first to leave.

Watching from the walls, Knox wrote, "We have the pleasure to see several bodies of Canadians filing off towards Charlesbourg and Beauport, and others down the south country, that have found means to get a-cross the river; hence we flatter ourselves that M. de Levis is going to raise the siege."[8]

VAUQUELIN'S BATTLE

The Royal Navy was nothing if not aggressive. The day after he reached Quebec, Swanton lunged up the river above the city to attack Vauquelin's warships, transports, and bateaux.

Outgunned and outnumbered, the French cut their cables and, propelled by the same tides that moved Swanton's ships, withdrew upriver. The *Pommone* went aground off the Anse au Foulon and was taken and burned by the British. Vauquelin ordered the bateaux and small transports to take refuge in the Cap Rouge River to land their cargoes, then he continued upriver in *l'Atalante*. "We kept on going up and firing on the two frigates that were chasing us; but finally, seeing the advantage they had over us and expecting that they would... catch up very soon, I decided that it would be best to find a place to run the frigate aground to save the King's sailors, who were very necessary to the colony and were in short supply."

After seeking the advice of his pilot, Vauquelin made his last stand off Pointe-aux-Trembles. "We arrived there at 7:30 [p.m.], with the [British] frigates one and half musket shot behind us, and ran around about twenty fathoms from the mill on that point. The two enemy [vessels] anchored... a half cannon shot away and maintained the heaviest possible fire... We too continued to fire... at 9:30 we found ourselves out of powder... and under the disagreeable obligation of watching the enemy fire without being able to reply."

Vauquelin managed to land most of his crew before the British boarded. Although taken prisoner by the British, he never formally surrendered and never lowered his flag. Once *l'Atalante* was in British hands, Deane sent the remaining French wounded ashore.[9] Of all the ships that had come to Quebec with Lévis, only one small vessel, *La Marie*, managed to escape upriver.

But if Vauquelin had lost the battle, he gained a certain vicarious revenge. Navigation on the St. Lawrence was complex and dangerous. Accidents happened. Now a prisoner aboard HMS *Lowestoft*, Vauquelin may have felt a certain satisfaction later when that vessel managed to ram HMS *Diana*. Three days later, in Knox's words, the *Lowestoft* "unfortunately ran upon some unknown rocks, and instantaneously went to the bottom."[10]

LÉVIS' RETREAT

The French siege did not end well. Lévis ordered his troops to drop the heavier guns into the river near the Anse au Foulon, passed out the remaining food, and carried off the field guns. Some of the regulars deserted. The Huron-Wendat returned to Lorette.

French soldiers posted at the Anse au Foulon depot broke into the stores after Cadet's clerks abandoned their posts, found Barthélemy Martin's brandy, and proceeded to drink themselves insensible; warriors looted the provision stores. Only the troops in the trench and the grenadiers remained under discipline. When they attempted to restore order, a scuffle turned violent, resulting in the deaths of one warrior and one grenadier, and the wounding of a second grenadier. At 10:00 p.m. on 17 May, the army marched for Fort Jacques Cartier, which they reached after a two-day march.

Lévis left Dumas and a force of about 1,800 regulars, militia, and warriors at Fort Jacques Cartier, Deschambault, and Pointe-aux-Trembles to keep an eye on the British at Quebec. Most of the rest of the army went back into winter quarters, to await the summer campaign.[11]

BRITISH PURSUIT

As the French withdrew, a British detachment, which included the officer of the 35th, set off after them. "We pursued some miles, took several wagons, with wounded men & some baggage, but could not come up with the [main] body; we only took care of [seized] the baggage. The wounded we let proceed." Along the way, some soldiers took advantage of the opportunity to loot. Their prizes included "church plate [altar vessels] which fell a prey to some of our Light Infantry, who thought it no sacrilege, to secure it, and apply it to their own use."[12]

Prisoner of war

Henry Hamilton, last seen surrendering himself on the Sainte-Foy battlefield, provides the only account of the news of the British relief of Quebec reaching Montreal.

When Lévis lifted the siege, Hamilton was living the good life as a prisoner of war in that town. "We were lodged together," he wrote, "in the convent of the Recollets, were treated with great kindness, and invited to the table of the Governor the Marquis de Vaudreuil [and] the Intendant M. Bigot."

Along with invitations to dinner, French officials kept their prisoner-guests up to date on current events. Towards the end of May, "The Marquis de Vaudreuil sent to us to attend at the Chateau— We went, he informed us that the siege was raised but gave us to understand that the country was still tenable from its natural defences."

The British officers, gentlemen all, responded to news of the French reverse with tact and courtesy. "We shrugged like Frenchmen, & not to hurt the mortifyed Governor, used some of the trite sayings, as . . . 'Fortune de la guerre.'"

This may have come naturally to Hamilton's fellows. But he himself only just managed to be civil. "I could scarce refrain from a broad grin of satisfaction."[13]

Humanitarian assistance

When Giraudais took the Bordeaux convoy into the Restigouche River, which flows into the Gulf of St. Lawrence south of the Gaspé Peninsula, he had planned to remain there for an indefinite period. One of his first actions was to send a detachment ashore to establish batteries to cover the ships in case of British attack and to set up an oven to bake fresh bread for his sailors and soldiers.

Captain François-Gabriel d'Angeac of the troupes de la marine, formerly of the Louisbourg garrison, now senior officer of the reinforcements for Canada, commanded the detachment. But when he set foot ashore, he stepped into an unfolding human catastrophe. "I discovered during that excursion more than fifteen hundred souls, exhausted . . . and dying of hunger."[14]

The 1,500 souls were refugees from the ethnic cleansing of Acadia that had begun in 1755 and continued as the British, determined to expel the entire French population from the Atlantic region, hunted down fugitives until the end of the war. Thorough, implacable, and ruthless, British forces had taken time after the siege of Louisbourg to push up the St. John River into what is now the New Brunswick interior to destroy a refugee centre, round up and expel the Acadians from what is now Prince Edward Island, and send James Wolfe to burn tiny fishing villages on the Gulf of St. Lawrence.

The refugees on the shores of the Restigouche represented the last concentration of Acadians in the region. Over the winter of 1759–1760, wrote Lieutenant Jean-François Bourdon de Dombourg of the troupes de la marine, Acadian refugees had been "reduced to eating cowhides, beaver skins, and dogs."[15] Giraudais arrived just in time to save them from final disaster.

Unable to take part in the defence of Canada, Giraudais and his subordinates turned to providing humanitarian assistance to the Acadian refugees. D'Angeac, responsible for operations ashore, took charge of this effort. "I arranged to provide a daily ration of a half-pound of flour and a quarteron of beef. . . This small assistance kept them from the gates of death."

Supplemented by provisions acquired by Acadian privateers preying on British merchant ships supplying the garrison of Quebec, d'Angeac's distributions ended the crisis and allowed the Acadians to survive another season.

Towards the end of June, a British naval force arrived and, following a series of engagements lasting over a week, destroyed Giraudais' ships. But d'Angeac continued to issue rations until October, when a second British expedition rounded up the remaining French forces on the Restigouche River.[16]

THE HALIFAX SQUADRON AT QUEBEC, 18 MAY

At Quebec on 18 May, Murray's troops moved out of their tents along the walls and returned to their billets. A merchant brig arrived from Philadelphia laden with provisions, which Murray purchased for his troops. The soldiers began to salvage the provisions, artillery, and munitions left behind by the French.[17]

On the same day, Colvill reached Quebec. En route, he had taken steps to secure the St. Lawrence for British shipping by posting one warship at Île-aux-Coudres and four at the Traverse channel. "I think," he wrote, "that [the Traverse is] the properest station to defeat the purposes of any squadron of the Enemy's ships, which may be determined to attempt to pass us."[18]

CONVERSATIONS WITH JAMES MURRAY

Malartic, left behind in hospital when the French army withdrew, noted that on the same day "Admiral Colvill arrived with the ships that had wintered in Halifax. I dined with M. de Murray."

They spent much of their time discussing Sainte-Foy. Murray praised Lévis' conduct of the battle and the courage of the French army. "After dinner," continued Malartic, "he did me the honour to ask my opinion of his motives in deciding to march out with his garrison on the twenty-eighth. I replied that it looked like he had hoped to be as lucky as on 13 September, and to have the glory of taking Canada without the assistance of the other English generals. He laughed and thanked me.["19]

Murray may have laughed, but Malartic knew his generals. Shortly after this dinner, Murray met with Captain Guillaume Léonard de Bellecombe of the Royal Roussillon regiment. In the subsequent conversation, he offered to grant the French easy terms if they capitulated to him immediately.

Bellecombe replied, very politely, that "if he [Murray] wanted the rest of Canada, he was going to have to fight for it.["20]

PART 4

MONTREAL

CHAPTER 24

LATE MAY AND JUNE

HIATUS

The end of the spring campaign left the war for Canada in a state of temporary equilibrium. The French held Canada between the Jacques Cartier River and Montreal. French regulars had gone back into winter quarters in Canadian homes, where they would be fed by their hosts to conserve government stocks of provisions; the Canadian militia and warriors of the Seven Nations and Acadia had gone home.

The British held Quebec and advanced posts on Lake Champlain and Lake Ontario. Before they could take the offensive, they would need months to move troops and supplies to the frontiers and allow the Quebec garrison to recover from the rigours of winter and battle.

Until then, the armies would remain at rest. But the initiative in Canada had changed hands. In April, the French and Seven Nations had set the pace and forced the British to react to them. In the coming summer, it would be the British who decided when and how campaigning would resume and Canada's defenders who responded as best they could.

SUPPLY LINES

No sooner had Lévis lifted the siege than the British at Quebec found themselves under pressure from another direction. Just to survive, let alone launch an offensive against Montreal, they needed a steady stream of supplies from the American colonies such as the cattle aboard the *Swallow* from Boston and the flour carried by the *Success* from Philadelphia. These supplies were already reaching Murray's garrison. "Ships," wrote Knox on 20 May, "are working up, by every tide, with stores, liquor, and provisions of all kinds."[1]

But too many of these vessels never made it to Quebec. "The squadron," reported Colvill, "was followed by many trading vessels from the colonies; some of which were taken by small privateers of the enemy near the Kamouraska Islands."[2] Colvill did not explain, and perhaps did not know himself, whether the privateers were from Acadian refugee camps at Restigouche, French colonies in the Caribbean, or metropolitan France.

His response was nonetheless prompt and effective. He had already left HMS *Pembroke* as a guardship at Île-aux-Coudres, upriver from Kamouraska. Now, he called on Captain Samuel Wallis, a veteran of the 1759 campaign and future Pacific Ocean explorer who, in 1767, would command the first European ship to visit Tahiti.[3] Wallis took charge of a squadron consisting of his own HMS *Prince of Orange*, the frigate *Eurus*, a schooner, and two sloops, and took them to Les Pèlerin, five islands about two hundred kilometres downriver from Quebec, near the Kamouraska Islands.

The master's log of HMS *Prince of Orange* chronicles Wallis' campaign against the privateers. Arriving off Les Pèlerin on 1 June, the squadron's sailors and marines established an encampment ashore for woodcutting, brewing beer, and housing invalids from the squadron in tents made of sails. The same day, in pursuit of an unidentified vessel that may have been a privateer forced to run aground, "the Eurus tender [a boat or small ship used to support a larger vessel] went on shore, after wch we saw a great smoake attended with an explosion."

For more than three weeks, the squadron remained on station near Les Pèlerin. The big ships guarded the main channel, challenging all vessels sailing up and down the river, most of which proved to be British and American merchant ships en route to Quebec along with a convoy escorted by Royal Navy warships. British shipping on the St. Lawrence was so dense that hardly a day went by without log entries such as "between 1 & 2 pm saw 9 sail to the Et wd coming up before the wind" and "1/2 past 2 sent our boat onboard them, 2 ships 1 snow 1 Brig from England 1 Brig from Philadelphia 1 schooner from Louisbourgh & 3 sloops from New Engd for Quebec."

While the ships patrolled the shipping channel, the sloop, schooners, longboats, and sailing boats—called shallops—hunted down privateers. On

5 June, "Between 8 & 9 the Eurus' tender set fire to a sloop on the s[outh] shore in a sml creek, wch had been an Engh [English] vessel taken by the French"; on 11 June "PM anchord here a prize schooner taken in the River Saguini by our shallop & tendr." In total, the squadron recaptured a sloop from Boston, burned two sloops, and captured a schooner that two boats from the *Prince of Orange* had pursued up the Saguenay River.⁴

As a sequel to the chase of the schooner up the Saguenay, "Captain Wallis," wrote Colvill, "explored this river with our small cruisers, and took a considerable quantity of fur, from a post [probably Chicoutimi] that did belong to the King of France, thirty leagues above Tadoussac, or the mouth of the river."⁵ The furs, logged aboard the *Prince of Orange*, included sixty-five bundles of white (or winter) beaver pelts, seven bundles of black beaver pelts, and an assortment of otter, wildcat, and martin pelts.

On 23 June, Wallis' privateer hunt ended when HMS *Rochester* arrived from Quebec with new orders. "At 3 PM," recorded the master of the *Prince of Orange*, "[we] began to unmoor, got the small bower [anchor] up & . . . the best bower. . . all our boats employ'd in bringing our men casks tents &c" from shore. "At 1/2 past 1 AM fired a gun a signal to weigh at 3 weighed [anchor] with the Rochester & Eurus." The squadron sailed downstream to conduct operations in the Gulf of St. Lawrence.⁶

They left behind a lower St. Lawrence that was a secure British waterway. Towards the end of June, when Ashley Bowen reached Île-aux-Coudres aboard the schooner *Swallow*, his only concern was fending off overly solicitous efforts to assist British mariners. This proffered assistance came from HMS *Pembroke*, the same ship he had served aboard as one of the "New England volunteers" during the British siege of Quebec in 1759.

A boarding party, led by the *Pembroke*'s purser, offered the *Swallow* a French pilot. Bowen, already familiar with navigation on the St. Lawrence, wasn't having any of this. "I said I came [as a] pilot from Boston and would take charge of said schooner."

The purser was not pleased. He "said if any accident should arise by not taking a French pilot, as there was one offered, the vessel must make all damages good."

Ignoring this financial threat, Bowen guided his ship upriver and arrived safely at Quebec. On the last day of the month, he took the *Success* downriver to the parish of Saint-Jean-de-l'Île-d'Orléans, where the British had evidently made arrangements to pasture imported livestock. There, the crew spent the afternoon "landing all our cattle in good order."[7]

The delivery of this cargo represented a small but significant victory in Britain's battle for Canada. Every ship that reached Quebec made the British that much stronger and the day Murray would sail for Montreal that much closer.

MURRAY'S REVENGE

While Wallis chased privateers in the lower St. Lawrence, Murray cracked down on the Canadians of the Quebec area. They had served against the British during the French siege. Now, he was going to make them pay.

Prior to the French retreat, Lévis had written a letter to Murray in which he did his best to protect the Canadians of the Government of Quebec from retaliation. As summarized by Knox, Lévis assured his British counterpart that "he was so tender of the people who had taken the oath to his Britannic Majesty, that he did not insist on their taking up arms, though he had compelled them to work for his army, which, he said, he had a right to do, in this or any other country, by the rules of war."[8]

Unimpressed, Murray compelled residents of Beauport to level the French trenches and batteries on the Buttes-à-Neveu, "as a punishment for their distinguish'd forwardness in assisting the French army during the siege."[9] More seriously, on 29 May he had militia captain Joseph Nadeau hanged in his own parish. Nadeau, wrote Knox, had "exerted his utmost endeavours to spirit up his countrymen to revolt, and drawing several of his own company, he being a captain of militia, to join the late French army."[10]

A week later, Knox added that "A priest and two or three Jesuits, are brought in as prisoners, and sent on board the ships in the bason; they have been too active in spiriting up the Canadians to a revolt."[11]

From a British perspective, these actions formed part of the necessary process of reasserting legitimate authority over British territory inhabited by people who had taken an oath of allegiance to the British Crown. Viewed from Fort Jacques Cartier, Murray's measures appeared in a much harsher light.

"I learn," wrote Dumas to Vaudreuil, "that the English have robbed and badly mistreated the residents of the Quebec area, and that people fear that neighbouring parishes will be burned very soon . . . the captain [of militia] of Saint-Charles [has been] hanged."[12]

Other Quebec-area residents, he reported, were subject to arrests aimed at forcing them to act for the British against the French. "Mr. de Murray has displayed a tendency towards violence that frightens and intimidates everyone, he has only to have people arrested under some pretext, [and] from that moment on to prove to him that they are not our spies, they become his, and by that means he knows everything that goes on in the colony."[13]

But if Murray employed force and fear to recruit Canadians, Dumas could still rely on loyalty and patriotism. "Mr. de Murray's severity intimidated everyone; nonetheless we still have people who pass on the news."[14]

Sometimes too much news. Dumas did his best to keep a precise account of the British vessels at Quebec, but he found himself buried under a flood of contradictory accounts from his agents. "I hear from various reports that 14 ships arrived at Quebec on 6 May, but they do not agree at all on the number that are currently in harbour. Some say from twenty-two to twenty-five and others 33 . . . But they all agree in saying that there were no troops [aboard], only one soldier of the Berry Regiment, who departed from the hospital, has said the opposite."[15]

FINANCIAL COLLAPSE

The end of the spring campaign left the French in a desperate situation. They had thrown everything they had into the siege of Quebec. The victorious Battle of Sainte-Foy had decimated the French army; abandoning Quebec had cost much of their remaining stock of artillery and munitions. "We are," wrote Lévis, "no longer able to remain in the field, lacking provisions, munitions, and generally everything. It's amazing that we manage to survive at all."[16]

In mid-June, the colony received a devastating blow when two messengers arrived overland from Acadia with news of the diversion of the Bordeaux convoy to the Restigouche River. Bad news, but hardly unexpected, giving the convoy's non-appearance at Quebec in May.

Infinitely worse and completely unexpected, they revealed that the French Crown had repudiated its Canadian debts. The stroke of a pen had flung thousands of individuals and families into bankruptcy. No one who was owed payment for providing goods or services to the Crown and its agents during the war could expect to be paid. The result, wrote Lapause, was "general consternation. . . as much among the merchants as the soldiers and Canadians."[17]

Consternation aside, this news had an immediate and very practical effect on the war effort. In July, Cadet sent his agents out into the countryside, seeking to buy peas and wheat for the troops. They failed, as Canadian farmers refused to exchange their crops for worthless paper. In the end, Vaudreuil, Lévis, and Bigot had to personally guarantee payments to farmers for their crops and livestock.[18]

Planning for all contingencies

The Seven Nations had their own take on the evolving strategic situation.

Genteel captivity in Montréal had introduced Henry Hamilton to a society where Seven Nations leaders, like British officer prisoners, were "used to admittance to the homes of traders and some of the first people."[19] This proximity allowed him to catch a revealing glimpse of alliance politics in action.

When the Seven Nations joined with the French in attacking Quebec, they had been well aware that this enterprise represented a last roll of the dice for their European allies. Before the French left Montreal, a Kanesetake Mohawk leader produced a precise appreciation of the French situation. "If they [the French] do not succeed in their last effort against Quebec, it would be in vain to make any further opposition against the English."[20]

Now that the expedition had failed, a delegation of Seven Nations leaders approached Vaudreuil with a blunt, realistic assessment. Hamilton was present at their conversation. "About this time," he wrote, "the Marquis had an interview with some Savages, they insisting that fortune had deserted the French Standard, expressed themselves as though the English should get possession of the Country."

Vaudreuil responded with bland assurances that all would be well. "The governor said by his interpreter, Jamais [Never]."

This response—essentially the same declaration that Vaudreuil had made to his British guests a few days before, "that the country was still tenable from its natural defences"—did not go over well. "The Indian by the same interpreter returned Oh Toujours jamais [Forever never]!"[21]

Nonetheless, the maintenance of the French alliance remained a key foreign policy priority for the Seven Nations. Throughout the Seven Years' War, they had chosen to support their French allies. But with a British army and fleet inside the colony at Quebec and other armies mustering on Lake Champlain and Lake Ontario, Seven Nations leaders had to balance the benefits of continued support of a longstanding alliance against the probable consequences of remaining in arms against the invaders.

Given previous British hostility to Amerindians, including the recent attempt by Robert Rogers to exterminate the Abenakis of Saint-François, the Seven Nations feared the worst. Two escaped British prisoners who passed safely through Kahnawake on 10 June made a concise report on the political situation among the Mohawks. "The Cocknawaga Indians are divided, one half proposes to go to Sir William Johnson, the other into the woods."[22] Aughneeta, a "principal chief" at Kanesetake, later referred to his community as divided between "some of our Young Men [who] were still headstrong and wou'd not believe that the French General wou'd be obliged to quit America" and "a great many of our People" who believed that a French defeat was inevitable and their best chance lay in coming to terms with the British.[23]

For the moment, the Seven Nations could temporize. But sooner or later, they were going to have to make a decision.

Murray's plan

Thus far, 1760 had not gone well for James Murray. He had watched his army almost collapse from scurvy, lost a major battle and fled ignominiously back into Quebec, seen his garrison break down in drunken chaos, endured a siege, had his residence blown up, and been rescued by the Royal Navy. His post-siege attempts to persuade the French to surrender to him had failed.

But Murray had a fleet of small warships, transports, and boats, he had what remained of his army, and he had a plan. Instead of just sailing up the river to Montreal to wait for Amherst, he intended "to do what I can to facilitate the entire reduction of Canada."

Confronting Lévis' army directly hadn't worked out so well in April. Murray consequently decided to eliminate its militia component, which had proved so effective at Sainte-Foy, piece by piece.

With most of Canada's population concentrated along the banks of the St. Lawrence and thus vulnerable to attacks from the river, Murray could oppose his entire military and naval force against a few militia companies at a time. By the end of the campaign, he expected to have entirely neutralized the militia, leaving Lévis with just a small force of regulars.

"The moment I arrive in Montreal," he informed the prime minister:

> I shall be probably master of the whole country; the Chevalier de Lévis must assemble his army for the defence of that capital; if the Canadians do not join him, his force will not greatly exceed mine; if they do, their country is abandoned to my mercy, my motions having the current of the river in my favour must always be four times quicker than theirs consequently it will be impossible for the Canadians to save their harvest this year if they assemble in arms for the country is no where inhabited or cultivated above two miles from the river.[24]

Despite this confidence, Murray's watchword throughout the campaign was caution. Before leaving, he discussed his intentions with Cramahé, who later reminded him of this conversation. "If you persist in the wise and prudent resolution you have laid down not to hazard anything, all will go well. Why risk, when you may attain all your ends by patience. Time as you rightly say, fights for you."[25]

LÉVIS' PLAN

But if Murray had a plan, so did Lévis. His moment of despair when the Royal Navy relieved Quebec had passed. And he still had a colony to defend and a career to advance.

Quebec remained in British hands, but the French still enjoyed the advantage of the central position. They might face invasion by three armies come summer, but these armies would be advancing from Quebec on the St. Lawrence River, Fort Crown Point on Lake Champlain, and Fort Ontario on Lake Ontario. "If our enemies do not coordinate their movements, we will attack the first of their armies to arrive. This is the only chance left to us."[26]

CHAPTER 25

MURRAY'S ADVANCE

QUEBEC TO THE RICHELIEU RAPIDS

By the second week of July, an improved diet and the passage of time had allowed enough convalescents to return to active duty to give Murray an effective field force, enough provisions had been accumulated to feed them all, and enough ships had arrived to carry the troops to Montreal, 140 nautical miles upriver.[1] Murray, confident that he could win the war all by himself if only he could reach Montreal ahead of Amherst, didn't waste any time. On 13 July, he ordered Captain Joseph Deane, formerly of HMS *Lowestoft*, now commander of the river fleet, to embark 2,500 troops. A garrison of 1,700 remained behind in Quebec. Reinforcements from Louisbourg were on the way. When they arrived, they would follow Murray upriver.

Murray's army embarked aboard a fleet consisting of the frigates *Diana* and *Penzance*, the sloops *Porcupine* and *Hunter*, and nine gunboats ("floating batteries"), escorting thirty-three transports and twenty-two flat-bottomed boats.[2]

The next day, wrote Murray, "Resolv'd to take the advantage of the tide, & get up as fast as possible . . . I immediately made the signal weigh'd anchor, and all the fleet got under sail."[3] Guided by French pilots, the fleet set off with HMS *Diana*, Deane's flagship, in the lead and HMS *Penzance* bringing up the rear.

When the fleet reached Fort Jacques Cartier, the British kept on going.

"At 8 past by the Fort of Jackhartier [Jacques Cartier]," wrote the master of the *Penzance*, "they fired several shott at us which fell short."⁴

By the fifteenth, the British had sailed past Cap Santé and reached the Point au Platon at the foot of the rapids, 115 nautical miles from Montreal.

The next morning, the *Porcupine* led the gunboats, most of the flat-bottomed boats, and half the transports up the Richelieu Rapids. A battery at Deschambault opened fire. The British responded with five broadsides. The French kept on firing until the ships were out of range.⁵

But before the rest of the fleet could follow, the wind changed, trapping the *Hunter*, the *Penzance*, and the rest of the transports below the rapids at Point au Platon.

Waiting for an east wind, Murray kept busy. That evening, he took several sloops and flat-bottomed boats back down the rapids and opened operations against the Canadian militia. Lookouts had sighted what appeared to be five hundred French regulars marching up the north shore from Jacques Cartier. Protected by the river and unwilling to risk an unnecessary engagement, Murray ignored them. With the north shore out of bounds, he turned to the south shore, where the French military presence was limited to a small party of colonial regulars at Point au Platon in the parish of Lotbinière.

On the night of 17–18 July, Murray slipped a detachment of rangers and regulars ashore under cover of darkness. At dawn, they attacked and dispersed the French force. With a beachhead secured, Murray disembarked his troops at Point au Platon "to refresh the men & get them greens [green vegetables]."⁶

The grenadiers and rangers made a thirty-kilometre circuit around the countryside and discovered that most of the local residents had abandoned their homes. Some of those who remained came out to hand over their muskets and attempt to convince the invaders to leave them alone. They declared, wrote Knox, that "it was with the greatest reluctance on their part that we met with any opposition from them; that they hope the contest will be decided in our favour this year, that they may remain at peace and quietness; moreover, they were rejoiced at our landing, as it furnished them an excuse to return to their habitations, and cease all further hostilities."⁷

With communications thus opened, the Canadians began to trade with the British, offering butter, eggs, and milk in exchange for salt pork. Before long, these informal transactions in the countryside had been replaced by a regular market on the point.[8]

In the meantime, British patrols posted manifestos on doors of the parish church and abandoned houses, "inviting," wrote the master of HMS *Diana,* "the inhabitants to come in & lay down their arms promising them the peaceable enjoyment of their lands."[9]

In response to this manifesto and the presence of British troops in overwhelming strength, more local families began to return to their homes and surrender their weapons. The captain of militia from the neighbouring parish of Saint-Croix came aboard the *Diana.* He received his own copy of the manifesto and orders to return the next day at 4:00 p.m. with the adults of Saint-Croix and the muster roll of his company.

At the appointed time, fifty-five men from Saint-Croix and seventy-nine from Lotbinière came to Point au Platon to turn in their weapons and take an oath of allegiance to the British Crown.[10] Knox watched the ceremony. "The men stand in a circle, hold up their right hands, repeat each his own name, and then say, 'Do severally swear, in the presence of Almighty God, that we will not take up arms against George the Second, King of Great Britain, &c. &c. or against his troops or subjects; nor give any intelligence to his enemies, directly or indirectly: So Help me GOD.'"[11]

After that, Murray addressed the crowd and made the case for getting out of a war they couldn't win, ending with an oblique threat to destroy the homes and crops of anyone who resisted. "Who can carry on or support the war without ships, artillery, ammunition, or provisions? At whose mercy are your habitations, and that harvest which you expect to reap this summer, together with all you are possessed of in this world? Therefore consider your own interest and provoke us no more."[11]

Oaths of allegiance in hand, Murray compelled the surrendered parishes to support the British garrison of Quebec. On 22 July, he wrote to the captains of militia ordering them to set the men of their parishes to work cutting firewood and bringing it into Point au Platon, along with sawn boards from local sawmills.[12] From there, the boards and firewood would be shipped to Quebec to improve and heat the garrison's winter quarters.

Above the rapids, the British were just as busy. The *Porcupine* sent boats to sound (measure the depth of) the channel for four nautical miles upriver. Colonel William Howe took the troops of his brigade ashore "to refresh the men."[13] Trade and surrenders began. On 23 July, the people of Deschaillons sent in a message offering to lay down their arms and take the oath. Howe sent an officer ashore to receive their submission.[14]

Finally, on 26 July, an east wind that could, with the assistance of a rising tide, propel ships up the rapids, began to blow. The second division sailed upriver; the rangers marched along the south shore.

Up ahead, two boats guided by a French pilot sailed upriver to Trois-Rivières, sounding as they went. The channel ran so close to land on the south bank that they were able to talk with a body of Canadians on the shore. The Canadians were armed, but instead of opening fire, they opened a conversation, calling out in English: "What water have you, Englishmen [referring to the depth of the channel]?"

The British reply was not entirely generous. "Sufficient to bring up our ships, and knock you and your houses to pieces; if you dare molest us, we will land our troops, burn your habitations, and destroy your country."

Another Canadian spoke up. "Let us alone, and you shall not meet with any annoyance, if your officers chuse to come a-shore and refresh themselves, I will be answerable for their being at liberty to return, when they please."

The British, a long way from the fleet, refused. The Canadians nonetheless took the precaution of demonstrating their goodwill by sending out two canoes loaded with "greens and salading."[15]

Despite the slowdown at the rapids, Murray's advance was proceeding according to plan. His physical progress up the river, though, was less important than what was happening around him. The grand plan to dismantle the French army by striking at the militia, parish by parish, was working. And Murray was just getting started.

FOLLOWING THE FLEET

When Murray passed Fort Jacques Cartier, Dumas ordered his gunners to fire a few rounds at the British. Then he pulled in his outposts, left a token garrison behind, formed up his detachment, and set off to "follow on land as the enemy moves on the river."[16]

At the Richelieu Rapids, Dumas' troops prevented Murray from landing on the north shore, but the three-gun battery at Deschambault failed to interfere with the British ascent of the rapids. When the fleet moved on, Dumas pursued, heading for Trois-Rivières.[17]

FLOATING FORTRESS

Not all of Deane's ships continued up the river with Murray. HMS *Penzance* remained below the rapids to keep that stretch of the river and the surrounding territory under British control and secure for British shipping.

The *Penzance*'s first days on station passed quietly. The captain had the ship's boats rowing guard at night to prevent surprises from the shore and kept a detachment of marines on Point au Platon. These measures were prudent, but this part of the St. Lawrence was now very much a British river. On the twenty-eighth, an unescorted supply ship arrived from Quebec with provisions, including two live bullocks for fresh meat. On the twenty-ninth, a flotilla of flat-bottomed boats passed downriver to help bring up reinforcements from Louisbourg. The ship's company made the river safer for navigation by "laying down buoys of water casks in the channel," and conducted routine operations such as exercising with small arms, cleaning the ship between decks, maintaining the rigging, and tarring the ship's sides.[18]

In the first week of August, HMS *Sutherland*, a ship of the line, replaced the *Penzance* at Point au Platon. The frigate sailed upstream and took station above the rapids.

Here, the *Penzance* returned to playing a more active role in the war. Landing parties of sailors and marines searched unsuccessfully for boats belonging to Canadians and collected sawn boards and firewood to send down the river to Quebec. The ship cannonaded small parties of French regulars and stood guard as British convoys and individual vessels shuttled between Québec and the fleet.

On the afternoon of 18 August, the *Penzance* came up against the limits of naval power when the captain "sent a flag of truce ashore to [the parish of] Grondines [on the north shore] desiring the inhabitants to deliver up their arms." The next morning, however, "a party of French regulars came and took post at Grondine to prevent the inhabitants from coming in to take the oaths."

By the end of August, the crew had evidently consumed the last of the beer ration. In a navy that drank beer and used water for cooking, this posed a problem. Over the next week, three log entries record some variation of "sent the longboat and shallop down to Quebec with 12 empty casks for beer." These voyages testify to both the firm control of the river that allowed small boats to travel at will and the reluctance of British sailors to resort to drinking water.[19]

THE RICHELIEU RAPIDS TO LAC SAINT-PIERRE

Near Champlain and Gentilly, ninety nautical miles from Montreal, the tide ceased to affect the river. This was bad news for the troops and sailors; human muscles would have to substitute for tidal power. "When you get half way up ..." the St. Lawrence, recalled James Miller, "the tide fails, and oars are hardly sufficient to stem the current, without a good breeze of wind, the labour of pulling against the stream, was excessive." There were, however, compensations. "The beauty of the prospect, made amends for the fatigue of body[,] being beautiful beyond description."[20]

At Batiscan on 29 July, the fleet came under fire from cannon on the north shore, supported by the militia. The British responded by cannonading the French positions for half an hour. Knox, thoroughly impressed, observed that "the spirited Canadians boldly sallied down within reach of musketry, fired upon the vessels, and retired: this was repeated, until at length a shot took place among them, killed one man, and disabled two others; then they thought proper to desist."[21]

Unwilling to lose a favourable wind by stopping to retaliate, Murray took other measures. He sent a schooner downriver carrying orders for Lieutenant Colonel Rollo and the reinforcements from Louisbourg "in case (and in that case only) the wind shou'd not be fair, to land a party at Batiscan, and burn the houses of the inhabitants who had join'd the French army."[22]

Other Canadians were more cooperative. On 3 August, wrote an anonymous naval officer who kept a journal of the campaign, "the captain of militia from Gentilly [on the south shore] was brought off, who reports his parish at home, that they received orders [from the French], but did not obey them, and is to have this all tomorrow to deliver up their arms & take the oaths."[23]

When a detachment landed at Bécancour (also on the south shore) to cut firewood, the local captain of militia came up and informed the senior officer that the people of his parish were at home and ready to take the oath. On 5 August, Knox wrote that "the inhabitants of the south coast came on board our ships without reserve, supplying us with vegetables, poultry, eggs, and whatever else they can spare, in exchange for salt pork and beef."

The fleet passed Trois-Rivières, seventy-five nautical miles from Montreal, on 8 August. The French garrison stood to arms; Murray ignored them and kept on going, leaving HMS *Diana* behind to watch the river. Murray and Deane shifted to a new flagship, the transport *True Briton*.

Knox admired the scenery. "In fine, their troops, batteries, fair-looking houses, their situation on the banks of a delightful river, our fleet sailing triumphantly before them, with our floats drawn up in line of battle, the country on both sides interspersed with neat settlements, together with the verdure of the fields and trees, afforded, with the addition of clear pleasant weather, as agreeable a prospect as the most lively imagination can conceive."[24]

Leaving this pastoral paradise behind, the fleet set forth across Lac Saint-Pierre, where the water was so shallow, wrote the Naval Officer, that the larger vessels were "plowing the ground [of the lake bed] the whole way, so that you might trace the ships way thro' the water."[25]

FROM LORETTE TO SOREL

Murray didn't know it, but he was being followed. As he sailed upriver aboard a warship bristling with artillery and surrounded by soldiers armed to the teeth, the Huron-Wendat of Lorette—men, women, and children— followed along behind, keeping out of sight and out of trouble.

By July of 1760, the Huron-Wendat had quietly taken themselves out of the war. Ouiharalihte, then a teenager who had been a fascinated spectator at the Battle of the Plains of Abraham in the previous year, explains. "We were unwilling latterly to take any active part in the War by opposing the English,—our council of Chiefs thought our force too small to effect much for our own safety, they determined upon being neutral."

When Lévis' army lifted the siege, the Huron-Wendat returned to their homes at Lorette, planning to follow later. By the time they were ready to leave, Murray was already on his way, and the St. Lawrence was filled with British ships. "The English Army had started before us in batteaux, and we travelled with our wives and children in our canoes, and on land; following as close to them as we could."

On Lac Saint-Pierre, the Huron-Wendat managed to slide past the British and "crossed over to the Islands of Sorel, and we *cabined* ourselves... [and] placed four warriors on the look out."

Here, in this apparent refuge, the trouble the Huron-Wendat had evaded all the way from Quebec finally caught up with them.

> A day or two after, a boat with six men and an officer came near the Island with an intention to land; our warriors shewed themselves at the approach of the boat, which they meant as a sign of peace, for we might have killed them all before they could have seen us. Our chiefs had ordered us to follow the English army without firing upon them. Those in the boat were very much alarmed when they saw us, and immediately turned about their boat. One of those men however fired at the most advanced of our warriors, who received no injury, but was so exasperated that he returned the fire, and shot the man.
>
> We afterwards found out that the Officer was Major [Samuel] Holland, who was always a very great friend to us, and often spoke to us about this affair.[26]

Huron-Wendat fears to the contrary, the British backed off after the shooting, allowing the refugees to continue on their way towards Montreal.

MURRAY AT SAINT-FRANÇOIS

On 10 August, Murray planned a routine landing at Saint-François du Lac, sixty nautical miles from Montreal, to give the troops some time ashore, trade salt beef and pork for fresh vegetables, and cover the departure of a detachment of rangers who would travel overland to make contact with the British force on Lake Champlain. The next morning, a small but powerful amphibious force, covered by gunboats and composed of grenadiers, light infantry, and rangers, set off for the south shore.

Murray ordered the detachment "to send a flag of truce to summon the Parish of St. Francis to surrender themselves," but "not to land on any account, if he thought there was the least risque" of facing the French army.

This proved to be the case. When the troops approached the beach, "they observ'd several partys of regulars . . . and the coast too difficult to land at, it being wood down to the water, they came off again."[27]

Not very heroic, but extremely pragmatic. Having lost one battle, Murray had no intention of losing even a skirmish. Leaving Saint-François du Lac undisturbed, the fleet continued on its way up Lac Saint-Pierre.

DUMAS' PURSUIT

When Murray sailed from the head of the Richelieu Rapids, Dumas followed on shore. The cavalry took the lead, followed by the infantry, two field guns, a few covered wagons, and thirteen carts.[28] Although unable to engage the British, their mere presence, combined with Murray's reluctance to risk another battle, at least succeeded for the moment in keeping the north shore of the St. Lawrence in French hands.

Marching hard, Dumas pursued Murray to Trois-Rivières, where he took up position, constructed entrenchments, and waited for an attack that never occurred. The British passed by and a frustrated Dumas set forth once more.[29]

"We have," declared Lévis, "reached the critical moment." With Murray above Trois-Rivières and British armies known to be mustering on Lake Champlain and Lake Ontario, "there is no doubt that they will coordinate their movements so as to act at the same time."

Normally confident and aggressive, Lévis briefly turned pessimist. "We lack the means to stop them. We have entrenched the islands at the head of Lac Saint-Pierre, but, since there are so many channels and we lack both cannon and powder, this is only a gesture we are making to slow down their march."[30]

CHAPTER 26

THE FOUR-FRONT WAR

For a month after his departure, James Murray had been advancing on Montreal all by himself and doing pretty well. Left to his own devices, he just might have fulfilled his grand ambition and captured Montreal in time to welcome Major General Amherst to Britain's newest colonial possession.

But that wasn't going to happen. In mid-August, the British Lake Ontario and Lake Champlain armies and Seven Nations and Haudenosaunee delegations began to move. Now the action was taking place on four fronts, three military, one diplomatic, separated in the beginning by hundreds of kilometres but all interacting as events on one front shaped developments on the others.

Unlike the spring campaign, when entire armies slammed into one another, holding nothing back, the four-front war in August would feature more movement than combat and minor engagements, quiet diplomacy, and individual decisions about continued participation in the war. New players entered the battle as British armies besieged French frontier forts and reinforcements arrived from Louisbourg and sailed up the St. Lawrence to join Murray. And Murray's troops and Deane's sailors, who had hitherto maintained civil and correct relations with Canadian non-combatants, began to target civilians.

ÎLE SAINT-IGNACE

On 12 August, Deane's ships passed from the open waters of Lac Saint-Pierre into the Archipel du Lac Saint-Pierre (Ouiharalihte's "Islands of Sorel"), an intricate network of islands and waterways extending all across the river. The British continued upriver until they encountered a boom of heavy logs stretched across the main channel. While sailors cleared the boom, Knox, who could never pass a romantic landscape without reaching for his pen, rhapsodized at length.

> I think nothing could equal the beauties of our navigation this morning, with which I was exceedingly charmed: the meandering course of the channel, so narrow that an active person might have stepped a-shore from our transports, either to the right or left; the awfulness and solemnity of the dark forests with which these islands are covered, together with the flagrancy of the spontaneous fruits, shrubs, and flowers; the verdure of the water by the reflection of the neighbouring woods, the wild chirping notes of the feathered inhabitants, the masts and sails of ships appearing as if among the trees.[1]

That evening, the fleet anchored above the town of Sorel at the mouth of the Richelieu River, fifty nautical miles from Montreal, and paused to let the Louisbourg division catch up.

On the thirteenth, a boat from the fleet rowing past Île Saint-Ignace, an island of the archipelago, picked up an escaped British prisoner of war who had been captured near Quebec during the winter. Safe aboard the *True Briton*, he informed Murray "that the Inhabitants [by which he meant the adult males] at the Isle St. Ignace had all left their houses and join'd the army at the Isle aux Noix."

The Canadians in question were French subjects who had neither surrendered to the British nor taken the oath of allegiance, obeying the lawful orders of French officers and officials. That didn't count for Murray. As far as he was concerned, surrendered or not, Canadians owed allegiance to the British Crown and would act accordingly or pay the price. "I resolved to make an example of the inhabitants of this Island who had left their houses & order'd Major [James] Agnew to collect all the cattle, sheep and greens, to be distributed to the whole army."[2]

The British had every expectation that this would be a profitable as well as a punitive venture. As Knox explained three days later, "The people of this country have not so much the appearance of poverty, as those in the neighbourhood of Quebec... I have been in a great many farmhouses since I embarked on this expedition, and I may venture to advance, that in every one of them, I have seen a good loaf, two, or three, according to the number of the family, of excellent wheaten bread."[3]

Murray's account of the landing was brief and circumspect, portraying a brisk, efficient operation. "Blew hard, the Granadiers landed at seven, the 500 men to cut fascines an hour after, rain'd hard all day, the cattle &c were taken off the island & distributed to ye men."[4]

Knox provides a less restrained version of events. Once ashore, a substantial proportion of the troops and sailors ran wild, looting and firing at will. Grenadiers and rangers, still under discipline, "picked up a great number of seamen and disorderly soldiers, who had been plundering the inhabitants," together with a crowd of sailors who were responsible for "shots being wantonly fired... at horses," and marched them back to the landing site.

The next day, Murray and Deane issued general orders that strongly suggest that the actions of soldiers and sailors had gone beyond mere looting. If Murray's journal entry had been prudent in the extreme, his order of the day, as paraphrased by Knox, contained a specific reference to attacks on Canadian women. "The General," wrote Knox, "has declared, that, if any soldier presumes to plunder, or offer any violence to the women on the island, he will be instantly hanged; Captain Deane has issued the like order to all the seamen."[5]

Tough words, to be sure. But neither Murray nor Deane chose to back them up with immediate action sending a clear message that this kind of behaviour would not be tolerated. Back in May, Murray had restored order in the Quebec garrison by hanging one soldier as an example. This time, the employment of the future tense amounted to an amnesty for crimes committed against the women of Île Saint-Ignace, and the lack of punishment provided a clear hint that further transgressions might be tacitly condoned, if not actually endorsed.

From a British perspective, in any event, robbery and violence against women had a positive impact upon the adult males of Île Saint-Ignace. On 16 August, when Murray landed his entire army on the island to cut firewood for cooking aboard ship: "I went ashore found ye inhabitants waiting for me, with their arms. I ordered them to be sworn & their arms to be sent on board the fleet, several left the enemys post at Sorrell that morning, others came from the army on the North shore. More Canadians came in from the parish of Berthier [now Berthierville], on the north shore, and the nearby islands of Dupas and Ile aux Castors."[6]

The presence of militia from Berthier was particularly significant. Lévis had his headquarters there, and a strong force of French regulars and Canadians guarded the parish. The local militia nonetheless crossed the river to Île Saint-Ignace to make their peace with the British.[7]

CROSSING LAKE ONTARIO

Lieutenant John Grant of the 42nd Highlanders, last seen enjoying a comfortable winter in the province of New York, returned to the war when the snow melted and the rivers unfroze. "In the beginning of May we returned to Schenectady and we camped on a hill near the town for a week till boats were ready. We then embarked 20 in a boat and retraced our route to Fort Stanwix [on the Mohawk River, along the route to Lake Ontario]."[8]

By the first week of August, Grant's battalion had reached Fort Ontario and joined the main British army led by Major General Jeffery Amherst in person. Amherst had previously commanded the land forces at the siege of Louisbourg in 1758. Success at Louisbourg led to his appointment as commander-in-chief of the British forces in North America. In 1759, while Wolfe attacked Quebec, Amherst had led an attempted invasion of Canada that advanced towards the outlet of Lake Champlain. Partway down the lake, he received word of the capitulation of Quebec. Rather than continuing on to Montreal and attempting to complete the conquest of Canada, he turned around and returned to British territory. The chief achievement of his campaign had been the construction of a massive fortress at Crown Point to defend New York against a French invasion.

In 1760, however, there would be no mistakes and no retreats. Amherst would invade Canada in overwhelming force—5,586 British regulars, including John Grant's 42nd Highlanders, 4,479 New York, New Jersey, and Connecticut provincials, and 706 warriors, mostly Haudenosaunee—fifteen of whom were Oswegatchies from the Seven Nations of Canada—supported by other British armies on Lake Champlain and the St. Lawrence River.[9]

Only two obstacles stood between Amherst and Montreal: Fort Lévis, on what is now Chimney Island, just below the present site of the Prescott-Ogdensburg International Bridge, and the rapids between Fort Lévis and Montreal.

THE HAUDENOSAUNEE WAR

Although longstanding allies of the British, the Haudenosaunee were deeply concerned that a British conquest of Canada would upset the balance of power in northeastern North America. As Saoten, a Seven Nations emissary, reported on his return to Canada, "the... [Six] Nations [Haudenosaunee] were beginning to reflect, and feared that as soon as there were no more Frenchmen, the English would want to destroy them; that at present they were closed in by all of their forts."[10]

No more able than the French or Seven Nations to halt the British juggernaut, the Haudenosaunee planned their own invasion of Canada, travelling alongside the British, but pursuing their own objectives. The Haudenosaunee contingent, declared the members of a party of Onondagas and Oneidas on 22 July, would be "coming expressly to prevent anyone [which is to say, the British] from harming the Natives."[11]

In the first week of August, the Haudenosaunee sent two envoys to the Seven Nations. In conference on the tenth in the presence of Pierre Pouchot, commandant of Fort Lévis, the emissaries reported that a British army would be on the upper St. Lawrence within a week. They strongly suggested that the Seven Nations "remain neutral, and allow the whites, who would soon be making peace, to fight."[12]

Speaking openly in front of Pouchot, the French allies made a cautious reply, suggesting that the delegates should go on to Montreal to make their case. In private, they accepted the Haudenosaunee proposal. Three days later, Captain Jelles Fonda, one of William Johnson's officers, noted in his own brand of English that "in the morning I heard from our Indians that the Indians who was gone to swegatia was retorned and said whould cep themselves nuteral when we whould come there." [In the morning I heard from our Indians that the Indians who had gone to Oswegatchie had returned and said they would keep themselves neutral when we would come there.][13]

At the same time, debates among Seven Nations leaders in Canada had ended in a decision to seek a diplomatic solution with the British. A high-level delegation representing the "several Nations & Tribes of Indians inhabiting the country about Montreal"[14] set off to meet the British and Haudenosaunee at Oswegatchie. When the main British army arrived, the Seven Nations would meet them not as enemies, but as neutrals and potential allies.

SAMUEL JENKS GOES TO WAR

John Grant's counterpart on Lake Champlain was New Englander Samuel Jenks, a man with a mission. In the spring of 1760, the twenty-eight-year-old blacksmith from Chelsea, just north of Boston, became Captain Jenks of the Massachusetts provincials.

The first entry of his campaign diary, written on 22 May, is precise and to the point. "Then set out on a campaign for the total reduction of Canada."

Happily married and gainfully employed, Jenks had endured defeat at the hands of the French at the Battle of Carillon in 1758. But in 1760 he came back for more. Why? He was going to war, he wrote, to play the man for the city & people of our God." In expressing this sentiment, Jenks was typical of mid-eighteenth-century New Englanders, whose concepts of masculinity centred on a British American identity, hostility to Catholicism, and military service in imperial conflicts.[15]

On 16 June, this personal crusade brought him to Lake Champlain and the army of Brigadier William Haviland. Haviland, who had already taken part in two campaigns on Lake Champlain, was overseeing the completion of Fort Crown Point and mustering an army to undertake an invasion of Canada.

Jenks began his time at Crown Point playing military tourist. "Went to view the works, which I think, when finished, may be justly stild [styled] the strongest place the English has on the continent. Here, I bleive, is our station for this campaign, for there is an immense sight of work to be done before these forts are completed."

Three days later, he added that "great numbers are at work in preparing cartridges & other necessaries for the expedition which I believe will be formed here against the fortified island [Fort Île-aux-Noix] & St. Johns."

After that, the captain-blacksmith settled into the routines of military life. Over the next two months, he supervised his troops as they cut timber for firewood, worked on the fortifications, and fired at targets. In his off hours, he complained to his diary about the rarity of mail from home and the shortcomings of the army's spiritual life. "I have not had the luck of hearing one sermon since I left home."

Which is not to say that Massachusetts had fielded an army of Puritans. Every Saturday night, Jenks met with fellow officers and "followed the old custom of drinking to wives & sweethearts." Given time off duty, he "spent part of the day with Capt Hart in his tent & several other gentlemen disputing on the carriage & deferent disposition of the fair sex."

But none of this conviviality could quite compare to the pleasure of receiving news from home on 11 July. "To day I recd a letter from my own partner, the only one I have recd from her since I left home." This pleasure was repeated on 6 August when a New England officer arrived carrying a letter from Chelsea, which "brought me the most agreeable news I have heard in camp; that is, I mean the news of my wife & friend being in health."

The letter came just in time. Within days, Haviland ordered his 3,300 regulars and provincials to prepare to embark for Fort Île-aux-Noix. "Saturday 9 August. . . this morning all my men recd one dollar a peice that desird it, to git them sum necessarys to carry with them down the lake. I have been packing up mine & giting sum stores for me on the lake."

On Monday 11 August, the army began to move. "This morning at 10 oclock A.M., we struck our tents & marcht down to the battoes, in order to imbarque for St. Johns. The Brigadier led the whole of the Massachusetts troops. At noon we sett of in three columns; the wind blood [blowed] prety fresh a head. We rowd till about sunsett when the signall was made to form on the left, or west, shore, & then we landed and the pequit [picket—troops on outpost duty] made the guard. We have come about six miles."[16]

THE LOUISBOURG DETACHMENT

When Lieutenant Colonel Andrew Rollo arrived in Quebec with two battalions from the Louisbourg garrison, he found instructions to follow Murray up the river towards Montreal. Along the way, he was to "disarm, and swear the inhabitants of the north shore, whenever it could be done without retarding his junction with me."[17]

In so doing, Rollo could build upon his previous experience in pacifying French territory in North America. In 1758, he had taken part in the siege of Louisbourg and led the detachment that occupied Île Saint-Jean (now Prince

Edward Island). There, he deported 2,200 Acadians and built Fort Amherst on the site of modern Charlottetown.[18]

Malachi James, mate of the American schooner *Success* and prolific diarist, became the unofficial historian of Rollo's expedition upriver. James had watched from the harbour on 31 July when at "11 AM the *Sutherland* Man of War & 11 sail of transports arrived from Louisbourgh."

Once at Quebec, Rollo lost no time in getting under way. On 3 August the expedition, including the *Success*, which had been assigned to Rollo's force, started up the river riding the flood tide. Five days later, the flotilla reached the foot of the Richelieu Rapids. Rollo scouted upriver. On his return, wrote James, the sailors "gave him 3 chears."

On the eighth, they rendezvoused with the frigate *Diana* above the rapids, and Rollo began to play his role in breaking the Canadian militia by landing five hundred troops at Champlain parish. Canadian families fled into the forest; Rollo threatened to burn their homes. After this persuasion, wrote James, "the inhabitants brought in their arms & took the oath of allegiance to King George without any resistance to our people. At 4 PM the troops all embarked on board their respective ships."

Over the next three days, the parishes of Champlain, Batiscan, and Sainte-Magdalene submitted to the British.[19]

By 14 August, the Louisbourg division had reached Trois-Rivières where, in James' words: "My Lord Rowle's ship & a brig run up the North Channail close aboard the town where the enemy began a very heavey fire on them from 2 batteryes wounded 1 officer & severall men on board My Lord's ship."[20]

Knox, although not present, paints a broader picture. "After they had passed the batteries, a field-piece was dragged along shore, which was vigorously played until the ships were out of reach, while the Indians and Canadians, like a parcel of water-dogs, ran almost up to their waists in water, discharging their small arms."[21] By the time the flotilla reached safety in Lac Saint-Pierre, the French artillery had inflicted several casualties and torn up the ships' rigging.[22]

After this excitement, the ships crossed Lac Saint-Pierre without incident. On 16 August Rollo was off to Sorel where, wrote James, "at 4 PM saw Genl Murreys fleet to our Great Joy."[23] On the seventeenth, Rollo linked up with Deane and Murray, who promoted Rollo to the local rank of brigadier.

Rollo's arrival increased the strength of Murray's army to a total of 3,807 regular infantry, seventy-six rangers, and one hundred gunners.[24] No sooner had they arrived than Murray sent Rollo's battalions "to row in their Boats to the Sorrell as if they were going to attack it to draw out the enemy, and see where their strength might be." The boat crews rowed; the French lined their entrenchments. As far as the British could tell, the garrison consisted of about fifty regulars and a crowd of Canadians.

Deeply unhappy by this latest demonstration of the willingness of local residents to fight for their country, Murray, who had no problem with using British civilians from the transport crews to support his regulars, decided to do something about it.

> I resolv'd to convince them, the French army could not protect their houses, or hinder them from being burnt, I therefore orderr'd a battalion of the Louisbourg Division to land, half a mile below the enemys post at Sorrell with 100 light infantry a league below that again, to burn all before them, till they met in the centre, and then to reimbark and bring off some prisoners if possible, sent a Manifesto, informd them they was thus punished, for carrying arms before my face, that I intended to attack the Sorell, and if one of them was found in arms, I shou'd put them to the sword.[25]

On 22 August, Murray put his intentions into action as a flotilla of flat-bottomed boats left the fleet and dropped downriver. Malachi James provides a pithy account of the day's events. "12 AM the Light Infantry landed to a small village below the fleet & burnt houses & barns destroying all before them. At 10 . . . return'd to their respective vessels."[26]

Knox concluded his own account of the day's events by blaming the Canadians. "This disagreeable procedure affected the General extremely, but the obstinate perseverance of the inhabitants in arms made it necessary, as well for their chastisement, as *in terrorem* to others."[27]

BERTHIER AND SOREL

On 12 August, Bourlamaque, recovered from his wounds, was at Sorel. Commanding 350 regulars and 350 militia, he watched as the British threaded their way among the Archipel Lac Saint-Pierre, then reported to Lévis.

"Twenty-seven or twenty-eight vessels just sailed up the ship channel . . . along with a great number of gunboats."

Faced with a force this strong, Bourlamaque wrote to Lévis requesting instructions. "I'm not sure what I should do." But when Murray sailed past Sorel, where Deane's warships fired a few shots at French workers constructing entrenchments, Bourlamaque abandoned his position and followed the flotilla up the river, leaving a small detachment to guard the town.[28]

Lévis wasn't pleased. "It is essential," he wrote back, "to prevent them from entering the Chambly [Richelieu] River and to hold the post at Sorel to the last extremity."[29] Expanding on this order the next day, he explained that "you know how necessary it is to prevent the enemy from reaching the Chambly [Richelieu] River and joining their Lake Champlain army. I hope that before my letter arrives, you will have returned to Sorel."[30]

On 14 August, Lévis himself travelled to Berthier, on the north side of the river almost opposite Sorel, where he joined Dumas in watching Murray's ships. He stayed there until the seventeenth, when a courier arrived with news that the British were on the move on both Lake Champlain and the upper St. Lawrence. Faced with three converging armies, Lévis "planned, [as British armies] approached Montreal, to unite his forces and attack whichever enemy army arrives first."[31]

OFFICERS AND FAMILY MEN

But while Lévis contemplated his steadily diminishing options, his army was melting away. On 12 August, having reoccupied Sorel, Bourlamaque had reported "no morale among the habitants. [They] all hope that I will not take away a single one of those who are below [downriver from] the English."[32] On the fourteenth, as he attempted to rally the local militia to defend the town, he added that "the habitants of [Yamaska] have refused to march; forty-two came in from Saint-François [du Lac], of whom twenty have already left . . . fifty or sixty Canadians, sent from Montreal as boat crews, have abandoned their boats in the river and gone home . . . I am overwhelmed with fatigue, there is no one I can rely on and I never sleep."[33]

Three days later, he still had four hundred militia in his force, "but they are deserting in packs, and yesterday's rain completed their discontent. I lost many today; more than two hundred have already deserted."[34]

Behind these desertions lay the growing divisions between those elements of the French army whose interest lay in a fight to the firing of the last round and the breaking of the last bayonet and those who believed they could best protect their interests by withdrawing from the war and making some accommodation with the British. Professionals from France could afford to keep fighting; Canadians could not.

French officers were salaried employees of the Crown. Their families, property, and homes were safe in France, where they were not exposed to British depredations. For them, every day they could prolong the defence of Canada enhanced their career prospects and increased their chances of promotion, pensions, and honours.

Canadians on the other hand, lived alongside invasion routes within reach of British forces that had never hesitated to burn, destroy, and deport. They had been prepared to risk everything in battle to cast the British out of Quebec. But once the spring campaign was over and all realistic hopes for a French victory had vanished, so did their willingness to fight for a government that could no longer defend them.

Simply speaking, the Canadians placed a higher priority on the safety of their homes and families than on fighting for a few more days or weeks to preserve the honour of French arms. "The habitants," confessed Lévis, "are terrified of the fleet; they're afraid that their houses will be burned."[35]

CHAPTER 27

SIEGES

SAMUEL JENKS AT ÎLE-AUX-NOIX

By 15 August, Samuel Jenks, along with the rest of Haviland's army, was closing on Île-aux-Noix. "Expect to be amongst bad neighbours before night. God grant we may behave ourselves like men . . . & let him do as seamest him best."[1]

On the sixteenth, while armed vessels fired on the French forts and ships "to feavour our landing," Jenks joined the army in storming ashore, "after which we marcht up & formd a line, & set out our pequits. The land we marcht through exceeding wett & mirey. I went sum times almost to my middle in mud & water, & obliged to run most of the way to keep up with the front."

The landing marked an important step in the campaign, but it was still a Saturday and Jenks and his friends didn't skip their weekly gathering. "We haveing a little rum, we made sum toddy to keep up the custom of Saturday night health." A few rounds of drinks to absent loved ones, however, were not enough to keep Jenks from spending a miserable night. "I lodged last night on the ground without my blanket, only a few bushes to cover me, & as wett as could well be."[2]

With the siege underway, the provincials set to work. They built roads, cut down and transported timber, worked on the batteries, moved provisions, munitions, and artillery, and mounted guard. Here, Jenks lays out a typical day's work.

To day I am ordred to assist the engineer; I have a party of 150 men, 2 subs, 4 sergts in carrying timber to the batterys; there is 800 of the provincials of us on fatigue in building battrys to day ... The enemy kept a constant fire on us most part of the day, firing 12, 9, & 6 pound shot ... they wounded 10 men, 5 of which, I beleive, mortally, the other not bad. I escaped my self narrowly several times. I think it very remarkable that the enemy have not killd great numbers, when we are so much exposed.[3]

On 23 August, the British batteries opened fire. Five days later, the siege came to an abrupt end. "This morning we found that the enemy had deserted & left ye island... the granadiers & light infantry went over & took possession of that fortress."

Infinitely more important for Jenks, the next day he "hapned to hear of a gentl going to New England. Immediately wrote a letter to my partner at home." Just a few hours later, "in the afternoon had all my things pact up in order to imbarque for St. Johns. I hear Genl Amherst is got nigh to Montreal, & we shall soon be there, if the enemy dont hinder us."[4]

LÉVIS PLANS A COUNTERSTRIKE

When Lévis learned that Haviland had invested Île-aux-Noix, he resolved to strike back hard. He sent Brigadier Roquemaure to Fort Saint-Jean with a force of 1,403 regulars and militia. Roquemaure carried orders to link up with a Seven Nations contingent, then march through the bush to Île-aux-Noix, smash Haviland's army, and break the siege. On the twenty-first, 474 warriors arrived.

When Roquemaure invited their leaders to join the expedition, however, they made a very careful response. Instead of an unconditional acceptance, which might have threatened their negotiations with the British, or a blunt refusal, which would have alienated the French, they temporized. After meeting among themselves, they informed Roquemaure that "they would only march alongside 5000 [French] men."[5] Furthermore, before committing themselves, they planned to send a scouting party consisting of one warrior from each nation to reconnoitre Île-aux-Noix and make their own observations of conditions there.

Three days later, the regulars, militia, and warriors were still at Fort

Saint-Jean when a messenger from Oswegatchie arrived with word that the Haudenosaunee had agreed to mediate between the British and the Seven Nations. With their war about to end, the warriors took their leave. The attempt to relieve Île-aux-Noix collapsed. On 29 August, the French burned and abandoned Fort Saint-Jean and withdrew towards Montreal.[6]

DEFENDING ÎLE-AUX-NOIX

When the rest of the French army had sailed off to Quebec in April, Lieutenant James Johnstone of the troupes de la marine, a former Scottish rebel, former soldier of the garrison of Louisbourg and former aide-de-camp to Louis-Joseph de Montcalm, found himself assigned to the caretaker winter garrison of Fort Île-aux-Noix, under the command of Louis-Antoine de Bougainville. While Lévis' army fought the Battle of Sainte-Foy and besieged Quebec, Johnstone wrote dramatic accounts of events he never witnessed and guarded Canada's Lake Champlain frontier against an attack that never came. By August, however, the war was coming his way again as Île-aux-Noix changed from a strategic backwater into the guardian of a crucial gateway to Canada.

Johnstone described the fort, located on the Richelieu River fifteen kilometres north of the outlet of Lake Champlain:

> The Ile-aux-Noix is about twelve hundred fathoms long and one hundred fifty to two hundred fathoms across. M. de Bourlamaque entrenched there and built very regular earthworks [in 1759]. At the same time he blocked the two arms of the river, formed by the island, with two booms made with large logs attached end to end with iron hoops and staples... Thus, for as long as we hold the Ile-aux-Noix, the English cannot invade by way of Lake Champlain.[7]

To defend Île-aux-Noix, Bougainville commanded a garrison of 830 regulars, 435 militia, and 188 gunners, clerks, bakers, sailors, labourers, and servants.[8] This was not nearly enough for Bougainville, who worried about both the size of his garrison and the quality of the defences. "There are very few people for such a large island. The outworks are incomplete; the old entrenchment won't last a day under cannon fire; nonetheless, we will do our best."[9]

These weaknesses were somewhat balanced by the presence of a number of small French warships and gunboats. This flotilla prevented the British from landing on the island or bypassing the fort by way of the river and maintained communication with the French outposts at Chambly and Saint-Jean. Lapause, present as Lévis' personal observer, reported on the operations of the last French naval force on the North American lakes. "Every night we send a ship behind the boom on the south channel, the enemy being active there, the other [ships] are just below the island, anchored a pistol shot from shore, to prevent the enemy from landing there."[10]

On 16 August, the British arrived and the siege began. Johnstone did not enjoy the experience.

> The enemy having many cannon, mortars, and howitzers, they established batteries on the other side of the river to take us in the flank, in the rear, and from all sides, so no part of the island is sheltered from their artillery. Under these conditions, the garrison endured a continuous cannonade, very intense and without a moment's pause, one of their batteries was so close to us, near the south boom, that they killed many soldiers with musket shots. We had no bunkers to protect our troops.[11]

Finally, the British succeeded in destroying or capturing Bougainville's tiny fleet on the morning of the twenty-fifth. Lashed by a heavy bombardment that killed many of the officers and sailors, the survivors abandoned their vessels, which drifted ashore in British-held territory.[12]

Without the ships and gunboats, Île-aux-Noix became untenable. Bougainville, who had received one letter from Vaudreuil giving him permission to capitulate and evacuate his garrison if necessary and another from Lévis ordering him to hold out until the last extremity, called a council of war.

Johnstone, typically, recorded the council as if he were the only one present. "How could we reconcile the contradictions in the two letters? M. de Bougainville showed them to me and asked my opinion. I saw no alternative to attempting a retreat, since we would be forced to surrender in two days when our provisions ran out . . . and making a final effort under the walls of Montreal . . . It was thus decided to retreat."[13]

JOHNSTONE'S RETREAT FROM ÎLE-AUX-NOIX

The French retreat from Île-aux-Noix began as a quiet, orderly exercise. Beginning at 10:00 p.m., Bougainville's troops boarded boats and canoes and slipped away from the island. Behind them, an officer of the troupes de la marine remained with forty soldiers to fire off the remaining munitions to cover the evacuation. They held out until 1:00 p.m. the next day, then negotiated a capitulation.

Johnstone and the remainder of the garrison crossed to the mainland without incident, then lost their way in the same semi-aquatic terrain that had caused Jenks so much misery. They were frequently up to their waists in water and at one point almost blundered into a British camp. For twelve hours, the fugitives did "nothing but unwittingly walk in circles, because our guides didn't know the way and we had no Natives with us."

For Johnstone, the retreat became a nightmare. "I have often found myself in painful and dangerous situations, but I have never suffered as much as I did during that cruel journey... I was so stricken with fatigue and so totally exhausted, hardly able to drag my legs, that I thought a thousand times that I would remain here for the rest of my life."

Finally, at 4:00 p.m., they paused in a field a league and a half from Fort Saint-Jean. "There I saw a boat about to leave for Fort Saint-Jean, and I had just enough strength left to fling myself aboard."

By the time he reached the fort, Johnstone had reached the very limits of his endurance. "I was so tired that I could hardly speak. It was a fine day and very warm. I left the boat and threw myself fully dressed into the water, not having the strength to remove my clothes that were covered in mud; where I stayed, with just my head out of the water, for over an hour."

After dinner with the commandant and a good night's sleep, Johnstone set off the next morning and walked to La Prairie, where he crossed the river to Montreal.[14] He travelled through a land shaken by the events on Lake Champlain. "The retreat from Ile aux Noix," wrote Lapause, "has so alarmed the habitants that almost all of them have deserted. Our married soldiers and many others... in all the battalions... follow their example."[15]

JOHN GRANT AT FORT LÉVIS

By 18 August, Amherst's army had crossed Lake Ontario in a flotilla of bateaux, escorted by small warships, and travelled down the St. Lawrence to Fort Lévis. There, he deployed his forces, established three batteries on two nearby islands and a peninsula, and prepared to unleash the same kind of savage barrage that had shattered Fort Île-aux-Noix.

For Lieutenant John Grant, however, his most memorable experience during the siege was falling asleep.

> I was ordered on picquet where we had to construct abbatis for defence against the Indians who were hovering about—No sooner that duty done than I was ordered on duty to the trenches. So that I was nealy [nearly] three days with scarce sleep—I was so tired at last that when the work was finished just before daybreak (of the fourth day of our arrival) I leant against the parapet of the battery and fell fast asleep.

This in itself would have made an amusing story for Grant to tell his children, but there was more to come. To understand what happened next, it's important to remember that the death of a lieutenant opened up an opportunity for the promotion ("a step") of an ensign.

> My party leaving me went of[f] before dawn to avoid the fire of the fort on the island which was heavy and reported me killed or missing. When I awoke 2 hrs after dawn, the batteries had opened and had been firing but so sound was my sleep as not to disturb me the veteran. The Regts ensigns looked disappointed taking me for a step.[16]

THE LA CORNE EXPEDITION

The French position on Lake Champlain had collapsed, but Lévis still had hopes for the Lake Ontario frontier. "We expected," he wrote, "that Fort Lévis would hold out for a long time, given the strength of its position."[17]

Should his confidence prove misplaced, Lévis had a backup plan. Beyond the fort, a series of dangerous rapids blocked the way to Montreal. Here, the presence of an active, aggressive French force could temporarily stop the British in their tracks. Lévis accordingly ordered Luc de La Corne and four hundred militia "to harass the [British] army of Lake Ontario if they attempt to descend [the St. Lawrence] and give us the time to assemble a stronger body of troops, assuming that circumstances permit us to take them from other frontiers."[18]

Moving quickly, La Corne advanced to within sight of Fort Lévis, only to discover that the fort had already fallen. When the British moved down the river, La Corne travelled ahead of them, maintaining contact and reporting to Lévis, but unable to do anything to interfere. Along the way, his detachment disintegrated as the militia returned home.[19]

DEFENDING FORT LÉVIS

In March of 1760, Captain Pierre Pouchot of the Béarn regiment, a forty-eight-year-old military engineer who had served in North America since 1756, took command of Fort Lévis. Located on Orakointon, now Chimney Island, about 180 kilometres from Montreal, Fort Lévis stood squarely in the path of any invasion of Canada by way of the upper St. Lawrence. While the dramatic events of the Quebec campaign played out in the east, Pouchot and his garrison of three hundred regulars and militia strengthened their fort's rudimentary fortifications and waited for a British attack.

On 18 August, Pouchot's sentries looked out to see the river covered by hundreds of bateaux carrying thousands of soldiers, escorted by gunboats and four small warships. "It made," he wrote, "a very pretty sight."

Pouchot expected them to come straight on and land on the island. Instead, the British slipped along the north shore, keeping a safe distance from the fort. Pouchot's batteries fired 150 shots without slowing them down.

The invaders might have been enemies, but they weren't strangers. Writing in the third person, Pouchot observed that since he "was acquainted with many of the officers of that army, many of them called out greetings as they passed, others asked him to let them pass, since they were his friends."

On 20 August, the British commenced construction of their siege batteries. Pouchot's gunners attempted to interrupt the work but lacked the munitions to generate an extensive barrage. Two days later, British ships and shore batteries began to bombard the fort with a mix of shells and roundshot. All of these batteries were served with great enthusiasm, without interruption, until noon, blasting the fort into flying shards and splinters. Everyone stayed under cover, all at their posts, with only the sentries watching the movements of the enemy.

Pouchot became one of the first casualties. "A piece of wood ten feet long and fourteen inches square, sent flying by a twelve inch mortar shell, gave M. Pouchot a massive bruise in the lower back, which did not prevent him from doing his duty."

Thinking the British were about to make an amphibious assault, Pouchot deployed 150 troops—half his garrison—along the shore and opened fire with five guns. Although few in number, the French cannon were very effective. They forced three British ships to run aground, all badly damaged. One crew surrendered and became prisoners of war. Troop-carrying bateaux that had emerged from behind an island, heading for the fort, prudently withdrew.

But if the French had won a minor victory, the bombardment continued. On the twenty-fifth, the French hit back with a counter-battery strike against the most effective siege batteries by the last three guns facing these positions. They inflicted only minor damage but provoked a vigorous response from the British. Pouchot wrote:

> That afternoon, they [the British] redoubled the fire of all their batteries, and fired red hot shot and firebombs. That was too much for this miserable fort, which was nothing but a heap of lumber and fascines. The red hot shot set fire to the long fascines lining the interior facing of the bastion, right at the bottom, where we put it out. This made us realize how badly the rampart had been damaged. Firebombs twice more ignited the ruins of the fort. We managed to extinguish these fires, with water from shell holes.

With his fort falling into ruins all around him, Pouchot surrendered that same day. The next morning, he wrote, "when enemy troops entered, they were very surprised to see only a few soldiers scattered at their posts... and about sixty militia with handkerchiefs on their heads, all in their shirts... They [the British] asked M. Pouchot where his garrison was. He replied that they were seeing it all."[20]

CONFERENCE AT OSWEGATCHIE

As the British besieged Fort Lévis, Seven Nations envoys came to nearby Oswegatchie to meet in council with William Johnson.[21] Aughneeta of Kanesetake later summarized the conference from his perspective. "The principal men of our village as well as those from the other villages attended on Sir

William Johnson at Oswegatchie where he received the submission of all the Deputies from Canada, and there in a full council granted us protection in the King's name, & confirmed to us our lands as granted by the King of France, and the free exercise of our religion."[22]

Speaking in 1770, Seven Nations representatives portrayed the terms as an exchange of guarantees. The Seven Nations would grant the British free passage to Montreal. The British would respect the land and religious rights of the Seven Nations. "If we did not assist the French, but permitted you to descend the River; without interruption, we should be placed among the number of your friends, and enjoy our rights and possessions and the free exercise of our Religion forever."[23]

Immediately upon agreement of these terms, the Seven Nations sent messengers to carry the news to their communities and those of their warriors who were still in the field. Ten Akwesasnes went so far as to join thirty-six French deserters from Fort Lévis in guiding the British through the rapids to Montreal.

As for the Haudenosaunee, now that they had achieved their objective of protecting the interests of the Seven Nations in general and their relatives in Oswegatchie, Akwesasne, Kahnawake, and Kanesetake in particular, they left the British at Fort Lévis and returned to their communities. Only 175 travelled on to Montreal with Amherst.[24]

FROM SOREL TO MONTREAL ISLAND

With the Berthier and Île Saint-Ignace areas terrorized into submission, on 23 August Murray's fleet set off once again, sailing up to the parish of Lanoraie, thirty-five nautical miles from Montreal. French columns on both banks of the river followed along until cannon fire from the fleet killed some of the light cavalry horses.[25]

Here, on 26 August, the fleet received a sharp reminder of the navigational hazards of the St. Lawrence. While the fleet remained off Lanoraie, the captain and master of HMS *Porcupine* sounded the channel upriver. They "found it very intricate... [with] rocks not larger than a boat on which is 10 11 & 12 feet,"[26] too shallow for the *Porcupine* and the larger transports. Just a few days' travel from Montreal, Murray's troops might have had to disembark from the ships and walk if the British had been forced to find their way on their own.

The fleet, however, had been guided up the river by a number of French pilots. These pilots may have been traitors who had accepted payment from the British to guide the flotilla upriver to Montreal, but they knew their business. Accompanied by Murray and Deane, they sounded a channel five metres deep up to Contrecoeur and marked rocks and shoals with the ships' boats.[27]

On the twenty-seventh, the fleet threaded its way up the channel. The *Porcupine* touched ground a few times and three transports ran ashore and had to be hauled off, but that night the fleet anchored off the eastern tip of the island of Montreal, between Île Sainte-Thérèse and the parish of Varennes on the south shore of the St. Lawrence, fifteen nautical miles from Montreal.[28]

Murray elected to halt at that point, to await solid information regarding Amherst and the main British army. On 28 August, the fleet shifted position and anchored off Pointe-aux-Trembles on the eastern end of the island of Montreal. At 2:00 p.m., the French force that had shadowed the fleet all the way from Fort Jacques Cartier appeared on the shore. A second body of French troops marched down the road from Montreal and occupied Pointe-aux-Trembles.[29]

That night, a British soldier from the 17th Regiment, taken prisoner six weeks before on Lake Champlain, escaped from Montreal and paddled a canoe out to the fleet. Once aboard, he gave Murray a good deal of military intelligence, along with an account of the contrasting reactions of Canadians and French regulars to the apprehended fall of the colony. He reported, wrote the Naval Officer, "that yesterday the women were all in tears, but the troops very merry, as they suspect it will be soon over, & they gett home."[30]

CHAPTER 28

VARENNES

FLOATING OFF THE NORTHEASTERN tip of Montreal Island, Murray now turned his attention to Varennes.

On 29 August, Murray and Deane crossed the river on the transport *Duke* for a look at that parish. He sent seven rangers on ahead to land and take a prisoner for intelligence, but that didn't work out. "The inhabitants," wrote Knox, "jealous of such a design, fired upon them before they made the shore, and obliged them to sheer off."[1]

On the thirtieth, the *Duke* sailed once more to Varennes, where Murray observed "about 200 Canadians with a few regulars shewing themselves about the Church of [Sainte-Anne de] Varennes." Rather than seeing these troops as legitimate defenders of Canada, Murray characterized them as occupiers, imposing the will of the French Crown by force and "keeping the country in subjection."[2]

Murray thereupon decided to smash this force and occupy Varennes. "I orderr'd 4 companies of Grenadiers, 4 of light infantry & the Rangers to hold themselves ready to land & take possession of it."[3] At 2:00 a.m. on the thirty-first, the troops embarked from Île Sainte-Thérèse in flat-bottomed boats.

First ashore were two companies of grenadiers and two of light infantry, eight hundred metres upriver from the church. A French force opened fire; the British drove them back. No British soldiers or sailors were hurt. Eight of the defenders were killed or wounded; twenty were taken prisoner. Their position secured, the British occupied several houses and launched three signal rockets.[4]

Murray saw the rockets and led the rangers, remaining grenadiers, and light infantry ashore just downriver from the church. While two grenadier companies occupied houses near the landing site, Murray led the light infantry and rangers in a rapid advance to the church. After a brisk skirmish, wrote Murray, the British "possessed ourselves of the Church, at day break without the loss of a man."[5] They captured twenty-four more prisoners, three of whom were French regulars, out of a force of sixty regulars and 320 militia.[6]

With the heart of the parish secured, Murray set off to examine his capture. "I reconnoitred the country, wch I found to be very open & proper to take post with my army, till I could procure intelligence of General Amhersts Motions."[7]

While Murray reconnoitred, his troops began to loot. On Île Saint-Ignace, British soldiers had had orders to steal the island's livestock on behalf of the Crown; at Varennes, they acted on their own.

For Knox, once again, this was all the fault of the Canadians for defending their homes. "Scouts were sent out, who procured some cattle and poultry, which the inhabitants had here in plenty; and, by their obstinacy, they [the Canadians] lost the best part of their wearing apparel and other effects."[8] Standing on the deck of the *Success*, Malachi James watched as "the soldiers brought a vast quantity of plunder."[9]

Around 8:00 a.m., Murray departed, along with most of his troops. He left behind two companies of light infantry and the rangers to fortify the church and guard the beachhead.[10]

In the early afternoon, the French launched a counterattack against this detachment. "A body of about fourscore [eighty] Canadians," wrote Knox, "came down, divided themselves into small parties, and attacked the rangers at Varenne." When the militia attempted to occupy a barn near the church, the rangers broke cover, advanced on the Canadians, and set fire to the barn. The Canadians switched targets. "Under cover of the smoke and flames," they attacked the British in the church. The rangers and light infantry drove them back.

A running fight ensued, Knox continued, as "the rangers, covered by a company of light infantry, pursued them in their flight for near a mile, in which they had three men killed and scalped near the chapel, and we had only three who were lightly wounded."[11] Listening to the musket fire across the water, James noted that the French "continued [to fire] 1/2 an hour then retreated."[12]

Following his return to the fleet, Murray registered his disapproval at the comprehensive looting of Varennes parish. But once again, instead of taking action, he issued a sharp order of the day. "Every Officer will exert himself to inforce a due obedience of orders, and to prevent marauding, or any other abuse being offered to the Canadians."[13]

Murray refrained from specifying what "any other abuse" might be. The anonymous Canadian author of the *Mémoire du Canada* was more informative, using language that is clear and unmistakeable. Yet at the same time, the author is careful to qualify his depiction of events by reminding readers that what happened at Varennes was unique and unexpected, and thus not characteristic of British behaviour in general.

British accounts all suggest that redcoats and sailors directed their violence solely at the local militia in open battle before turning their attention to seizing property. The *Mémoire du Canada* declares that on the afternoon of 30 August, British combatants at Varennes progressed from employing military violence against armed men to sexual violence against women and children. "M. Murray, warned of the approach of these two armies [of Lake Champlain and the upper St. Lawrence] had 400 men land at a place named Varennes. Since the inhabitants of that place fired on them, he allowed his troops to loot. They even raped girls and women, something that had never happened before in all of the war."[14]

The *Mémoire* was a private narrative, but a reference to this event also appears in French official correspondence. In a report to the minister of marine and colonies on 2 September, François Bigot said of the British at Varennes that "this detachment has raped, robbed and burned houses and barns and committed other disorders."[15]

VIOLENCE AND RAPE

From Quebec to Lac Saint-Pierre, interaction between British soldiers and sailors and Canadian non-combatants occurred in pacified areas where the local militia had laid down their arms and taken the oath of allegiance. From a British perspective, the Canadians along this stretch of the river were behaving rationally and appropriately, acting as neutrals in the war between the French and British Crowns and accepting their new role as British subjects.

On Île Saint-Ignace and at Varennes, on the other hand, the British confronted Canadians who had been living in French-controlled territory and had never taken the oath of allegiance to the British Crown. Instead, they acted as French subjects bound to obey officers and officials of the French Crown. This applied particularly to adult males, who continued to serve as soldiers in the militia. As far as Murray was concerned, this persistent loyalty to France was one step away from treason.

Thus, the Saint-Ignace expedition was explicitly punitive and directed against the general population, which had been defined as enemies. Murray's troops had orders to confiscate private property, which gave them a licence to rove and loot. The Canadians, trapped on an island, had nowhere to run.

When the British described the fighting at Varennes, they wrote as if they had been facing opponents who had no right to resist. Seizing an entire parish involved skirmishing in extended order over a large area, taking the troops out from under the eyes of their officers. Pillaging the Varennes parish scattered them even farther and brought them into contact with female non-combatants.

Under these conditions, British troops at Île Saint-Ignace and Varennes could do pretty much what they pleased, and it pleased them to "offer... violence to... women" and to rape women and girls.[16]

Chapter 29

THE LAST DAYS OF THE
WAR FOR CANADA

John Grant runs the rapids

Amherst and his troops spent six days making repairs to the former Fort Lévis, now Fort William Augustus. Then they were on their way again, heading downriver towards the rapids that formed the last obstacle before Montreal.

"We got about 40 miles the first day," wrote Grant, "in the best manner we could without meeting any rough water or rifts as they were called. The next day the same. The country still uninhabited."

The following morning, after receiving assurances that "we had no rapids to fear," the boats set off once more. After several hours of uneventful progress along the smoothly flowing river, the British ran into trouble. In Grant's words:

> On a sudden I saw the boat a head of me suddenly disappear, and felt the suction of the water immediately divined the cause,
>
> I jumped up called out "A Rapid" and to keep to the right, & to pass the word, instantly turn the head of the boat, clapped two to the oars and pulled hard... The boat was whirled about and filled with water. The casks floated & one struck me a blow on the side that almost stunned me.
>
> We however got down safe & saw several boats upset, and poor fellows drowning and struggling in the eddies below the falls and calling piteously for help. I ordered some men to haul out the boat with the camp kettles,

which I followed into the bottom of [the] fall and succeeded in saving 13 of my regt. The other boats from having timely notice got down safe & two or three came in time to save a few more but 50 or 60 found a watery grave. Bonnets casks baggage also floating about in the eddy.[1]

The British sorted themselves out and continued on their way.

SAMUEL JENKS ON THE RICHELIEU RIVER

On 30 August, Haviland's army, Samuel Jenks included, sailed northward down the Richelieu River towards Fort Saint-Jean and Fort Chambly, the last French outposts between their army and Montreal. As they approached, Jenks wrote, "we espyed a great smoak at a great distance & one not so large pretty nigh us." This smoke turned out to be rising from the two French forts, which had been abandoned and burned by their garrisons. For Jenks, this was a sign from God. "The enemy are gone to Montreal; thus Heaven apparantly fights for us."

The invaders continued down the Richelieu to Île Sainte-Thérèse (Murray had landed on another Île Sainte-Thérèse in the St. Lawrence River), where Jenks' company was assigned to construct a field fortification. This stop gave him time to reflect on the hardships of a soldier's life. "Last night I lay out with the picquit to keep them alert, now we are in an enemys country. I lay down under the breastwork to git a little sleep. I could not help thinking what lodging I have exchanged for this, which is not half so good or convenient as we generally provide for our swine at home."

As work on the entrenchment progressed, Jenks and his fellows came into amicable contact with local residents. "The French about here are busy giting in their harvest, & sum of our men are helping them; so we are very good neighbours at present."[2]

On 7 September, the army was on the move once more. The war seemed very far away, as Jenks and his comrades passed through a countryside that seemed as if it could have been at peace. "This afternoon we marched off for Montreal... There is great numbers of the inhabitants come takeing their oaths... & they are very helpfull in carrying our stores, artellery, & baggage. there is near a 100 waggons of them, & the finest horses for draught that I ever saw in my life any where."[3]

END OF AN ALLIANCE

Inside the diminishing perimeter of French-controlled territory, the French army was falling to pieces. "Desertion," reported Roquemaure, "was universal in the army, even among the grenadiers, who left a half-dozen at a time."[4]

Lévis, however, was not even close to giving up the fight. He planned to unite the former garrisons of Sorel and Saint-Jean with as many fighters of the Seven Nations as he could assemble, then attack Haviland's Lake Champlain army.

To that end, on 2 September he crossed the St. Lawrence to La Prairie to meet with four hundred warriors of the Seven Nations. The French general was still speaking when a messenger arrived carrying the "news that the English had accepted the peace proposed to them on their [the Seven Nations'] behalf by the Natives of the Five Nations [the Haudenosaunee]."[5] The Seven Nations leaders ended the meeting and led their warriors home.

With Amherst now within striking distance of Montreal, Lévis evacuated the remaining French troops across the St. Lawrence to Montreal Island.

THE HURON-WENDAT AND JAMES MURRAY

Following their narrow escape in the Archipel Lac Saint-Pierre, Ouiharalihte and the Huron-Wendat found sanctuary in the Mohawk community of Kahnawake. "We went there," recalled Ouiharalihte, "and found the Village deserted like our own, there was nobody in it. We took possession of the houses; but sent some of our young men in search of the Iroquois."

A few days later, word arrived of the successful negotiation of neutrality between the Seven Nations and the British at Oswegatchie. With three aggressive British armies closing on Montreal, the Huron-Wendat and other Seven Nations representatives moved quickly to inform the nearest British commander of their change of status. Ouiharalihte noted that:

> Before many days had passed, we heard that the War was at an end. Our chiefs immediately on hearing the news mounted their horses and went to Laprairie where the English General [Murray] was. Upon their arrival at the quarters of the General, their horses were taken care of by the soldiers; the Officers took our Chiefs by the army and led them to their General. As soon as he saw them he cried out "These are the Hurons! Why did you

leave your Village? You have nothing to fear from us, go back to your Village you are safe," and he turned round to some one near him and gave an order. We received the next morning a paper from him, which we understood to mean that Peace was made.[6]

Varennes to Longueuil

Murray did not allow the atrocities at Varennes to interfere with his advance on Montreal. The next morning, he released twenty-four prisoners who had taken the oath of allegiance and sent them home carrying copies of his latest manifesto. This document gave Canadians five days to desert from the French army, return to their homes, and submit to the British or face the consequences.[7] Knox provided a summary:

> If they will surrender and deliver up their arms, he will forgive them; if not, they know what they may expect, from the examples which he has hitherto reluctantly given them; and, as for such Canadians as have been incorporated in the battalions of regulars, if they will surrender by a day limited, his Excellency will not only reinstate them in their settlements and lands, but likewise enlarge and protect them; but, if, after all, they shall still persist, they must expect to share the fate of the French troops, and be transported with them to Europe, &c.

The manifesto, he continued, "has had a happy effect on these brave unfortunate people."[8] Over the following days, five companies of militia from Varennes handed in their muskets and took the oath. Four more companies came in from Boucherville. Messengers from Sorel, Yamaska, and Verchères arrived, announcing the imminent arrival of their own militia units.

The Canadians from Boucherville had a message for Murray regarding French regulars who preferred to remain with their families in Canada under British rule than go back to France following a capitulation. "Some of them inform'd me, some of the French soldiers had land in the country, and wou'd desert, if they were assured of being received. I immediately sent an order, specifying, I would receive them all, and they shou'd have liberty to continue in the country. . . a great many soldiers deserted from the French army to us, upon my message."[9]

By now, it was apparent that the campaign was all but over and French resistance had ceased. On 4 September, Murray noted that "Crowds of Canadians are surrendering to us every minute, and the regulars, worn out with hunger and despair, desert to us in great numbers."[10] Four hundred Canadians from La Prairie came to Varennes to lay down their arms. The captain of militia of Yamaska, who had collected all the muskets in his company and stored them in his home until the British sent for them, came in to submit on behalf of his parish.

On the fifth, Murray took the grenadiers and light infantry to Longueuil. On the way, he met two hundred Canadians from that parish, on their way to surrender. Once there, he held a council with the Seven Nations delegation from Kahnawake. Murray, wrote the naval officer, "received them under his protection, upon the same terms with the Canadians, allowing them the free exercise of their Religion, their customs, and the liberty of trading with the English garrisons."[11]

JOHN GRANT REACHES MONTREAL

On 4 September, Amherst's army landed on Île Perrot, where his troops spent two days preparing to push on to Montreal Island. They re-embarked on the morning of 6 September. John Grant recorded the spectacle. "At daybreak therefore the whole army were embarked with 2 days provisions in their haversacks but without their luggage. Mustered in divisions, colours deployed drums beating pipers playing. The river was like glass, the morning beautiful, it was a glorious sight. We landed in a few hours at Lachine."

Once ashore, the army headed for Montreal with the Black Watch in the lead. At this point, with French resistance all but absent, one might have expected a bold, triumphal march. Instead, Grant recalls a cautious, almost fearful advance across the island.

> The 42nd Regt was immediately ordered to advance. We pushed along at double quick along a narrow path bounded by brushwood, only 4 abreast, but were afraid of a surprise. It was 9 miles and within less than two hours we had debouched from it and formed on the plain in front of Montreal. Our situation was not pleasant as we expected an attack every moment and were not sure of a support. However we could always retreat on the wood. We remained under arms till sun set, when the rest of the army arrived.

Within sight of Montreal, Amherst's soldiers endured one last ordeal. "We had no tents," continued Grant, "and spent but a miserable night our bodies... [worn out] by our rapid march and the hot day and chilly night dew and the dampness... [on] the ground... Next day we stood to our arms, but the Capitulation of the Canadas was signed."[12]

MONTREAL ISLAND

By 7 September, the French regulars guarding the shore of Montreal Island opposite Murray's fleet had departed; the captain of militia of Pointe-aux-Trembles assured the British, wrote Murray, that "his people had all deserted the French army, and wanted to lay down their arms."[13] Murray sent thirty rangers to seize a beachhead and requisition horses and wagons for the army.

At 1:00 p.m. the landing began; an hour later, the entire army was ashore. With the rangers screening the landward side, the army marched along the river towards Montreal. Progress was slow, since the French had burned every bridge along their way. The Canadians proved more cooperative. "The country-people," wrote Knox, "brought horses to draw our artillery, and others saddled, for the officers to ride, besides carts for our baggage. We marched through a delightful country, and a pleasant village... the roads were lined with men and women, who brought pitchers and pails of milk and water for the refreshment of the soldiers."[14]

At 5:00 p.m. Murray halted at Longue Point, one-and-a-half nautical miles from Montreal. As the army camped for the night, a French officer arrived with word that negotiations for surrender were under way. The next morning, Murray advanced to within musket shot of the eastern gate of Montreal, where he received word from Amherst that Canada had capitulated.[15]

Murray was not entirely pleased by this development. As far as he was concerned, Amherst might have signed the surrender, but there was no question as to who had won the victory. A month later he wrote to William Pitt, gently reminding the prime minister of "how fortunate the garrison of Quebec were in reducing the French army by obliging the Canadians to abandon it to a man, and how effectually we cleared the route for the junction of the three Corps, by taking post at Longueuil, and driving Monsieur de Levis to the Island of Montreal before the other two corps were heard of."[16]

Yet if he had not received the credit he thought he deserved for the final conquest of Canada, Murray had one consolation. When the first dispatches from London arrived in the spring of 1760, he had been able to inform Amherst that "I find his Majesty has appointed me Colonel of the 2d Battn of R. Americans [the 60th Regiment]. I am very thankful to him for it."[17]

JENKS' VICTORY

On 8 September, Jenks and the Lake Champlain army reached the St. Lawrence River.

> Last evening we set out from Shamble, & marcht on through a fine, pleasant country, thick of inhabitants; sum of them lookd very easy & chearfull, others lamenting the fate of their country. Our army marcht in as sevill [civil] a manner to the inhabitants as if they had been in our own country... This morning we set out again before sunrise, & it was extreme bad walking occasioned by the rain last night.

Haviland's troops travelled so fast and so light that they left their transport far behind, an unfortunate development for a hungry Jenks. Ever resourceful, and more than willing to take advantage of the power of an invading army, he wrote:

> I went into a French house determined to git sum refreshment or stay till the waggons come up. I got sum sower milk, & drank very hearty of it, & then the master of the house came in & asked if we would eat any soup, whch I told him we would. They then set before us a fine dish of it; & some pieions [pigeons] stewd heads & all on, I here made a fine feast. Had not I met with this nourishment, I could not a held out to march 1/2 mile further. I then set out for the regt, who had got about 2 miles start.

He caught up with the army at the river. "Just as I joynd the regt I saw Col Vaverland [Haviland] put off to go over to Genl Amherst in a whale boat who calld to shore & told us that the city had surrendred this morning, & that we had done fighting... I desire to bless God we have all Canada now under our command without any more blood shed."[18]

CAPITULATION

On 6 September, French lookouts spotted Amherst's flotilla heading from Île Perrot to Montreal Island. Lévis sent the cavalry to reinforce La Corne, but the British "boats moved faster than our horses [and] they arrived at Lachine at the same time."

The cavalry withdrew towards Montreal, pursued by the British advance guard. Around 11:00 a.m., the British main body advanced to within 1,200 metres of Montreal.

The French army was now reduced to a remnant of about two thousand regulars, mostly single and unattached. Married soldiers had already left to join their Canadian families. The Seven Nations had made their own peace with the British. As for the local militia, wrote Lapause, "the residents of Montreal refused to take up arms. . . and accused us of wanting to sacrifice them."[19]

That evening, Vaudreuil called a council of war in the Château Vaudreuil, his Montreal residence, built by his father, a previous governor general of New France. Lévis summarized the results. "Everyone thought, like the Marquis de Vaudreuil, that the general interest of the colony demanded that things not be pushed to the last extremity, and that a capitulation, advantageous for the people and honourable for the troops, who would be preserved for the King, would be preferable to a stubborn defence that would not delay the loss of the country by two days."[20]

The next day passed in negotiations with the British and recriminations among the French. Citing alleged war crimes by the French and their Amerindian allies, Amherst refused to grant Montreal's defenders the honours of war. Lévis demanded that Vaudreuil suspend negotiations and fight to the last to preserve the honour of French arms. Montreal, he declared, was "secure against a coup de main and could not be taken without cannon. It would be unheard of for the troops to submit to such harsh, humiliating conditions without having been cannonaded."[21]

Vaudreuil responded with a curt note on the eighth. "Given that the interest of the colony does not permit us to refuse the conditions proposed by the English general, which are advantageous to the colony whose fate has been entrusted to me, I order M. le Chevalier de Lévis to accept the present capitulation and have his troops lay down their arms."[22] Later that day, first Vaudreuil, then Amherst signed the capitulation, bringing the war for Canada to an end.

Vaudreuil's willingness to place the welfare of the Canadians over the demands of the regular army and his own career did not pass unnoticed. Even the anonymous author of *Mémoire du Canada*, a bitter critic of the governor general, praised "M. le marquis de Vaudreuil's sacrifice of his reputation for the public good."[23]

Under the terms of the capitulation, Canadians became British subjects, with the security of their property and religion guaranteed. The British Crown would recognize the Seven Nations' rights to their lands and religion. French regulars would be transported back to France by the British, and not serve again in the current war. The militia were permitted to return home.

With the capitulation signed, the British took possession of Montreal. An anonymous diarist recorded the event. "The capitulation being finished the grenadiers and light infantry marched into the town . . . in yᵉ following order of proceeding &c a 12 pounder wᵗʰ a flag and a detach[ment of the] Royal Artillery, 2ⁿᵈˡʸ: ye grenadiers of the line . . . 3ʳᵈˡʸ: ye Light Infantry of yᵉ line . . . each with a band of Musick be fore them."[24]

JOHNSTONE IN HIDING

While Lévis worried about his honour and Vaudreuil about the Canadians, James Johnstone worried about James Johnstone. A fugitive from British justice ever since he had taken part in the Jacobite Rebellion of 1745, Johnstone had attempted to flee the colony with Kanon's fleet in the fall of 1759. Vaudreuil, however, preferred that he remain to take part in the 1760 campaign.

Now, Johnstone was more than a little concerned about his fate. "During the negotiations for the capitulation at Montreal I was very uneasy, since I didn't know what treatment I would receive from the English." At Lévis' suggestion, he began to call himself "Monsieur de la Montagne" (i.e., Montagnard or Highlander) and went into hiding.

But changing his name and going underground was not enough to conceal Johnstone from the British. A few days after the British took possession of Montreal, he wrote, "I had a dreadful shock. Someone banged loudly on my bedroom door at 7:00 a.m., and when I opened it I was appalled to see a large young man, almost six feet tall, in an English uniform."

The formidable officer asked if he was indeed speaking to the Chevalier Johnstone. "Although I thought that he had been sent with a detachment to arrest me, seeing no chance of escape I replied that I was, and asked him what he wanted."

Johnstone's visitor proved to be a cousin from Scotland serving as a captain in the Royal Artillery. He had come with an innocuous invitation to travel with him back to Quebec and to stay in his rented house in Beauport until Johnstone could board a ship for France.

Johnstone, still believing himself to be the object of a manhunt, explained his delicate situation; his cousin went off to speak with James Murray. Two hours later, the cousin returned with the deflating news that hunting down Johnstone was not a high priority for the British army. The British, in fact, seemed not to care. Murray had declared that "he, along with all the rest of the English army, had known for a long time that I was in Canada; that I could remain quietly and safely with him [Johnstone's cousin]; that he [Murray] was not looking for me any more; and that he sent his compliments."

Fooling no one, but continuing to hide under the alias "Chevalier de la Montagne," Johnstone travelled from Quebec to Montreal with a boatload of French gunners. Once there, he took up residence in Beauport, where he spent three weeks waiting for a ship. The time passed swiftly, as Johnstone was "always socializing with numerous English officers... These officers paid me many compliments, and took care to always call me M. Montagne, although they knew very well my story, no one seemed surprised that I spoke English so well."

Johnstone remained with his cousin until 16 October, when the convoy carrying the French regulars sailed from Quebec for France.[25]

THE TREATY OF KAHNAWAKE

Unlike their French allies, the Seven Nations were never defeated and never surrendered. Instead, their representatives had met at Oswegatchie with Haudenosaunee and British representatives and negotiated neutrality, while at the same time maintaining their connections to the French until the last possible moment.

On 15 and 16 September, they met again with the Haudenosaunees and British at Kahnawake and converted neutrality into alliance. The Seven Nations formally terminated their relationship with the French by announcing that they would "bury the French hatchet we have made use of, in the bottomless pit" and formed a new alliance with the British by taking hold of "the old Covenant Chain [symbolizing the British alliance]... and we in the name of every nation here present assure you that we will hold fast of the same, for ever hereafter."

The Seven Nations furthermore agreed to return their British prisoners and support the British in war; the British agreed to permit the Seven Nations to travel freely to Albany to trade and to allow Catholic priests to remain in Seven Nations' communities.[26]

The British may have overcome the French allies of the Seven Nations, whom they valued, and occupied the St. Lawrence valley, which they had fought hard to prevent. But Seven Nations leaders had successfully managed a peaceful transition from being independent allies of the French to independent allies of the British and, in so doing, had secured the safety of their families and communities.

FORT JACQUES CARTIER

Montreal had fallen, but the last French outpost in Canada held out for a few more days.

When James Murray sailed for Montreal in July, he left behind 1,700 members of his army who were still recovering from the hardships of the winter or wounds from Sainte-Foy. If all had gone according to plan, Colonel Simon Fraser, commander of the Quebec garrison, would have used these troops to capture Fort Jacques Cartier early in the campaign. This should have been easy. According to Murray's spies, "The enemy's situation in your district cannot be formidable, fifty men is all they have left at Jacques Quartier."

Fraser's garrison, however, was in no state to undertake even so minor a mission. "I am sorry," Murray added, "to find the garrison does not recover, for you are weaker than when I left you. I had sanguine hopes that the warm weather & your attention to the wants of the sick, would have soon enabled you to satisfy your ambition [to take Fort Jacques Cartier]."

Murray then attempted to console his subordinate. "I beg you will not be distressed about Jacques Quartier... the 50 men will continue where they are till we appear before it, & then they will retire thro' the woods, after having set fire to the houses &c."

For the moment, Murray reiterated an order to establish an outpost at Pointe-aux-Trembles between Quebec and the Jacques Cartier River, "if that can be done with ease to your garrison. If not to burn ye country after the harvest is gathered in, from the River Jasque Quartier to the very banks of the Cap Rouge, that the inhabitants of that Quarter may be drove back upon the Upper Canada for sub^ce [subsistence]."[27]

Not until September were enough members of the Quebec garrison back on their feet for Fraser to launch his attack on Jacques Cartier. Fraser, the chief of Clan Fraser, who, like James Johnstone, had taken part in the 1745 rebellion, had raised the 78th Highlanders to demonstrate his renewed loyalty to the British Crown. He had taken part in the siege of Louisbourg and been wounded at the battles of Montmorency and Sainte-Foy. On 8 September, he assembled 1,200 infantry and gunners, two cannon, one howitzer, and seven mortars, loaded them aboard ships, and headed upriver.[28]

Awaiting him was Ensign François-Marie Balthazara d'Albergati-Vezza of the troupes de la marine. D'Albergati-Vezza's decision to seek his fortune serving the French Crown had taken him from his birthplace in Bologna, Italy, into the heart of North America.

In the course of his North American adventure, d'Albergati-Vezza had been wounded fighting George Washington at Fort Necessity and taken part in two attacks on Fort William Henry and the battles of the Plains of Abraham and Sainte-Foy. On the Plains of Abraham, he had commanded a detachment of Canadians that turned back a British charge and helped to cover the escape of the French regular battalions.

But when he wrote out a statement of his services, d'Albergati-Vezza gave pride of place to the final action of his career in Canada. "Although only an ensign, during the last two months of the war in this country I had the honour to command a fort. . . named Jacques Cartier."[29]

The triangular fort occupied a natural strongpoint, described by Knox as "a bold commanding eminence [hill]," shielded on two sides by the Jacques Cartier and St. Lawrence Rivers. As to its defences, Knox recorded the observations of a paroled British officer who visited the fort on his way to Quebec. "The fortress of Jacques Cartier, by reason of its elevated situation, appears very difficult of access but, by all he could perceive, the works of the place consist only of a rampart of earth and fascines, with a ditch to the country side, and some picket work [stockades]."

Moreover, the fort had been built to accommodate significant numbers of troops, making it so large that Knox estimated that a proper defence would have required a garrison of 1,500.[30]

D'Albergati-Vezza, on the other hand, commanded just thirty-six regulars and a few local militia, along with eighteen small cannon and thirty livres of gunpowder. This was barely enough to mount a token defence, but he did his best.

On 10 September, Fraser's force landed about three kilometres upriver and followed the Chemin du Roi towards the fort. D'Albergati-Vezza led a detachment out of Fort Jacques Cartier and opened fire with field guns.

The officer of the 35th recorded the results. "We reciev'd some cannon shot on the road, from a few guns they had planted in different places."[31]

When this failed to delay the British, d'Albergati-Vezza pulled his troops back to the fort. Joseph Lamotte, a Canadian from Le Grand-Bois-de-l'Ail, just up the Jacques Cartier River, noticed that one gun had been left behind. Loaded and ready for action, it could be turned against the French. Under fire from the British, who were drawing steadily closer, Lamotte ran back, pounded a spike into the touchhole, then fled for the fort. Greeted by comrades who thought he had been killed, Lamotte replied, "You can see, my friends, that my last hour has not come yet."[32]

Next, d'Albergati-Vezza tried to stall for time. He sent out an officer who met the British on the road and asked for a two-day ceasefire until word arrived regarding the status of Montreal. Fraser rejected the truce and demanded an immediate surrender. D'Albergati-Vezza refused; the British marched on.

When the British advance guard reached the fort, the garrison stood to arms. Fraser made a second demand for surrender. D'Albergati-Vezza replied "that he would defend that post to the last extremity" and backed up his defiance with cannon shot.[33]

Fraser thereupon deployed his mortars and opened fire, flinging shell after shell into the fort. At the same time, he deployed his infantry in three columns and prepared to advance. British ships, which had dropped down-river from the landing site, hovered ominously offshore. Outnumbered, outgunned, and with very little ammunition and only a few calves, pigs, and chickens for provisions, d'Albergati-Vezza decided that the time had come to surrender.

Having done all that *ancien régime* military propriety required against a vastly superior enemy force, Canada's last defenders laid down their arms. The officer of the 35th briefly narrated the surrender. "We march'd into it [the fort] the same day we landed. Found but 3 officers & 25 soldiers... The Marquis said he had the Honour of surrendering the last place in all Canada."[34] The regulars became prisoners of war. The militia took the oath of allegiance to the British Crown and returned to their homes.

Vaudreuil, endorsing d'Albergati-Vezza's conduct, praised "the very honourable surrender of the place."[35]

PART 5

CONCLUSION

CHAPTER 30

OCCUPIED CANADA

MONTREAL ISLAND

Whatever their private feelings towards their British occupiers and the conquest of their colony, many Canadian families living in areas untouched by the war entered the British era leading reasonably comfortable lives. Residents of the parish of Sainte-Geneviève, on the north shore of Montreal Island, are a case in point. Safely distant from combat zones and military lines of communication, they did not encounter British troops at home until after the capitulation.

Their isolation ended in September when John Grant and the second battalion of the 42nd Highlanders marched to their designated winter quarters in Sainte-Geneviève. "We were billeted on the best houses," wrote Grant, "we were on a river half a mile broad [Rivière des Prairies] opposite the Isle Jesus." Grant himself moved in "with a Lieutenant of Militia and his family. The houses consisted only of two rooms with a cooking place and were of logs, one of the rooms I had. A stove was between the two rooms warming both and also a fire place."

Grant had nothing to say regarding how his involuntary hosts responded to the appropriation of half of their home by an enemy soldier. But he did portray the Canadians as well provided with food and willing to exchange "beef mutton, poultry enough for our mess, for several months" for salt. The officers bought the meat in the form of live animals, "which are killed at the beginning of the winter and remain frozen during it, cutting off a piece when wanted."

The Canadians of Saint-Geneviève furthermore had enough livestock to trade with the troops as well as the officers. "Our men were well off. Two were quartered in every house, and the Canadians who prefer pork and scarcely eat at that time any other meat, exchanged poultry & beef for the men's rations."

The Canadians seem to have been less willing to part with their vegetables. Grant observed them consuming large quantities on a regular basis, writing that "one of their dishes every day, pieces of pork boiled down in a mass of cabbage, and then slices of bread put in—Spruce beer was the common drink." Among the British, on the other hand, "we were badly off for vegetables, there being none but onions, garlic and cabbage, and but little of them."

Overall, Grant had a good winter. He suffered from a lack of reading material, "having but few books," but "the priest was a pleasant man. We went about in sledges, sometimes on snow shows [snowshoes]. We went sometimes to dine with the priest, lived well & plenty of liqueurs and burgundy & champagne." Dancing, however, was out of the question, as "priests forbade the young women from joining the parties."[1]

BERTHIER, QUEBEC, AND SAINT-PIERRE

The priests needn't have worried. Following the capitulation, Chaplain Robert Macpherson of the 78th Highlanders had been billeted in Berthier (now Berthier-sur-mer) on the south shore of the St. Lawrence, opposite Île d'Orléans. In 1761, he wrote to his brother that:

> We have the good fortune of being in the neighbourhood of three or four Ladies of Quality, such as this country affords of that rank. As each of us has his horse and sledge we pay them frequent visits and generally have them once a fortnight to dine and sup with us, when the Entertainment always ends with a dance, or what the New Englanders call a frolic. The French ladies in general are very witty and sprightly, indeed the truth is they never are silent . . . [but] they are just as virtuous . . . as any of our precise Prim ladies at home.

Macpherson, whose perspective, it goes without saying, was very different from that of a Canadian farm family, added that agricultural production in the vicinity of Quebec was beginning to recover from the ravages of war.

The goodness of this distant country is such that the Canadians have already recover'd from the disasters they were reduced to by the entire depreciation of their paper money or colony bills, almost the only species of currency they made use of, from the miserable effects of ten years' war during which they were oblig'd to leave a great part of their land uncultivated, and from what was the worst of all, having the one half of their country burnt and plunder'd the first campaign we came amongst them [in 1759]. The markets are now very well supplied and produce opens at a moderate enough price. The Poor Canadian lives more plentifully and much more delicately than most of the Fer Baill's ["township men," or farmers] in the Highlands.

The Canadians were also having an impact on their occupiers, as Britons adjusted to life in a French-speaking colony. Macpherson, who had preached in the chapel of the Ursuline convent of Quebec in the winter of 1759–60, further informed his brother that "An acquaintance I made with, and correspondence I carry on with the Nuns at Quebec, since winter [of] 1759, have principally contributed to my speaking French tolerably and understanding it very well."[2]

James Thompson, billeted nearby in Saint-Pierre (now Saint-Pierre-de-la-Rivière-du-Sud), had a similar experience.

When we got to Saint Pierre, [Sergeant Alexander] Ferguson and myself have the good-luck to get a billet upon another *Capitaine* [captain of militia], and his name was [Michel] José Blais. Here we were treated with the greatest civility, and almost adopted as children of the family. I had now pick'd up as much of the French language as to understand almost everything that was said to me, and I myself could manage to gabble tolerably.[3]

Île d'Orléans

Other Canadians endured trauma, hunger, and hardship that did not end with the capitulation. They included survivors of rape at the hands of Murray's soldiers and families whose parishes had been ravaged by British troops in 1759 and 1760. These families now lived in a wilderness devoid of houses and farm buildings and had lost personal possessions and livestock that could not easily be replaced. Families from Quebec returned to homes that had been damaged or destroyed by bombardment, cannonade, and fire during the 1759 siege.

Residents of Île d'Orléans were afflicted by both war and nature. Prior to the arrival of British forces in 1759, the French had evacuated the island. Following the capitulation of Quebec, Murray allowed local families to return to their farms. Two petitions from the parish priests of the island to Murray told their story.

High winds and the advancing season in the fall of 1759 prevented the islanders from harvesting more than a third of their crops. To avoid starvation, they purchased wheat from less devastated parishes on the mainland. Over the winter, their situation deteriorated when Murray compelled them to use their horses to haul firewood for the garrison. The heavy work crippled the horses, which, wrote the priests, "made it impossible for them to work as usual: each inhabitant could only sow a third as much as he was accustomed to do."[4]

The coming of summer in 1760 just made matters worse. "The excessive heat of summer, combined with a frightening number of grasshoppers and grubs, utterly devastated our fields."[5] By the fall of that year, the curés lamented "the sad situation of the residents of that island, some of whom have already eaten up their entire harvest and are living on roots and vegetables, while others have only enough for the next two or three months, and nothing for the winter; let alone enough to be able to sow their fields next spring without considerable assistance.[6]

Life was even worse for residents of the east end of the island nearest to Quebec, who endured the depredations of both nature and British sailors and Canadians from the mainland. One curé wrote, "Everything conspired to contribute to our misfortune, the sailors and Canadians who cut wood for the King in this area robbed us and every night carried off. . . poultry, sheep, vegetables, and other provisions that we expected to sell or exchange in the city for other, more necessary, food."[7]

James Murray could be just as ruthless as James Wolfe and just as willing to make war upon the civilian population. But he balanced willingness to employ terror as a military tactic with humanity and sympathy for former enemies after hostilities ceased.

Over the winter of 1760–61, Murray would take steps to alleviate the worst of the suffering. He sent provisions, beginning with four hundred bushels of dried peas and four hundred more of oatmeal, gave the islanders permission to salvage what they could from a wrecked ship carrying 1,300 barrels of flour, and made plans to import wheat from the Montreal area or British America. British merchants and officers in Quebec raised five hundred pounds for famine relief; private soldiers contributed one day's rations per month over the winter.[8]

This display of humanity notwithstanding, Murray continued to treat Canadians as potential adversaries in a future French-British war. Until a peace treaty ended hostilities, whether Canada would remain under British rule or return to French control remained uncertain. Murray consequently chose to withhold advice on farming that he thought might reduce the possibility of future crop failures and thereby strengthen New France against a future British assault. "Humanity and sound policy dictate the preservation, at least of these unhappy wretches, tho' there will be no necessity to point out to them improvements until we know the state of their country at the peace."[9]

CHAPTER 31

LOOKING BACK FROM THE TWENTY-FIRST CENTURY

VIEWED FROM A DISTANCE of more than 250 years, our past appears engraved in stone. Whatever happened, happened. Long-term processes and random events occurred; the world moved on. But up close, history is considerably more fragile.

The Battle of the Plains of Abraham remains the single most important military event in Canadian history. In the short term, it led to the surrender of Quebec, giving the British control over Canada's sole Atlantic seaport and a base for offensive action against Montreal. Over the long term, the battle shaped the future of North America and the world.

No one knew that at the time, however, and Vaudreuil, for one, refused to accept defeat. Within moments of the collapse of the French regular battalions at the Battle of the Plains of Abraham, he began his attempts to reverse the battlefield verdict. He supported the Canadian militia and Amerindian warriors, who held off the British until the French battalions escaped, tried to persuade the French regulars to face Wolfe's army once again, and brought Lévis from Montreal to lead the French army back to Quebec. Only the first of these efforts succeeded, but Vaudreuil continued to see the Battle of the Plains of Abraham as a setback from which the French could recover. In the spring of 1760, he sent Lévis downriver to recapture Quebec.

It is hard to say just how close Lévis actually came to breaking Murray's army at Sainte-Foy and taking Quebec without heavy artillery from France. Perhaps a tiny incident—one misunderstood order—saved the British from catastrophe and cost Lévis a decisive victory. Perhaps it didn't. Battles are messy events, and history is seldom that neat.

It is even harder to say what would have happened if the French had taken Quebec and reduced James Wolfe's 1759 triumph to a historical footnote. Canada's defenders would still have faced heavy odds on the Lake Champlain and Lake Ontario frontiers.

Nonetheless, Canada's geography would have handed the French some significant advantages. The wide belt of mountains and forests that separated Canada from New York could be crossed by large armies only along the Mohawk River-Lake Ontario-upper St. Lawrence and Lake Champlain-Richelieu River waterways. This channelled British attacks, allowing the French to concentrate their resources along two corridors instead of defending a frontier extending for hundreds of kilometres. Internal lines of communication along these waterways would have allowed the French to shift troops from frontier to frontier to respond to the threats or take advantage of the weakness of Amherst's forces.

The French, moreover, would have been able to mobilize militia and provisions from all of Canada instead of just the Montreal area. While the British spent months concentrating troops and supplies at Fort Oswego and Crown Point, captured munitions and heavy artillery from Quebec could have strengthened Forts Lévis and Île-aux-Noix while regulars, militia, and Amerindians reinforced garrisons, disrupted British supply lines, and conducted spoiling attacks to disrupt British offensives before they occurred. French soldiers and Canadian militia, whose morale had soared following the Battle of Sainte-Foy, would have faced a British commander-in-chief who, in 1759, had displayed a decided preference for fortifying British America over invading Canada.

None of which is meant to suggest that recovering Quebec would have guaranteed a French victory in the summer of 1760, just that it was not impossible. The British, possessed of command of Lakes Ontario and Champlain, huge quantities of supplies and munitions, and significant numerical superiority, might have rolled on regardless and taken Montreal in September. The Royal Navy would certainly have blockaded the St. Lawrence River and might even have carried battalions from the Louisbourg garrison, Nova Scotia, and New York to threaten Quebec.

But had Vaudreuil and Lévis been successful in both the spring and summer campaigns, consider the potential consequences. Canada might have held out for two more years and remained in French hands at the end of the war. The St. Lawrence valley might now be an overseas province of France, an independent Francophone-Amerindian North American nation, or an American state, in which case Canada as we know it would not exist. With a French threat remaining in the north, American Independence might have been deferred for generations or never occurred at all.

At this distance in time, these contemplations seem absurd, the province of alternative history science fiction. But in 1760, the future remained a world of unknown possibilities and opportunities, and Canadian militia, French soldiers, and the Seven Nations warriors expended a great deal of effort to shape what is to us our fixed and unchanging past.

That notwithstanding, when Lévis' army lifted the siege of Quebec, the French lost their last hope of recovering the city and preventing, or at least postponing, the British capture of Montreal and the capitulation of Canada.

Three years later, in 1763, the Treaty of Paris ended the Seven Years' War and redrew the map of North America. With the exception of the islands of St. Pierre and Miquelon, which remain French possessions today, all of eastern North America came under British control. Canada became the British colony of Quebec. Nova Scotia absorbed the former French territories in Acadia. Under a separate French-Spanish agreement, France ceded Louisiana west of the Mississippi River to Spain.

The Treaty of Paris made no provision for the return of Acadians who had survived expulsion by the British. They came back anyway and rebuilt their shattered society. Canadians continued to live their lives as Catholic Francophones under a British administration that retained many of the laws, practices, and personnel of the French colonial government. But the conquest had been a bitter blow for Canadians. "One cannot," wrote Canadian nun Marie de la Visitation, "express the sorrow and bitterness that has seized every heart."[1] One Canadian, fur trader Charles-André Barthe, a resident of Detroit, literally dreamed of the return of French rule.

On the night of 12–13 [December 1765], I dreamt that an Englishman told me that Canada, Acadia, and Montreal Point [now Windsor, Ontario], belonged to the King of France. Overcome with surprise, at the same time I heard people saying that Mr. Le Chevalier de Longueuil had been named

Governor of Detroit and Mr Bellestre, Major of that place; and that Mr. Duruisseau was going from door to door spreading this news, and at the end of my dream, I found myself at Lamothe's house in Montreal.[2]

Most Canadians likely harboured similar sentiments.

Never defeated during the Seven Years' War, Amerindian nations that had formerly been allied with France negotiated new alliances with the British. When the British failed to live up to their obligations as allies, many Amerindians of the Great Lakes and Ohio valley resorted to war in 1763. In a lightning campaign, they seized nine of eleven British outposts west of Fort Niagara. In 1764, several of these nations, together with others from the Atlantic to Hudson Bay, met with the British at Fort Niagara in 1764. Here, they accepted a renewed British alliance based on the Royal Proclamation of 1763, which included the first step towards Crown recognition of Aboriginal Title.

To the south, with France expelled from the North American mainland, many American colonists no longer felt the need for British military protection. During the Seven Years' War, Americans had come to see themselves as full partners in the British Empire. Afterwards, they rejected British attempts to treat them as subordinates by attempting to limit their westward expansion into Amerindian territory and compel them to accept taxation to help pay for the war. Angry and alienated, most of Britain's American colonies rebelled in 1775, formed the United States of America, and in so doing laid the foundations of the global superpower we know today. Other British colonies remained loyal to the Crown, defeated American invasions in 1775–76, and eventually united in 1867 to form the Dominion of Canada.

Decades after the event, French victories in the Seven Years' War remained a sensitive topic among the British in Canada. Even members of Canadian families with long records of loyalty to the British Crown had to tread carefully, reflecting their ambiguous status as Catholic and Francophone subjects of a fiercely Protestant and Anglophone state. When Philippe Aubert de Gaspé published his recollections of walking over the Sainte-Foy battlefield with his uncle, he added that "back then you could only speak in whispers [about the Battle of Sainte-Foy], or risk being taken for *French and bad subjects* [English and italics in the original]."[3]

With the passage of time, British sensitivities eased. Remembered in

Francophone Canada as a last triumph before the conquest, the Battle of Sainte-Foy quickly vanished from the mainstream of history, lost in the shadow cast by the titanic consequences of the Battle of the Plains of Abraham and the French cession of Canada at the Treaty of Paris. But it remains a standing reminder that neither our history nor the nations it created can ever be taken for granted.

ACKNOWLEDGEMENTS

WRITING IS A PROVERBIALLY solitary activity, but it's very hard to actually write a book alone. Over the past four years, I have benefited enormously from the assistance of many friends and colleagues willing to sacrifice their time and energy to help me produce a better book.

Tim Cook of the Canadian War Museum and Dean Oliver of the Canadian Museum of History reviewed the manuscript and saved me from any number of missteps. Tim Foran of the Canadian Museum of History and Mélanie Morin-Pelletier of the Canadian War Museum did the same for the final chapter.

R. Paul Goodman and Earl John Chapman were kind enough to pass along references to documents they had discovered in the course of their own research, most notably the anonymous "Journal of the Proceedings of the 35th Regiment of Foot." Stephen Brumwell generously offered to share his notes on the Eubule Ormsby court martial. Displaying considerable magnanimity in these cash-strapped times, the Stewart Museum provided both a high-resolution .jpeg of their portrait of François-Gaston de Lévis and the rights to use it as an illustration, free of charge. Equally magnanimous, Hélène Quimper of the National Battlefields Commission gave me a copy of LS-Philippe Picard's and Paul Gaston L'Anglais' *Découvertes archéologiques dans le Parc des braves à Québec*. Rick Broadbent, my agent, continues to be as wonderfully efficient and supportive as ever. Anna Comfort O'Keeffe, Daniela Hajdukovic, Lucy Kenward and the team from Douglas & McIntyre did some very fine work producing this volume. Arlene Prunkl performed a truly inspired edit.

ENDNOTES

PREFACE

1   W.J. Eccles, *The Canadian Frontier, 1534–1760*, revised edition (Albuquerque, 1983), pp. xi-xii. Bank of Canada Inflation Calculator, http://www.bankofcanada.ca/rates/related/inflation-calculator/. Accessed 17 March 2016.

CHAPTER 2

1   Wolfe to Walter Wolfe, 19 May 1759, Beckles Wilson, *The Life and Letters of James Wolfe* (London, 1909), p. 429.

2   Guy Le Moing, *La Bataille navale des "Cardinaux" (20 Novembre 1759)* (Paris, 2003), pp. 21–22; Frank McLynn, *1759: The Year Britain Became Master of the World* (London, 2004), pp. 99, 183–190; N.A.M. Rodger, *The Command of the Ocean, A Naval History of Britain, 1639–1815* (New York, 2005), p. 277; Nicholas Tracy, *The Battle of Quiberon Bay 1759: Hawke and the Defeat of the French Invasion* (Barnsley, 2010), p. 115.

3   Olaudah Equiano, *The Interesting Narrative of the Life of Olaudah Equiano, or Gustavus Vassa, the African*, 9th Edition (London, 1794), p. 96.

4   Rodger, *The Command of the Ocean*, pp. 277–278; Tracy, *The Battle of Quiberon Bay*, pp. 115–116.

CHAPTER 3

1   Earl John Chapman and R. Paul Goodman, "Quebec, 1759: Reconstructing Wolfe's Main Battle Line from Contemporary Evidence," *Journal of the Society for Army Historical Research*, vol. 92, no. 369 (spring 2014), pp. 1–59; D. Peter MacLeod, *Northern Armageddon: the Battle of the Plains of Abraham* (Vancouver, 2008), pp. 206–215.

2   Jean-Guillaume Plantavit de Lapause de Margon, "Relation des affaires du Canada depuis le 1er Xbre 1759 au [15 juin 1760]," *Rapport de l'archiviste de la province de Québec*, 1933–34, p. 140.

3   "An account of the guns, mortars, ammunition, and arms, &c. found in the city of Quebec upon its surrender to his Majesty's troops the 18th of September, 1759, viz.," *An Authentic Register of the British Successes* (London, 1759), p. 112.

4   Robert Eastburn, *A Faithful Narrative, of the Many Dangers and Sufferings, as Well as Wonderful Deliverances of Robert Eastburn, during His Late Captivity among the Indians: Together with Some Remarks upon the Country of Canada, and the Religion, and Policy of Its Inhabitants; the Whole Intermixed with Devout Reflections* (Philadelphia, 1758), reprinted in *Held Captive by Indians: Selected Narratives, 1642–1836*, ed. Richard Vanderbeets (Knoxville, 1973), pp. 168–169.

5   Jemima Howe, "The Captivity and Sufferings of Mrs. Jemima Howe, Taken Prisoner by the
     Indians at Bridgman's Fort, in the Present Town of Vernon, Vt. Communicated to Dr. Belknap
     by the Rev. Bunker Gay, 1755," in *North Country Captives: Selected Narratives of Indian Captivities
     from Vermont and New Hampshire*, ed. Colin G. Calloway (Hanover, 1992), p. 95.

6   W.J. Eccles, "Pierre de Rigaud de Vaudreuil de Cavagnial, Marquis de Vaudreuil," *Dictionary
     of Canadian Biography, vol. IV, 1771 to 1800*, ed. Francess G. Halpenny (Toronto, 1979),
     pp. 662–674.

7   Buying a regimental colonelcy was a major investment. During the 1740s Montcalm commanded
     an infantry regiment worth 40,000 livres. See W.J. Eccles, "Louis-Joseph de Montcalm, Marquis
     de Montcalm," *DCB, vol. III, 1741 to 1770*, p. 458.

8   W.J. Eccles, "François [François-Gaston] de Lévis, Duc de Lévis," *DCB, vol. IV*, pp. 477–482.

9   François Le Mercier, "Mémoire relatif à la situation du Canada, en se réduisant à l'indispensable
     pour conserver au Roy cette colonie jusqu'au printemps 1761," 7 January 1760, Library and
     Archives Canada, Manuscript Group 1, Archives des Colonies, C11A, vol. 105, ff. 267–269, reel
     F-105.

10   Ibid.

11   Vaudreuil to Berryer, 7 November 1759, in Alfred Barbier, "La Baronie de la Touche-D'Avrigny et
     le Duché de Chatellerault sous François 1er," *Mémoires de la société des antiquaires de l'ouest*, vol. IX,
     second series (1880), p. 370; Gilles Proulx, Le dernier effort de la France au Canada: Secours ou
     Fraude, *Revue d'histoire de l'amérique française*, vol. 36, no. 3 (December 1982), pp. 415–416.

12   Vaudreuil to Berryer, 7 November 1759, in Barbier, "La Baronie de la Touche-D'Avrigny,"
     Mémoires de la société des antiquaires de l'ouest, vol. IX (1880), p. 369.

13   D. Peter MacLeod, "The Canadians Against the French: The Struggle for Control of the
     Expedition to Oswego in 1756," *Ontario History*, vol. LXXX, no. 2 (June 1988), pp. 143–157.

14   Bourlamaque to Lévis, 1 November 1759, LAC, MG18-K8, Fonds Chevalier de Lévis, vol. 7,
     Lettres de M. de Bourlamaque à Monsieur de Lévis, no. 44, p. 2, reel C-364.

15   Jacques Kanon, "1759. Campagne d'Amérique. Kanon (Jacques) Lieut. de frégate commande
     la frégate le Machault (Canada)," December 1759, LAC, MG2, Fonds de la Marine, Série B4,
     Campagnes, vol. 91, f. 41, reel F-1304; James S. Pritchard, "Jacques Kanon," *DCB, vol. III*,
     pp. 321–322.

CHAPTER 4

1   Durell, "Journal," entry of 27 May 1759, LAC, MG12, Great Britain, Public Record Office,
     Admiralty Papers, ADM 50, Admirals' Journals, vol. 3, Philip Durell, f. 231, reel B-19.

2   Jonathan R. Dull, *The French Navy and the Seven Years' War* (Lincoln, 2005), pp. 158–163;
     Le Moing, *La Bataille navale des "Cardinaux,"* pp. 87–157; Rodger, *The Command of the Ocean*,
     pp. 279–283; Geoffrey Marcus, *Quiberon Bay* (Barre, MA, 1963), pp. 127–158; Tracy, *The Battle
     of Quiberon Bay*, p. 115.

3   Letter of Sebastien François Bigot de Morogues, 1759, in Michel Depeyre, *Tactiques et stratégies
     navales de la France et du Royaume-Uni de 1690 à 1815* (Paris, 1998), p. 103.

CHAPTER 5

1   "Journal of the Proceedings of the 35th Regiment of Foot," "A Few Notes Related to the
     Foregoing Journal," John Carter Brown Library, b6123117.

2   James Murray to George Murray, 11 October 1759, William Fraser, *The Earls of Cromartie: Their
     Kindred, Country and Correspondence* (Edinburgh, 1876), pp. 246–247.

3   Ibid.

4   John Knox, *An Historical Journal of the Campaigns in North America for the Years 1757, 1758, 1759, and 1760*, vol. II (London, 1769), p. 185.

5   Erica M. Charters, "Disease, Wilderness Warfare, and Imperial Relations: The Battle for Quebec, 1759–1760," *War in History*, vol. 16, no. 1 (January 2009), p. 5.

6   Knox, *Historical Journal*, vol. II, p. 102.

7   James Thompson, "Anecdote No. 23," in *A Bard of Wolfe's Army: James Thompson, Gentleman Volunteer, 1733–1830*, eds. Chapman and McCulloch (Montreal, 2010), pp. 191–192.

8   James Miller, *Memoirs of an Invalid*, Centre for Kentish Studies, U1350/Z9A, pp. 31–32.

9   Knox, *Historical Journal*, vol. II, pp. 260, 267, 269, 277; Charters, "Disease, Wilderness Warfare, and Imperial Relations," *War in History*, pp. 12–13.

10 Knox, *Historical Journal*, vol. II, p. 283.

11 Murray, "Journal of the Expedition against Quebec in the Year One Thousand Seven Hundred & Fifty Nine and from the Surrender Being the 18th Day of Sep[r] 1759 to the 17th May 1760, also a Journal Resumed from the 18th of May to the 17th of Sep[r] Following, with the Articles of Capitulation between His Excellency General Amherst Commander in Chief of His Britanick Majesty's Forces in North America, & His Excellency the Marquis Vaudreuil (Grand Croix of the Royal & Military Order of St. Louis Governor & L[t] Gen[l] for the King in Canada). Camp before Montreal, the 8th Sep[r] 1760," [hereafter Murray, "Journals"], LAC, MG23-GII1, Series 4, vol. 1, f. 88, reel C-2225.

12 In February, March, and April, Murray's separate columns for dead, killed, and wounded record eight killed in action, eight wounded, and 407 dead. "Monthly Return of His Majesty's Forces in the River St. Lawrence, under the Command of Brigadier Gen[l] James Murray, Quebec," 24 October 1759, 24 November 1759, 24 December 1759, 24 January 1760, 24 February 1760, 24 March 1760, 24 April 1760, LAC, MG11, Great Britain, Public Record Office, Colonial Office Papers, CO 5, Original Correspondence, Secretary of State, America and West Indies, vol. 64, between f. 99 and f. 101, reel B-2175.

13 MacLeod, *Northern Armageddon*, p. 212.

14 Murray to Amherst, 25 January 1760, LAC, MG11, CO 5, vol. 57, Part III, f. 75v, reel B-2171.

15 John Grant, "Journal," 1741–1763, pp. 15, 25, 53, Alexander Turnbull Library, National Library of New Zealand, MS-Copy-Micro-0491.

CHAPTER 6

1   Le Mercier, "Mémoire relatif à la situation du Canada," 7 January 1760, LAC, MG1, AC, C11A, vol. 105, ff. 267–269, reel F-105.

2   Berryer to Rostan, 15 February 1760, LAC, MG1, AC, B, Lettres envoyées, vol. 112, f. 53, reel F-317. See also Gustave Lanctôt, "Le dernier effort de la France au Canada," *Mémoires de la société royale de Canada*, Series III, vol. 13 (1918), pp. 41–54; Proulx, "Le dernier effort de la France au Canada," *RHAF* (December 1982), pp. 413–426.

CHAPTER 7

1   "Memoranda Book," LAC, MG19, Fur Trade and Indians, F1, Claus Family Papers, vol. 23, no. 2, ff. 69–71, reel C-1485.

2   MacLeod, *The Canadian Iroquois and the Seven Years' War* (Toronto, 1996), p. xi.

3   Stephen Brumwell, *White Devil: An Epic Story of Revenge from the Savage War That Inspired* The Last of the Mohicans (London, 2004), pp. 183–205; MacLeod, *The Canadian Iroquois and the Seven Years' War*, pp. 148–149, 152.

4   William Johnson, "Journal of Niagara Campaign," 26 July–14 October 1759, *The Papers of Sir William Johnson*, vol. XII, ed. Milton W. Hamilton (Albany, 1962), pp. 155–156.

5   "At a Meeting of the Deputies of the 6 Confederate Nations," 13–14 February 1760, LAC, MG11, CO 5, vol. 58, ff. 149–149v, reel B-2172.

6   Amédée Gosselin, ed., "Le journal de M. de Bougainville," *Rapport de l'archiviste de la province de Québec*, 1923–1924, pp. 259–260.

7   Ibid., p. 284.

8   Lapause, "Relation des affaires du Canada depuis le 1er X^bre 1759 au. . ." (21 May 1760), *RAPQ*, 1933–1934, p. 144; LAC, MG18-K8, Fonds Chevalier de Lévis, vol. 12, Journal des campagnes de Lévis au Canada, 1756–1760, f. 206, reel C-365; Anne-Joseph-Hippolyte de Maurès de Malartic, *Journal des campagnes au Canada de 1755 à 1760* (Paris, 1890), p. 307; Franklin B. Hough, *History of St. Lawrence and Franklin Counties, New York, from the Earliest Period to the Present Time* (Albany, 1853); reprinted (Baltimore, 1970), p. 183.

CHAPTER 8

1   Vaudreuil to the minister, 15 April 1760, LAC, MG1, AC, F3, Collection Moreau de Saint-Méry, vol. 16, f. 16v, reel F-392.

2   Ibid.

3   Nicolas Sarrebource de Pontleroy, "Mémoire et observations sur le projet d'attaquer les postes ennemis en avant de Québec, et sur celui de surprendre la place ou de l'enlever de vive force," 18 January 1760, LAC, MG18-K8, vol. 13, Guerre du Canada—Relations et Journaux de différentes expeditions en 1756–1757–1758–1759–1760, f. 236, reel C-929.

4   Vaudreuil to the minister, 15 April 1760, LAC, MG1, AC, F3, vol. 16, f. 16, reel F-392.

5   François-Gaston de Lévis, "Instructions concernant le dispositions et ordre de bataille qui doivent suivre toutes les troupes," LAC, MG18-K8, vol. 12, f. 195, reel C-365.

6   MacLeod, *Northern Armageddon*, pp. 206–215.

7   Lévis, "Instructions concernant l'ordre dans lequel les milices attachées à chaque bataillon seront formées pour camper et servir pendant la campagne," LAC, MG18-K8, vol. 12, f. 200, reel C-365.

8   Joseph Fournerie de Vézon, "Évènements de la guerre au Canada depuis le 13 7bre 1759 jusqu'au 14 juillet 1760," *RAPQ*, 1938–1939, p. 5.

9   Vaudreuil, order appointing Doucet captain of militia, 8 juillet 1760; Pierre Doucet, "Acadien réfugie au Canada, nommé capitaine de milices d'une compagnie d'Acadiens, à Montréal, 1760," AC, E, Dossiers personnels, vol. 137, reel F-826.

10 Lévis, "Journal," LAC, MG18-K8, vol. 12, f. 206, reel C-365.

11 Vaudreuil to the minister, 23 April 1760, LAC, MG1, AC, F3, vol. 16, f. 26, reel F-392.

12 Lévis, "Journal," LAC, MG18-K8, vol. 12, f. 190, reel C-365.

13 Cadet to Bigot, 6 January 1760, in Barbier, "La Baronie de la Touche-D'Avrigny et le Duché de Chatellerault sous François 1er," *Mémoires de la société des antiquaires de l'ouest*, vol. IX, second series (1880), p. 374; Bigot to Cadet, 7 January 1760; ibid., p. 375.

14 Vaudreuil to the minister, 28 June 1760, LAC, MG1, AC, C11A, vol. 105, ff. 117–117v, reel F-105.

15 Three hundred quarts. A French quart was equivalent to about 180 litres. To give a better idea of the volume of brandy this involved, quarts have been converted into wine barrels holding 226 litres. So three hundred quarts are roughly equivalent to 289 barrels. Marcel Trudel, *Initiation à la Nouvelle-France* (Montreal, 1968), p. 238; Lester A. Ross, "Système de capacité pour les liquides de Bordeaux," in *Archaeological metrology: English, French, American, and Canadian systems of weights and measures for North American historical archaeology* (Ottawa, 1983), p. 72.

16 Mémoire of B. Martin, 24 March 1760, LAC, MG1, AC, C11A, vol. 105, ff. 121–121v, reel F-105.

17 Vaudreuil to Dumas, 7 March 1760, LAC, MG18-K15, Fonds Jean-Daniel Dumas, Lettres de Vaudreuil, de Lévis, et de Dumas, f. 4.

18 Vézon, "Évènements de la guerre au Canada," *RAPQ*, 1938–1939, p. 5.

CHAPTER 9

1 Vaudreuil to Dumas, 1 June 1760, LAC, MG18-K15, Lettres de Vaudreuil, de Lévis, et de Dumas, f. 24.

2 Marie-Joseph Legardeur de Repentigny, Soeur Marie de la Visitation, *Relation de ce qui s'est passé au Siège de Québec, et de la prise du Canada; par une Religieuse de l'Hôpital Général de Québec: adressé à une Communauté de son Ordre en France* (Quebec, 1855), p. 14.

3 Murray to Samuel Martin, Secretary to the Right Honourable the Lords Commissioners of the Treasury, 28 August 1761, LAC, MG23-GII1, James Murray Collection, Series 1 (3), "Letters from and to General Murray, 1759–1789," f. 106, reel C-2225.

4 Murray, "Responses to complaints from British merchants in Canada," 1767, LAC, MG23-GII1, "Correspondence, n.d. 1765–1766," Letter Bundles #7–8, ff. 18–19, reel A-1992.

5 Ibid., ff. 19–20, reel A-1992.

6 José Igartua, "Barthélemy Martin," *DCB, vol. III*, p. 435; Alice Jean E. Lunn, *Développement économique de la nouvelle France, 1713–1760* (Montreal, 1986), p. 149.

7 Bernier to Bougainville, 30 October 1759, MG18-K8, vol. 9, "Lettres adressées à Lévis, 1756–1760," no. 14, ff. 1–2, reel C-364.

8 Murray, "Responses to Complaints from British Merchants in Canada," 1767, LAC, MG23-GII1, James Murray Collection, "Correspondence, n.d. 1765–1766," Letter Bundles #7–8, f. 19, reel A-1992; Thierry Claeys, *Les institutions financières en France au XVIIIe siècle*, vol. I (Paris, 2011), p. 808; Thierry Claeys, *Dictionnaire biographique des financières en France au XVIIIe siècle*, Troisième edition complete, tome 2, L–Z (Paris, 2011), pp. 2320–2323.

9 Murray, "Responses to Complaints," 1767, LAC, MG23-GII1, James Murray Collection, "Correspondence, n.d. 1765–1766," Letter Bundles #7–8, f. 19, reel A-1992.

10 Ibid., f. 20, reel A-1992.

11 "Mémoire sur l'état actuel de la commission etabli pour la liquidation des dettes du Canada," 1762, AC, C11A, vol. 105, ff. 387, 389; Murray, "Responses to Complaints," 1767, LAC, MG23-GII1, James Murray Collection, "Correspondence, n.d. 1765–1766," Letter Bundles #7–8, f. 20, reel A-1992.

12 Murray to Cramahé, 28 October 1765, LAC, MG23-GII1, vol. 1 (2), "Letter Book of General James Murray, 1763–1765," f. 270, reel C-2225; Igartua, "Barthélemy Martin," *DCB, vol. III*, p. 435.

13 Murray, "Journals," LAC, MG23-GII1, Series 4, vol. 1, ff. 86, 88–89, reel C-2225. On 18 April, Knox noted that "A report prevails today, that this garrison will actually, in a short time, be besieged by the whole force of Canada." Knox, *Historical Journal*, vol. II, p. 376.

14 Murray to Amherst, 30 April 1760, LAC, MG11, CO 5, vol. 58 (II), f. 33, reel B-2172.

15 Murray, "Journals," LAC, MG23-GII1, Series 4, vol. 1, ff. 88–89, reel C-2225.

16 Ibid.; Murray to Pitt, 25 May 1760, LAC, MG11, CO 5, vol. 64, ff. 19v–20, reel B-2175.

17 Knox, *Historical Journal*, vol. II, p. 284.

18 Murray to Amherst, 30 April 1760, LAC, MG11, CO 5, vol. 64, f. 15, reel B-2175.

19 Murray to Amherst, 25 January 1760, LAC, MG11, CO 5, vol. 57, Part III, ff. 75v–76, reel B-2171.

20 Murray to Pitt, 25 May 1760, LAC, MG11, CO 5, vol. 64, f. 20, reel B-2175.

21 Murray, "Journals," LAC, Murray Papers, Series 4, vol. 1, ff. 90–91, reel C-2225.

22 *Despatches of Rear-Admiral Philip Durell, 1758–1759, and Rear-Admiral Lord Colville*, ed. C.H. Little (Halifax, 1958), p. 28.

23 Amherst to Colvill, 4 March 1760, LAC, MG11, CO 5, vol. 57, Part III, f. 50, reel B-2171.

24 Letter of Colvill, 24 May 1760, *Despatches of Rear-Admiral Philip Durell, 1758–1759, and Rear-Admiral Lord Colville*, ed. C.H. Little, p. 15.

CHAPTER 10

1 Malartic, *Journal des campagnes au Canada*, p. 312.

2 Vaudreuil to Savard and Tramblé, 16 April 1760, LAC, MG18-K8, vol. 13, Guerre du Canada— Relations et Journaux de différentes expeditions en 1756–1757–1758–1759–1760, ff. 152–152v, reel C-929; Vaudreuil, "À MM. les commandants des vaisseaux de guerre ou marchands expédiés pour le Canada," ibid., 1 April 1760, ibid., ff. 160–160v; ibid., Vaudreuil, "Ordonnance du gouverneur général," 16 April 1760, ibid., ff. 168–169.

3 Lapause, "Mémoire et observations sur mon voyage en Canada," *RAPQ*, 1931–1932, p. 108.

4 Malartic, *Journal des campagnes au Canada*, p. 313.

5 Lapause, "Mémoire et observations," *RAPQ*, 1931–1932, p. 109.

6 Étienne Taillemite, "Jean Vauquelin," *DCB, vol. IV*, pp. 751–752.

7 Lévis, "Journal," LAC, MG18-K8, vol. 12, *Journal des campagnes de Lévis au Canada, 1756–1760*, f. 207, reel C-365.

8 "Journal de la campagne du S. Giraudais sur les N^re le Machault," LAC, MG2, Fonds de la Marine, Série B4, Campagnes, vol. 98, f. 6, reel F-1308; Proulx, "Le dernier effort de la France au Canada," *RHAF* (December 1982), pp. 413–426; Judith Beattie, Bernard Pothier, *The Battle of the Restigouche, 22 June–8 July 1760* (Ottawa, 1977), pp. 12–14; Gustave Lanctôt, "Le dernier effort de la France au Canada," *Mémoires*, SRC, Section I, 1918, pp. 41–42; La fédération québécoise des sociétés de généalogie, "Chendard/La Giraudais, François-Pierre," Fichier Origine, no. 280119. http://www.fichierorigine.com/detail.php?numero=280119.

CHAPTER 11

1 Malartic, *Journal des campagnes au Canada*, p. 314.

2 Lévis, "Relation de ce qui s'est passé en Canada depuis le 1er X^bre [1759] jusqu'au 1er juin 1760," LAC, MG18-K9 vol. 5, Fonds François-Charles de Bourlamaque, f. 330, reel C-363.

3 James Murray, "Ordinance," LAC, MG11, CO 5, vol. 64, f. 86, reel B-2175.

4 Knox, *Historical Journal*, vol. II, pp. 287–288.

5 Murray to Samuel Martin, Secretary to the Right Honourable the Lords Commissioners of the Treasury, 28 August 1761, LAC, MG23-GII1, James Murray Collection, "Letters from and to

General Murray, 1759–1789," vol. 1 (3), f. 106, reel C-2225; "Jean-Félix Récher," *Bulletin des recherches historiques*, vol. 9, no. 5, ed. Henri Têtu (May 1903), pp. 144–145.

6   Murray, "Journals," LAC, MG23-GII1, Series 4, vol. 1, f. 91, reel C-2225.

7   Malartic, *Journal des campagnes au Canada*, p. 314.

8   Lévis, "Relation de ce qui s'est passé en Canada depuis le 1er Xbre [1759] jusqu'au 1er juin 1760," LAC, MG18-K9, vol. 5, f. 331, reel C-363.

9   Ibid.

10   Lévis, "Journal," LAC, MG18-K8, vol. 12, *Journal des campagnes de Lévis au Canada*, f. 209, reel C-365.

11   Ibid., ff. 209–210, reel C-365.

12   Lapause, "Mémoire et observations," *RAPQ*, 1931–1932, p. 109.

13   Marie de la Visitation, *Relation de ce qui s'est passé au Siège de Québec*, p. 18.

14   Lapause, "Mémoire et observations," *RAPQ*, 1931–1932, p. 109.

15   Lapause, "Relation des affaires du Canada," *RAPQ*, 1933–1934, p. 142.

16   Knox, *Historical Journal*, vol. II, pp. 289–290.

17   Ibid.

18   Marie de la Visitation, *Relation de ce qui s'est passé au Siège de Québec*, p. 17.

19   Ensign John Désbruyères, 35th Regiment, to Townshend, 19 May 1760, LAC, MG18-M Northcliffe Collection, Series 2, George Townshend Papers, vol. XII, "Miscellaneous Documents Relating to the Campaign against Quebec in 1759 and the Battle of Sillery on 28 April 1760," f. 341, reel C-360.

CHAPTER 12

1   Murray, "Journals," LAC, MG23-GII1, Series 4, vol. 1, ff. 93–94, reel C-2225; Malcolm Fraser, *Extract from a Manuscript Journal, Relating to the Siege of Quebec in 1759, Kept by Colonel Malcolm Fraser, then Lieutenant of the 78th (Fraser's Highlanders) and Serving in That Campaign* (Quebec, 1866), p. 30.

2   Henry Hamilton, "Reminiscences," 1792, LAC, MG23-GII11, f. 85. "From the state of the roads, the French must have suffered much on their march & no doubt are entitled to great praise."

3   Knox, *Historical Journal*, vol. II, p. 291.

4   Murray, "Journals," LAC, Murray Papers, Series 4, vol. 1, ff. 93–94, reel C-2225.

5   Knox, *Historical Journal*, vol. II, p. 291.

6   Ibid., pp. 291–292; Murray, "Journals," LAC, MG23-GII1, Series 4, vol. 1, ff. 93–94, reel C-2225.

7   Lévis, "Relation de ce qui s'est passé en Canada depuis le 1er Xbre [1759] jusqu'au 1er juin 1760," LAC, MG18-K9, vol. 5, f. 332, reel C-363.

8   Malartic, *Journal des campagnes au Canada*, p. 315. See also Lévis, "Relation de ce qui s'est passé en Canada depuis le 1er Xbre [1759] jusqu'au 1er juin 1760," LAC, MG18-K9, vol. 5, f. 333, reel C-363.

9   Malartic, *Journal des campagnes au Canada*, p. 315.

10   Lévis, "Relation de ce qui s'est passé en Canada depuis le 1er Xbre [1759] jusqu'au 1er juin 1760," LAC, MG18-K9, vol. 5, f. 334, reel C-363.

CHAPTER 13

1   Têtu, ed. "Jean-Félix Récher," *Bulletin des recherches historiques*, vol. 9, no. 5 (May 1903), p. 143.

2   Lévis, "Journal," LAC, MG18-K8, vol. 12, ff. 212–212v, reel C-365; Lévis, "Relation de ce qui s'est passé en Canada depuis le 1ᵉʳ Xᵇʳᵉ [1759] jusqu'au 1ᵉʳ juin 1760," LAC, MG18-K9, vol. 5, ff. 334–335, reel C-363.

3   Joseph Bouchette, *Description topographique de la province du Bas Canada: Avec des remarques sur le Haut Canada et sur les relations des deux provinces avec les États-Unis de l'Amérique* (London, 1815), pp. 482–483.

4   Pehr Kalm, *Peter Kalm's Travels in North America: The English Version of 1770*, vol. II, ed. Adolph B. Benson (New York, 1966), p. 458.

5   "Proceedings of a General Court Martial, Held at Quebec, the First Day of June 1761, by Virtue of a Warrant from His Excellency Governor Murray, Dated the Thirtieth May of the Same Year, Major Thomas Oswald President," National Archives [United Kingdom], War Office, WO 71, Judge Advocate Generals' Office: Courts Martial Proceedings and Board of General Officers' Minutes, vol. 68, Marching Regiments, 1760 Oct.–1761 July.

6   Henri-Raymond Casgrain, *Wolfe and Montcalm* (Toronto, 1964), p. 257.

7   Notarial contract, 25 October 1734, cited in Philippe-Baby Casgrain, "Le moulin du Dumont," *Bulletin des recherches historiques*, vol. 11, no. 3 (March 1905), p. 66.

8   Jean-Baptiste Dumont, "To be sold or rented / À vendre ou à louer," *The Quebec Gazette / Le Gazette de Québec*, no. 711 (15 April 1779), p. 2 (English), p. 3 (French).

9   Gilles Deschênes and Gérald-M. Deschênes, *Quand le vent faisait tourner les moulins: trois siècles de meunerie banale et marchande au Québec* (Québec, 2009), pp. 162–173; Jacques Mathieu, Eugen Kedl, translated by Käthe Roth, *The Plains of Abraham: The Search for the Ideal* (Sillery, 1993), p. 100; Kathy Paradis, Laval Gagnon, *La tournée des vieux moulins à vent du Québec* (Quebec, 1999), pp. 13–22, 41; LS-Philippe Picard, Paul Gaston L'Anglais, *Découvertes archéologiques dans le Parc des braves à Québec* (Quebec, 2012), pp. 28–29.

10 Lévis, "Relation de ce qui s'est passé en Canada," LAC, MG18-K9, vol. 5, f. 334, reel C-363.

11 Lapause, "Mémoire et observations sur mon voyage en Canada," *RAPQ*, 1931–1932, p. 111.

12 Malartic, *Journal des campagnes*, p. 315.

13 Lévis, "Journal," LAC, MG18-K8, vol. 12, f. 213, reel C-365.

CHAPTER 14

1   Thompson, "Anecdote No. 28," in *A Bard of Wolfe's Army*, eds. Chapman and McCulloch, pp. 203–204. Thompson added that "This I myself had occasion to witness, from my having frequent business with the wounded men."

2   Christian Rioux, "James Thompson," *DCB*, vol. *VI, 1821 to 1835* (Toronto, 1987), pp. 768–770.

3   Thompson, "Anecdote No. 23," in *A Bard of Wolfe's Army*, eds. Chapman and McCulloch, p. 194.

4   Elizabeth Arthur, "Henry Hamilton," *DCB, vol. IV*, pp. 321, 324.

5   Henry Hamilton, "Reminiscences," 1792, LAC, MG23-GIII1, Henry Hamilton Papers, f. 86.

6   Désbruyêres to Townshend, 19 May 1760, LAC, MG18-M, Series 2, f. 342, vol. XII, f. 342, reel C-360.

7   John Johnson, *Memoirs of the Siege of Quebec and Total Reduction of Canada in 1759 and 1760*, LAC, MG18-N18, Siege of Quebec 1759 Collection, ff. 119–120.

8   Thompson, "Anecdote No. 23," in *A Bard of Wolfe's Army*, eds. Chapman and McCulloch, p. 194.

9   "Monthly Return of His Majesty's Forces in the River St. Lawrence, under the Command of Brigadier Genˡ James Murray, Quebec 24th April 1760," LAC, MG11, CO 5, 64, ff. 99–101, reel B-2175; Ian McCulloch, "'From April Battles and Murray Generals, Good Lord Deliver

Me!' The Battle of Sillery, 28 April 1760," in *More Fighting for Canada: Five Battles 1760–1944*, ed. Donald E. Graves (Toronto, 2004), p. 314a.

10 Thompson, "Anecdote No. 21, Captain McDonald: His Mode of Wetting Both Eyes, and His Cruel Death," in *A Bard of Wolfe's Army*, eds. Chapman and McCulloch, p. 197.

11 Knox, *Historical Journal*, vol. II, p. 200.

12 Richard Humphreys, "Rich Humphreys, His Journal, Commencing Cork May 1757 with Its Continuation, Quebec 1766," f. 79, British Library, Blechynden Papers, vol. LXXXV, Add. mss 45662.

13 Malcolm Fraser, *Extract from a Manuscript Journal*, pp. 31–32.

14 Lévis, "Journal," LAC, MG18-K8, vol. 12, f. 209, reel C-365.

15 Malartic to Bourlamaque, 28 September 1759, LAC, MG18-K9, vol. 4, f. 213, reel 362.

16 Bourlamaque, "Avantages d'une attaque sur Québec," 10 December 1760, LAC, MG18-K9, vol. 5, f. 345, reel C-362.

17 Johnstone, *Mémoires de James Johnstone dit le chevalier de Johnstone*, ff. 373–374, LAC, MG18-J10, Mémoires de James Johnstone dit le chevalier de Johnstone.

18 Marie de la Visitation, *Relation de ce qui s'est passé au Siège de Québec*, pp. 14, 17.

19 Bourlamaque to Bougainville, 3 May 1760, à Ste. Foix, "pour vous seul," LAC, MG18-K10, Fonds Louis-Antoine de Bougainville, vol. 2, ff. 287–288.

20 Lévis, "Journal," LAC, MG18-K8, vol. 12, f. 212, reel C-365.

21 Lapause, "Mémoire et observations sur mon voyage en Canada," *RAPQ*, 1931–1932, p. 111.

22 Malcolm Fraser, *Extract from a Manuscript Journal*, p. 30.

23 Murray to Amherst, 30 April 1760, LAC, MG11, CO 5, vol. 64, f. 15, reel B-2175.

24 Ibid.

25 Désbruyêres to Townshend, 19 May 1760, MG18-M, Series 2, vol. XII, f. 342, reel C-360.

26 Ibid., f. 341, reel C-360.

27 Knox, *Historical Journal*, vol. II, p 293.

28 Murray to Amherst, 30 April 1760, LAC, MG11, CO 5, vol. 64, f.16, reel B-2175.

29 Murray to Pitt, 25 May 1760, LAC, MG11, CO 5, vol. 64, f. 20v, reel B-2175.

30 Johnson, "Memoirs of the Siege of Quebec," LAC, MG18-N18, f. 117.

CHAPTER 15

1 Johnstone, *Mémoires de James Johnstone*, LAC, MG18-J10, ff. 378–379.

2 Lapause, "Mémoire et observations sur mon voyage en Canada," *RAPQ*, 1931–1932, p. 111.

3 Philippe Aubert de Gaspé, *Mémoires* (Montreal, 1971), pp. 83–84.

4 Patrick Mackellar, "Plan of the Battle Fought on the 28th of April 1760 upon the Height of Abraham near Quebec, between the British Troops Garrison'd in That Place and the French Army That Came to Besiege It," LAC, National Map Collection, 14081.

5 Thompson, "Anecdote No. 23," in *A Bard of Wolfe's Army*, eds. Chapman and McCulloch, p. 199; Mackellar, "Plan of the Battle Fought on the 28th of April," 1760, LAC, NMC 14081.

6 Knox, *Historical Journal*, vol. II, p. 293.

CHAPTER 16

1 "Extrait d'un journal tenu à l'armée que commandoit feu M. de Montcalm..." LAC, MG1, AC, C11A, vol. 104, f. 201v, reel F-104.

2 Malartic to Bourlamaque, 28 September 1759, LAC, MG18, K9, vol. 4, p. 214.

3 Murray to Amherst, 30 April 1760, LAC, MG11, CO 5, vol. 64, f. 15, reel B-2175.

4   Malcolm Fraser, *Extract from a Manuscript Journal*, pp. 30–31.

5   Ibid., p. 31.

6   Knox, *Historical Journal*, vol. II, p. 295.

7   "Journal of the Proceedings of the 35th Regiment of Foot," entry of 28 April 1760, John Carter Brown Library, b6123117.

8   Bourlamaque to Bougainville, 3 May 1760, à Ste Foix, "pour vous seul," LAC, MG18-K10, vol. 2, ff. 288–289.

9   Malartic, *Journal des campagnes*, p. 316.

10 Ibid., p. 319.

11 Macleod, *Northern Armageddon*, pp. 189–190.

12 Christopher Duffy, *The Military Experience in the Age of Reason* (New York, 1988), pp. 217–218.

13 Ralph Willett Ayde, *The Bombardier and Pocket Gunner* (London, p. 174; William Muller, *The Elements of the Science of War; Containing the Modern, Established, and Approved Principles of the Theory and Practice of the Military Sciences* (London, 1811), p. 151.

14 David G. Chandler, *The Campaigns of Napoleon* (New York, 1966), p. 358; Ayde, *The Bombardier and Pocket Gunner*, p. 255. The exact measure is 3.498 inches.

15 David McConnell, *British Smooth-Bore Artillery: A Technological Study to Support Identification, Acquisition, Restoration, Reproduction, and Interpretation of Artillery at National Historic Parks in Canada* (Ottawa, 1988), p. 319.

16 Adrian B. Caruana, "Tin Case-Shot in the 18th Century," *Arms Collecting*, vol. 28, no. 1 (February 1990), p. 11.

17 Ayde, *The Bombardier and Pocket Gunner*, p. 256; Muller, *The Elements of the Science of War*, pp. 155–156.

18 Henry Hamilton, "Reminiscences," 1792, LAC, MG23-GII11, f. 87.

19 Bernier to Berryer, 20 June 1760, LAC, MG4, AG, A1, vol. 3574, no. 53, p. 1, reel F-725.

20 Malcolm Fraser, *Extract from a Manuscript Journal*, pp. 31–32; Knox, *Historical Journal*, vol. II, p. 293; Johnson, "Memoirs of the Siege of Quebec," LAC, MG18-N18, f. 121; Henry Hamilton, "Reminiscences," 1792, NAC, MG23-GII11, ff. 92–93.

21 Miller, *Memoirs of an Invalid*, ff. 36–38, 21v, CKS, U1350/Z9A.

22 Thompson, "Anecdote No. 23," in *A Bard of Wolfe's Army*, eds. Chapman and McCulloch, pp. 194–195.

23 Thompson, "Anecdote No. 28," in Ibid., p. 204.

24 Malcolm Fraser, *Extract from a Manuscript Journal*, p. 31.

25 MacKellar, "Plan of the Battle Fought on the 28th of April, 1760," LAC, NMC 14081; "Plan de la bataille de Sainte-Foy du 28 avril 1760," Service historique de la Défense, GR, 6M, LIC 244, no. 4, in *La guerre de Sept Ans en Nouvelle-France*, eds. Laurent Veyssière & Bertrand Fonck (Paris & Québec: Septentrion, 2011); *Plan de la ville de Québec et de la bataille qui s'est livrée dans ses environs, le 28 avril 1760, entre les François commandés par le Marquis [sic] de Lévis, et les Anglois sous les ordres du Brigadier-Général Murrays*, MG18-K8, vol. 12, map no. 8, reel C-365; "Plan of the Action on the Heights of Abraham 28th of April 1760," in "Journal of the Proceedings of the 35th Regiment of Foot," John Carter Brown Library, b6123117.

26 James Murray to Rear Admiral George Murray, 19 October 1760, William Fraser, *The Earls of Cromartie*, p. 252.

27 Johnson, "Memoirs of the Siege of Quebec," LAC, MG18-N18, f. 121; MacKellar, "Plan of the Battle Fought on the 28th of April, 1760," LAC, NMC 14081.

CHAPTER 17

1   Lévis, "Journal," LAC, MG18-K8, vol. 12, f. 214, reel C-365. Lévis did not specify which two of the Royal Roussillon, Berry, and Marine brigades were "les deux brigades plus avancées qu'il ne l'avoit ordonné."

2   *Plan de la ville de Québec et de la bataille qui s'est livrée dans ses environs, le 28 avril 1760, entre les François commandés par le Marquis [sic] de Lévis, et les Anglois sous les ordres du Brigadier-Général Murrays*, MG18-K8, vol. 12, map no. 8, reel C-365.

3   Lévis to Vaudreuil, 28 April 1760, LAC, MG18-K8, vol. 11, Lettres du Chevalier de Lévis concernant la guerre du Canada, 1756–1760, ff. 351–352, reel C-364.

4   Bourlamaque to Bougainville, 3 May 1760, à Ste Foix, "pour vous seul," LAC, MG18-K10, vol. 2, f. 289.

5   Lévis, "Relation de ce qui s'est passé en Canada," LAC, MG18-K9, vol. 5, f. 335, reel C-363.

6   Mackellar, "Plan of the Battle Fought on the 28th of April, 1760," LAC, NMC 14081.

7   Bourlamaque to Bougainville, 3 May 1760, à Ste Foix, "pour vous seul," LAC, MG18-K10, vol. 2, ff. 289–290.

8   Lévis, "Relation de ce qui s'est passé en Canada," LAC, MG18-K9, vol. 5, ff. 335–336, reel C-363.

9   Vaudreuil to Berryer, 3 May 1760, LAC, MG1, AC, C11A, vol. 105, f. 14, reel F-105.

10 Malartic, "Journal des mouvemens qu'a fait le regt de Béarn, 1758–1759," LAC, MG4, AG, A1, vol. 3540, no. 128, ff. 80–81, reel F-724.

11 Malartic, *Journal des campagnes*, p. 319n.

12 La Visitation, *Relation de ce qui s'est passé au Siège de Québec*, p. 18.

13 Vaudreuil to Berryer, 3 May 1760, LAC, MG1, AC, C11A, vol. 105, f. 14, reel F-105.

14 Malartic, *Journal des campagnes*, pp. 316–317.

15 Ibid., p. 318.

16 Johnstone, "Campagnes de 1760 jusques à la capitulation generale pour cette colonie qui fût faite à Montréal le 7 Septre. 1760," *Mémoires de James Johnstone*, LAC, MG18-J10, f. 381.

17 Malartic, *Journal des campagnes*, pp. 316–318.

18 Johnstone, "Campagnes de 1760," *Mémoires de James Johnstone*, LAC, MG18-J10, f. 381.

19 Gaspé, *Mémoires*, p. 82.

20 Malartic, *Journal des campagnes*, p. 316.

21 Murray to Amherst, 30 April 1760, LAC, MG11, CO 5, vol. 64, f. 15v, reel B-2175.

22 Henry Hamilton, "Reminiscences," LAC, MG23-GII11, ff. 89–90.

23 Murray to Amherst, 30 April 1760, LAC, MG11, CO 5, vol. 64, f. 15v, reel B-2175.

24 "État des services du Sr. D'Ailleboust de Douglas fils de Gentilhomme âgé de 24 ans enseigne en pied dans les troupes détachées de la Marine en Canada, relatif à différentes opérations militaires qui sont faits dans cette partie de l'Amérique Septentrionale pendant la présente guerre," 19 August 1761, d'Ailleboust de Douglas, Enseigne des troupes de la Marine au Canada, 1738, MG2 Fonds de la Marine, Série C7, Dossiers individuels, vol. 3, reel F-660. See also Vaudreuil, "Ordre de marcher à une compagnie de Grenadiers," 16 April 1760, ibid.

25 Malartic, *Journal des campagnes*, p. 318.

26 Johnstone, *Mémoires de James Johnstone*, LAC, MG18-J10, f. 381.

27 Lévis, "Relation de ce qui s'est passé en Canada," LAC, MG18-K9, vol. 5, f. 336, reel C-363.

CHAPTER 18

1   Johnson, "Memoirs of the Siege of Quebec," LAC, MG18-N18, f. 121.

2   Murray to Amherst, 30 April 1760, LAC, MG11, CO 5, vol. 64, f. 15v, reel B-2175.

3   Murray to Pitt, 25 May 1760, LAC, MG11, CO 5, vol. 64, f. 21v, reel B-2175.

4   "Proceedings of a General Court Martial, Held at Quebec, the First Day of June 1761," TNA, WO/71/68.

5   Testimony of Lieutenant Thomas Mills, 47th Regiment, 3 June 1761, "General Court Martial Held at Quebec, 2 June 1761," TNA, WO/71/68, f. 190.

6   Deposition of Lieutenant Eubule Ormsby, 35th Regiment, "General Court Martial Held at Quebec, 3 June 1761," ff. 193–194.

7   Testimony of Lieutenant Weld, 35th Regiment, "General Court Martial Held at Quebec, 3 June 1761," f. 183.

8   Testimony of John Maxwell, 35th Regiment, "General Court Martial Held at Quebec, 1–2 June 1761," f. 182.

9   Testimony of Private John Bennet, 35th Regiment, "General Court Martial Held at Quebec, 2 June 1761," f. 183.

10 Testimony of Private John Stone of the 35th Regiment, "General Court Martial Held at Quebec, 2 June 1761," f. 181.

11 Testimony of Private John Maxwell, 35th Regiment, "General Court Martial Held at Quebec, 2 June 1761," f. 182.

12 Testimony of Private Francis Nailor [Naylor], drummer, 35th Regiment, "General Court Martial Held at Quebec, 2 June 1761," ff. 182–183.

13 Testimony of Private John Walsh, 35th Regiment, "General Court Martial Held at Quebec, 3 June 1761," f. 192.

14 Testimony of Private Joseph Scott, 35th Regiment, "General Court Martial Held at Quebec, 3 June 1761," f. 192.

15 Testimony of Lieutenant Weld, 35th Regiment, "General Court Martial Held at Quebec, 3 June 1761," f. 183.

16 Testimony of Private John Stone of the 35th Regiment, "General Court Martial Held at Quebec, 2 June 1761," f. 181.

17 Testimony of Lieutenant Weld, 35th Regiment, "General Court Martial Held at Quebec, 3 June 1761," f. 184.

18 Testimony of Lieutenant Fraser, 48th Regiment, "General Court Martial Held at Quebec, 2 June 1761," f. 190.

19 Testimony of Lieutenant William Johnson, Royal Artillery, "General Court Martial Held at Quebec, 3 June 1761," ff. 190–191.

20 Testimony of Thomas Wilkins, 35th Regiment, "General Court Martial Held at Quebec, 3 June 1761," f. 193.

21 Testimony of Lieutenant Eubule Ormsby, 35th Regiment, "General Court Martial Held at Quebec, 3 June 1761," f. 191.

22 Statement of Major Thomas Oswald, president of the court, "General Court Martial Held at Quebec, 3 June 1761," f. 195.

23 Lévis, "Relation de ce qui s'est passé en Canada," LAC, MG18, vol. 5, ff. 336–337, reel C-363.

24 "Charles-François Mézières de l'Épervanche entré au Service cadet sous le règne de Monsieur le Marquis de Beauharnois Gouverneur Général du Canada," c. 1760; "L'Épervanche, Charles-François Mézières de, officier des troupes du Canada," LAC, MG1, AC, E, vol. 278, reel F-797.

25 Lévis, "Journal," LAC, MG18-K8, vol. 12, ff. 214–214v, reel C-365.

26 Johnson, "Memoirs of the Siege of Quebec," LAC, MG18-N18, p. 127.

27 Thompson, "Anecdote No. 23," in *A Bard of Wolfe's Army*, eds. Chapman and McCulloch, p. 199.

28 Malcolm Fraser, *Extract from a Manuscript Journal*, p. 31.

29 Mackellar, "Plan of the Battle Fought on the 28th of April, 1760," LAC, NMC 14081.

CHAPTER 19

1   Lapause, "Mémoire et observations sur mon voyage en Canada," *RAPQ*, 1931–1932, p. 111.

2   Lévis, "Relation de ce qui s'est passé en Canada," LAC, MG18-K9, vol. 5, f. 337, reel C-363.

3   Lévis to Vaudreuil, 28 April 1760, LAC, MG18-K8, vol. 11, f. 353, reel C-364.

4   Ibid.

5   Lévis, "Journal," "Instructions concernant les dispositions et ordre de bataille qui doivent suivre toutes les troupes," LAC, MG18-K8, vol. 12, f. 196, reel C-365.

6   Lapause, "Mémoire et Observations," *RAPQ*, 1931–1932, p. 112.

7   Johnstone, *Mémoires de James Johnstone*, LAC, MG18-J10, f. 381.

8   Lévis, "Journal," LAC, MG18-K8, vol. 12, f. 215n, reel C-365.

9   Jean-Nicolas Desandrouins, "Recueil et journal des choses principales qui me sont arrivés, et de celles qui m'ont le plus frappés, depuis mon départ de France," in Charles Nicolas Gabriel, *Le maréchal de camp Desandrouins, 1729–1792: Guerre du Canada 1756–1760: Guerre de l'indépendance Américaine 1780–1782* (Verdun, Quebec, 1887), p. 35.

10 Lévis, "Relation de ce qui s'est passé en Canada," LAC, MG18-K9, vol. 5, f. 337, reel C-363.

11 Knox, *Historical Journal*, vol. II, p. 294.

12 Testimony of Francis Naylor, drummer, 35th Regiment, 2 June 1761, "General Court Martial Held at Quebec, 1 June 1761," TNA, WO/71/68, ff. 182–183.

13 Johnson, "Memoirs of the Siege of Quebec," LAC, MG18-N18, p. 121.

14 Thompson, "Anecdote No. 23," in *A Bard of Wolfe's Army*, eds. Chapman and McCulloch, p. 199.

15 Johnson, "Memoirs of the Siege of Quebec," LAC, MG18-N18, p. 121.

16 Lévis, "Journal," LAC, MG18-K8, vol. 12, f. 215, reel C-365.

17 Knox, *Historical Journal*, vol. II, p. 295.

CHAPTER 20

1   Malcolm Fraser, *Extract from a Manuscript Journal*, p. 31.

2   Thompson, "Anecdote No. 24," in *A Bard of Wolfe's Army*, eds. Chapman and McCulloch, p. 200.

3   Robert Macpherson to William Macpherson, 24 August 1760, *Letters from North America, 1758–1761: The Private Correspondence of Parson Robert Macpherson 78th Regiment of Foot (Fraser's Highlanders)*, ed. Earl John Chapman (Montreal, 2013), p. 55.

4   Thompson, "Anecdote No. 24," in *A Bard of Wolfe's Army*, eds. Chapman and McCulloch, p. 200.

5   Newte, Thomas [William Thomson], *A Tour in England and Scotland, in 1785. By an English Gentleman* (London, 1788), pp. 228–229.

6   Malcolm Fraser, *Extract from a Manuscript Journal*, pp. 31–32.

7   Johnson, "Memoirs of the Siege of Quebec," LAC, MG18-N18, p. 121.

8   Miller, *Memoirs of an Invalid*, pp. 37–38, CKS, U1350/Z9A.

9   Hamilton, "Reminiscences," ff. 88, 90–91, LAC, MG23-GIII1, Henry Hamilton Papers.

10 Marie de la Visitation, *Relation de ce qui s'est passé au Siège de Québec*, p. 19.

11 Journal of the Proceedings of the 35th Regiment of Foot," entry of 28 April 1760, John Carter Brown Library, b6123117.

12 Letter of Bonneau, New York, 12 July 1760, "de Bonneau, Le Sieur, capitaine au régiment de Guyenne au Canada," LAC, MG1, AC, E, vol. 39, reel F-802.

13 Lapause, "En 1760," *RAPQ*, 1933–1934, p. 159.

14 Thompson, "Anecdote No. 24," in *A Bard of Wolfe's Army*, eds. Chapman and McCulloch, pp. 199–200.

15 Mackellar, "Plan of the Battle Fought on the 28th of April, 1760," LAC, NMC 14081.

16 Humphreys, "Rich Humphreys, His Journal," f. 80, British Library, Blechynden Papers, vol. LXXXV, Add. mss 45662.

17 Malcolm Fraser, *Extract from a Manuscript Journal*, p. 32.

18 Hamilton, "Reminiscences," LAC, MG23-GII11, f. 94.

19 Désbruyères to Townshend, 19 May 1760, LAC, MG18-M, Series 2, vol. XII, ff. 342–343, reel C-360.

20 "État général des officiers et soldats tués ou morts de leurs blessures ou blessés à la bataille du 28 avril, au siège de Québec," LAC, MG18-K8, vol. 12, f. 217, reel C-365; Murray, "A return of the number kill'd, wounded, prisoners, etc. from the 27th April to the 24th May 1760, enclosed in Murray to Pitt, 25 May 1760, LAC, MG11, CO 5, vol. 64, ff. 65v–66, reel B-2175.

21 Marie de la Visitation, *Relation de ce qui s'est passé au Siège de Québec*, pp. 19–21.

22 "Mémoire," October 1767, LAC, MG1, AC, E, vol. 9, "Arnoux, André, Chirurgien-major du Roi à Quebec, sa veuve et ses enfants. . . 1746-an XII [1803]," reel F-811.

23 Arnoux, "Canada: Hôpitaux de l'Armée en 1760, Récapitulation des dépenses"; Arnoux, "Mémoire," October 1767; Veuve Arnoux, Mémoire, undated, LAC, MG1, AC, E, vol. 9, "Arnoux, André," reel F-811.

24 Raymond Douville, "André Arnoux," *DCB*, vol. *III*, pp. 18–20.

25 Hamilton, "Reminiscences" 1792, LAC, MG23-GII11, ff. 92–93.

26 Gaspé, *Mémoires*, pp. 81–82. Gaspé speculated that La Naudière kept silent regarding this part of his military career so as not to risk accusations of being anti-British. Nonetheless, Gaspé's other relatives seemed to have no inhibitions regarding talking about the Seven Years' War.

27 Murray, "Journals," LAC, MG23-GII1, Series 4, vol. 1, f. 98, reel C-2225.

28 Thompson, "Anecdote No. 28," in *A Bard of Wolfe's Army*, eds. Chapman and McCulloch, pp. 203–209.

29 Thompson, "Anecdote No. 23," in *A Bard of Wolfe's Army*, eds. Chapman and McCulloch, p. 195.

30 Lévis, "Journal," LAC, MG18-K8, vol. 12, f. 215, reel C-365.

31 Lévis, "Relation de ce qui s'est passé en Canada," LAC, MG18-K9, vol. 5, f. 342, reel C-363.

32 Malartic to Lévis, 17 May 1760, LAC, MG18-K8, vol. 11, f. 363, reel C-364.

33 Bourlamaque to Berryer, 26 June 1760, LAC, MG4, AG, A1, vol. 3574, reel F-725, no. 81, p. 2.

34 Bigot to Bougainville, 5 May 1760, LAC, MG18-K10, vol. 2, f. 297. Bigot was quoting a previous letter from Bougainville.

35 Knox, *Historical Journal*, vol. II, pp. 323–324.

CHAPTER 21

1 Lapause, "Journal de l'entrée de la campagne 1760 [II]," *RAPQ*, 1933–1934, f. 199.

2 Bernier to the minister of war, 20 June 1760, LAC, MG4, AG, A1, vol. 3574, f. 53–2, reel F-725.

3 Jean Vauquelin, "Extrait du journal de M. Vauquelin, commandant la frégatte l'Athalante, dans le fleuve St. Laurent, en 1760," LAC, MG18-K8, vol. 13, ff. 117–117v, reel C-929.

4 Lapause, "Relation des affaires du Canada," *RAPQ*, 1933–1934, p. 144.

5 Malartic, *Journal des campagnes*, p. 321.

6   Lévis, "Journal," LAC, MG18-K8, vol. 12, f. 224, reel C-365.

7   Gaspé, *Mémoires*, pp. 114–115.

8   Lévis, "Journal," LAC, MG18-K8, vol. 12, f. 224, reel C-365.

9   Malcolm Fraser, *Extract from a Manuscript Journal*, p. 35.

10   Knox, *Historical Journal*, vol. II, pp. 298, 301.

11   Murray, "Journals," LAC, MG23-GII1, Series 4, vol. 1, f. 99, reel C-2225.

12   Malcolm Fraser, *Extract from a Manuscript Journal*, p. 35.

13   Knox, *Historical Journal*, vol. II, pp. 305–306.

14   Ibid.; Murray, "Journals," LAC, MG23-GII1, Series 4, vol. 1, f. 98, reel C-2225; Humphreys, "Rich Humphreys, his Journal," Blechynden Papers, vol. LXXXV, Add. mss 45662, British Library, f. 82.

15   Murray, "Journals," LAC, MG23-GII1, Series 4, vol. 1, f. 98, reel C-2225.

16   John Johnson, "Memoirs of the Siege of Quebec," LAC, MG18-N18, Box 3, Memoirs, f. 124.

17   Miller, *Memoirs of an Invalid*, CKS, U1350/Z9A, pp. 40–41.

18   Knox, *Historical Journal*, vol. II, p. 308.

19   Ibid.; Murray, "Journals," LAC, MG23-GII1, Series 4, vol. 1, f.100, reel C-2225.

20   Têtu, ed. "Jean-Félix Récher" *Bulletin des recherches historiques*, vol. 9, no. 5 (May 1903), pp. 144–145.

21   Vaudreuil to Berryer, 3 May 1760, LAC, MG1, AC, C11A, vol. 105, f. 151, reel F-105.

22   Lévis' circular to Quebec area militia, 28 April 1760, LAC, MG4, AG, A1, vol. 3574, "Canada, 1760," f. 31-1, reel F-725.

23   Malartic, *Journal des campagnes*, p. 322.

24   Vaudreuil to the minister, 31 May 1760, LAC, MG1, AC, F3, vol. 16, f. 52v, reel F-392.

25   "Journal of the Proceedings of the 35th Regiment of Foot," entry of 17 May 1760, John Carter Brown Library, b6123117.

26   Vaudreuil to Lévis, 30 April 1760, LAC, MG18-K8, vol. 5, "Lettres du marquis de Vaudreuil à Lévis," no. 103, reel C-364.

27   Ibid., no. 102, reel C-364.

28   Vaudreuil to the minister, 31 May 1760, LAC, MG1, AC, F3, vol. 16, f. 53v, reel F-392; Lévis, "Journal," LAC, MG18-K8, vol. 12, f. 224, reel C-365.

29   Ibid., ff. 50–51v, 55v, reel F-392.

30   Letter of Bonneau, New York, 12 July 1760, LAC, MG1, AC, E, vol. 39, "de Bonneau, Le Sieur, capitaine au régiment de Guyenne au Canada," reel F-802.

31   Malartic, *Journal des campagnes*, p. 321.

32   Master's Log, HMS *Diana*, 1760, LAC, MG12, ADM 52, vol. 829, f. 12, reel C-12888.

CHAPTER 22

1   Lévis, "Relation de ce qui s'est passé en Canada," LAC, MG18-K9, vol. 5, ff. 342–342, reel C-363.

2   Lévis to Vaudreuil, 30 April 1760, LAC, MG18-K8, vol. 11, 1756–1760, f. 353, reel C-364.

3   Bigot to Lévis, 9 May 1760, LAC, MG18-K8, vol. 8, Lettres de Bigot à Lévis, no. 70, p. 3, reel C-364.

4   Malartic, *Journal des campagnes*, p. 323.

5   Knox, *Historical Journal*, vol. II, pp. 309–310.

6   Thompson, "Anecdote No. 24," in *A Bard of Wolfe's Army*, eds. Chapman and McCulloch, p. 201.

7   Knox, *Historical Journal*, vol. II, p. 315.

8   Malachi James, "Malachi James Diary, 1759–1761," Massachusetts Historical Society, P-218, entry of 8 and 26 May 1760.

9   Ashley Bowen, "Journal," *The Journals of Ashley Bowen (1728–1813) of Marblehead*, ed. Philip Chadwick Foster Smith (Boston, 1973), p. 51.

10   Bowen, "1760, A Journal or Memorandum of a Voyage from Boston to Canada in a Transport Schooner [*Swallow*] Belonging to Joseph Weare of Old York. We sailed from Boston May the 25 in year 1760. Sailed from Louisbourg June the 10. Arrived at Quebec the 28 of June. October 16 left Quebec bound for Mount Royal. November 14 arrived Mount Royal and sailed from Mount Royal the 22 and comes at Sorel the 30 November. Left Sorel April the 19, 1761. Arrived at Quebec April the 24. May the 6 left Quebec. May the 27 arrived at Boston. FINIS 1761," *The Journals of Ashley Bowen*, ed. Smith, p. 107.

11   Lévis to Vaudreuil, 13 May 1760, LAC, MG18-K8, vol. 11, f. 357, C-364; Lévis, "Journal," LAC, MG18-K8, vol. 12, ff. 227–228, reel C-365.

12   Lapause, "Mémoire et observations sur mon voyage en Canada," *RAPQ*, 1931–1932, p. 116.

13   Johnson, "Memoirs of the Siege of Quebec," LAC, MG18-N18, Box 3, Memoirs, f. 123.

14   Murray to Barrington, 7 October 1760, LAC, MG11, CO 5, vol. 64, f. 129v, reel B-2175.

15   Knox, *Historical Journal*, vol. II, p. 313n.

16   "Journal de la campagne du S. Girandais sur le N^{re} le Machault," LAC, MG2, Série B4, vol. 98, ff. 9–9v, reel F-1308.

CHAPTER 23

1   Knox, *Historical Journal*, vol. II, p. 316. Knox misidentified their adversaries as French grenadiers.

2   Lévis, "Journal," LAC, MG18-K8, vol. 12, f. 227, reel C-365.

3   Lévis to Bigot, 15 May 1760, LAC, MG18-K8, vol. 11, ff. 361–362, reel C-364.

4   Knox, *Historical Journal*, vol. II, p. 316.

5   Désbruyères to Townshend, 19 May 1760, LAC, MG18-M, Series 2, vol. XII, ff. 344–345, reel C-360.

6   Alexander Colvill, "Journal [Memoirs] of Vice Admiral Alex Colvill, 1732–1764," LAC, MG18-L1, Alexander Colvill Collection, p. 44.

7   Murray to "The Captain of any of His Majesty's Ships, or any commander of Squadron or convoy coming up the River St. Lawrence," 9 May 1760, LAC, MG23-GII1, James Murray Collection, Series 1, General Murray's Letters 1759–1760, f. 25, reel C-2225.

8   Knox, *Historical Journal*, vol. II, p. 318.

9   Vauquelin, "Extrait du journal," LAC, MG18-K8, vol. 13, ff. 118v–119, 119v, reel C-929.

10   Knox, *Historical Journal*, vol. II, p. 324.

11   Malartic, *Journal des Campagnes*, p. 326; Lapause, "Journal de l'entrée de la campagne 1760 [II]," *RAPQ*, 1933–1934, pp. 198–206; Lévis, "Journal," LAC, MG18-K8, vol. 12, ff. 230–232, reel C-365.

12   "Journal of the Proceedings of the 35th Regiment of Foot," John Carter Brown Library, b6123117, entry of 17 May 1760.

13   Henry Hamilton, "Reminiscences," 1792, NAC, MG23-GII11, ff. 94–95. In the first weeks of June, Hamilton and his fellow captives were exchanged and sent down Lake Champlain to rejoin the British army at Fort Crown Point. From there, Hamilton passed to New York and finally rejoined his regiment in Canada in the fall.

14 François-Gabriel d'Angeac, "Relations depuis notre depart de Royant jusqu'au jour de nôtre combat avec les Anglais le huit juillet mil sept cent soixante," LAC, MG2 Fonds de la Marine, Série B4, Campagnes, vol. 98, f. 15, reel F-1308.

15 Bourdon to the minister, 11 October 1760, LAC, MG1, AC, C11A, vol. 105, f. 219, reel F-105.

16 François-Gabriel d'Angeac, "Relations depuis notre depart," LAC, MG2, Série B4, vol. 98, ff. 15v–16, reel F-1308; Beattie & Pothier, *The Battle of the Restigouche*, in *Canadian Historic Sites: Occasional Papers in History and Archaeology*, no. 16, pp. 1–33.

17 Murray, "Journals," LAC, MG23-GII1, Series 4, vol. 1, f. 119, reel C-2225.

18 Colvill to Admiralty, 24 May 1760, *Despatches of Rear-Admiral Philip Durell, 1758–1759, and Rear-Admiral Lord Colville*, ed. C.H. Little, pp. 15–16.

19 Malartic, *Journal des campagnes*, p. 327.

20 Malartic to Lévis, 26 May 1760, LAC, MG18-K8, vol. 11, f. 382, reel C-365.

CHAPTER 24

1   Knox, *Historical Journal*, vol. II, p. 325.

2   Colvill to the Admiralty, 12 September 1760, LAC, MG12, ADM 1, Admiralty & Secretariat, vol. 482, Admirals' Despatches. North America 1759–1766. Admirals Colvill and Saunders, f. 133, reel B-1355.

3   Glyndwr Williams, "Wallis, Samuel (1728–1795)," *Oxford Dictionary of National Biography*, Oxford University Press, 2004; online edn., Jan. 2008, http://www.oxforddnb.com/view /article/28578, accessed 17 March 2016.

4   Master's Log, HMS *Prince of Orange*, 1759–1760, LAC, MG12, ADM 52, Masters' Logs, vol. 966, entries of 1, 5, 9, and 11 June 1760, reel C-12889.

5   Colvill to the Admiralty, 12 September 1760, LAC, MG12, ADM 1, Admiralty & Secretariat, vol. 482, Admirals' Despatches. North America 1759–1766. Admirals Colvill and Saunders, f. 133, reel B-1355.

6   Master's Log, HMS *Prince of Orange*, LAC, MG12, ADM 52, Masters' Logs, vol. 966, entries of 18 and 23 June 1760, reel C-12889.

7   Ashley Bowen, "1760 A Journal or Memorandum of a Voyage from Boston to Canada," in *The Journals of Ashley Bowen*, ed. Smith, pp. 109–110.

8   Knox, *Historical Journal*, vol. II, p. 321.

9   Murray, "Journals," LAC, MG23-GII1, Series 4, vol. 1, ff. 119–120, reel C-2225.

10 Knox, *Historical Journal*, vol. II, p. 336.

11 Ibid., p. 339.

12 Dumas to Vaudreuil, 31 May 1760, LAC, MG18-K15, "Lettres écrites à Mr. Le Général pendant mon commandement sur la frontière à Deschambault," p. 4.

13 Ibid., 2 June 1760, p. 7.

14 Ibid., 3 June 1760, p. 10.

15 Ibid., 9 June 1760, p. 21.

16 Lévis to Berryer, 28 June 1760, LAC, MG18-K8, vol. 11, f. 404, reel C-365.

17 Lapause, "Mémoire et observations sur mon voyage en Canada," *RAPQ*, 1931–1932, p. 119.

18 "A messieurs les commandants de bataillon," 24 July 1760, LAC, MG18-K8, vol. 11, f. 415, reel C-365.

19 Hamilton, "Reminiscences," 1792, LAC, Henry Hamilton Papers, MG23-GII11, f. 94.

20 Amherst to Johnson, 2 June 1760, LAC, MG13, Great Britain, Public Record Office, War Office Papers, WO 34, Amherst Papers, vol. 38, f. 115, reel B-2656. See also Amherst to Haviland,

11 June 1760, LAC, MG13, Great Britain, Public Record Office, War Office Papers, WO 34, Amherst Papers, vol. 52, B-2666, f. 47.

21 Henry Hamilton, "Reminiscences," 1792, LAC, Henry Hamilton Papers, MG23-GII11, f. 95.

22 Haviland to Amherst, c. June 1760, LAC, MG13, WO 34, vol. 51, f. 47, reel B-2666.

23 "Minutes of a Speech Addressed to Sir John Johnson Bar^t, Superintendent General & Inspector General of Indian Affairs, by the Principal Chiefs of the Village of Lake of Two Mountains, Assembled in Council," Indian Department Office, Montreal, 8 February 1787, LAC, MG11 Great Britain, Public Record Office, Colonial Office Papers, CO 42, Canada, formerly British North America, Original Correspondence, vol. 66, Quebec, October–November 1789, f. 53, reel B-46.

24 Murray to Pitt, 13 July 1760, LAC, MG23-GII1, Series 1 (3), ff. 40–41, reel C-2225.

25 Cramahé to Murray, 30 July 1760; LAC, MG23-GII1, Series 1 (3), f. 76, reel C-2225.

26 Lévis to Berryer, 28 June 1760, LAC, MG18-K8, vol. 11, f. 404, reel C-365.

CHAPTER 25

1   Quebec City–Montreal distances are from Transports Québec, "Outil d'estimation des distances routières." http://www.quebec511.info/fr/distances/index1.asp, accessed 18 March 2016.

2   Letter of James Murray, 13 July 1760, LAC, MG11, CO 5, vol. 64, ff. 110–110v, reel B-2175; Master's Log, HMS *Diana*, 1760, LAC, MG12, ADM 52, vol. 829, f. 12, reel C-12888; Knox, *Historical Journal*, vol. II, p. 344; Colvill, "A General Account of the Disposition of His Majesty's Ships and Vessels in North America under the Command of the Right Hon'ble the Lord Colvill," 8 September 1760, LAC, MG12, ADM 1, vol. 482, ff. 117–118, reel B-1355.

3   Murray, "Journals," LAC, MG23-GII1, Series 4, vol. 1, f 123, reel C-2225.

4   Master's Log, HMS *Penzance*, 15 July 1760, LAC, MG12, ADM 52, vol. 975, f. 12, reel C-12889.

5   Murray, "Journals," LAC, MG23-GII1, Series 4, vol. 1, ff. 123–124, reel C-2225; Knox, *Historical Journal*, vol. II, pp. 348–349.

6   Murray, "Journals," LAC, MG23-GII1, Series 4, vol. 1, f. 126, reel C-2225.

7   Knox, *Historical Journal*, vol. II, p. 352.

8   Ibid., p. 353.

9   Master's Log, HMS *Penzance*, 19 July 1760, LAC, MG12, ADM 52, vol. 975, f. 12, reel C-12889.

10 Knox, *Historical Journal*, vol. II, pp. 352–353.

11 Ibid., pp. 352–354.

12 Murray, "Journals," LAC, MG23-GII1, Series 4, vol. 1, f.124, reel C-2225.

13 Master's Log, HMS *Porcupine*, LAC, MG12, ADM 52, vol. 1409, f. 12, reel C-12890.

14 Murray, "Journals," LAC, MG23-GII1, Series 4, vol. 1, f. 124, reel C-2225.

15 Knox, *Historical Journal*, vol. II, p. 355.

16 Lapause, "Mémoire et observations sur mon voyage en Canada," *RAPQ*, 1931–1932, p. 120.

17 Lévis, "Journal," LAC, MG18-K8, vol. 12, f. 239, reel C-365.

18 Master's Log, HMS *Penzance*, 27–30 July 1760, LAC, MG12, ADM 52, vol. 975, f. 12, reel C-12889.

19 Ibid., 26 July–15 September 1760; N.A.M. Rodger, *Wooden World: An Anatomy of the Georgian Navy* (Annapolis, 1986), pp. 91–92.

20 Miller, *Memoirs of an Invalid*, ff. 42–43, CKS, U1350/Z9A.

21 Knox, *Historical Journal*, vol. II, pp. 356–357.

22 Murray, "Journals," LAC, MG23-GII1, Series 4, vol. 1, f. 138, reel C-2225.

23 "Diary of a Naval Officer at the Time of the Quebec Campaign," LAC MG18-N45, reel A-652, f. 11.

24 Knox, *Historical Journal*, vol. II, pp. 359–361; HMS *Diana* drew too much water to continue upriver. Colvill, "A General Account of the Disposition of His Majesty's Ships and Vessels in North America under the Command of the Right Hon'ble the Lord Colvill," 8 September 1760, LAC, MG12, ADM 1, vol. 482, ff. 117–118, reel B-1355.

25 "Diary of a Naval Officer at the Time of the Quebec Campaign," LAC, MG18-N45, Paulus Aemilius Irving fonds, f. 14, reel A-652. Knox made a similar observation: "We may rather be said to have plowed than sailed; for our largest ships mudded the water with the soft sand or slime at bottom, which was discernible in their stern-way." Knox, *Historical Journal*, vol. II, p. 362.

26 "Indian Lorette [II]" *The Star and Commercial Advertiser/ L'Étoile et Journal du Commerce*, no. 13, 27 February 1828.

27 Murray, "Journals," LAC, MG23-GII1, Series 4, vol. 1, f. 143, reel C-2225. For use of salt and salt provisions as trade goods, see Knox, *Historical Journal*, vol. II, p. 367.

28 Murray, "Journals," LAC, MG23-GII1, Series 4, vol. 1, f. 132, reel C-2225.

29 Lévis, "Journal," LAC, MG18-K8, vol. 12, ff. 240-241, reel C-365.

30 Lévis to Belle-Isle, 7 August 1760, LAC, MG18-K8, vol. 11, f. 417, reel C-365.

CHAPTER 26

1 Knox, *Historical Journal*, vol. II, pp. 365–366.

2 Murray, "Journals," LAC, MG23-GII1, Series 4, vol. 1, ff. 145, 146, reel C-2225.

3 Knox, *Historical Journal*, vol. II, pp. 369–370.

4 Murray, "Journals," LAC, MG23-GII1, Series 4, vol. 1, f. 147, reel C-2225.

5 Knox, *Historical Journal*, vol. II, pp. 368–369.

6 Murray, "Journals," LAC, MG23-GII1, Series 4, vol. 1, f. 148, reel C-2225; "Diary of a Naval Officer," LAC MG18-N45, ff. 21–22, reel A-652; Knox, *Historical Journal*, vol. II, pp. 370–371.

7 "Diary of a Naval Officer," LAC, MG18-N45, f. 22, reel A-652.

8 Grant, "Journal," NLNZ, MS-Copy-Micro-0491, pp. 15, 25, 53–54.

9 "Return of the Men, Women & Children of the Six Nations of Indians, under the Command of Sir William Johnson, Bart. at Oswego, August 5th 1760," LAC, MG13, WO 34, vol. 39, f. 158, reel B-2657; "Embarkation Return of His Majesty's Forces under the Command of Major-General Amherst from the Camp at Fort Ontario, 9th of August 1760," LAC, MG11, CO 5, vol. 59, part 1, f. 123, reel B-2173.

10 Pierre Pouchot, *Mémoires sur la dernière guerre de l'Amérique septentrionale, entre la France et l'Angleterre. Suivis d'Observations, dont plusieurs sont relatives au théâtre actuel de la guerre, & de nouveaux détails sur les moeurs & les usages des Sauvages, avec des cartes topographiques*, vol. II (Yverdon, 1781), pp. 236–237. See also Francis Jennings, *Empire of Fortune: Crowns, Colonies & Tribes in the Seven Years' War in America* (New York, 1988), pp. 415–416, 419.

11 Ibid., p. 248. Pouchot, recording this statement in his journal, added in a footnote that "This was correct."

12 Ibid., p. 255.

13 "Journal of Jelles Fonda," *Johnson Papers*, vol. XIII, ed. Milton Hamilton, p. 169.

14 Johnson to Pitt, 24 October 1760, *Johnson Papers*, vol. III, ed., James Sullivan, p. 272.

15 Samuel Jenks, *Diary of Captain Samuel Jenks during the French and Indian War*, 1760 (Cambridge, 1890), p. 19; Ann M. Little, *Abraham in Arms: War and Gender in Colonial New England*. (Philadelphia, 2007), pp. 10–11, 167.

16 Jenks, *Diary of Captain Samuel Jenks*, pp. 4–26; Amherst to Haviland, 12 June 1760, LAC, MG13, WO 34, vol. 52, f. 53, reel B-2666; Thomas Mante, *The History of the Late War in North-America, and the Islands of the West-Indies Including the Campaigns of MDCCLXIII and MDCCLXIV against His Majesty's Indian Enemies by Thomas Mante, Assistant-Engineer during the Siege of the Havanna, and Major of a Brigade in the Campaign of 1764* (London, 1772), pp. 340–341.

17 Murray to Pitt, 24 August 1760, LAC, MG11, CO 5, vol. 64, ff. 112v–113, reel B-2175.

18 John Humphreys, "Andrew Rollo, 5th Baron Rollo," in Francess G. Halpenny, *DCB, vol. III, 1741 to 1770* (Toronto, 1974), p. 565.

19 Malachi, "Malachi James Diary," MHS, P-218, entries of 31 July, 7 August, 9–11 August 1760.

20 Ibid., entry of 14 August 1760.

21 Knox, *Historical Journal*, vol. II, p. 372.

22 Mante, *The History of the Late War in North-America*, pp. 337–339.

23 Malachi, "Malachi James Diary," MHS, P-218, entry of 16 August 1760.

24 "[Wee]kly Return of the Corps of Troops in the River of St. Lawrence in the Field under the Command of Brigadier General Murray," 24 August 1760, LAC, MG11, CO 5, vol. 64, f. 116, reel B-2175.

25 Murray, "Journals," LAC, MG23-GII1, Series 4, vol. 1, ff. 151–152, reel C-2225.

26 Malachi, "Malachi James Diary," MHS, P-218, entry of 22 August 1760. See also "Diary of a Naval Officer," LAC, MG18-N45, f. 26, reel A-652; Knox, *Historical Journal*, vol. II, pp. 375–376; Murray, "Journals," LAC, MG23-GII1, Series 4, vol. 1, ff. 152–153, reel C-2225.

27 Knox, *Historical Journal*, vol. II, p. 375.

28 Bourlamaque to Lévis, 12 August 1760, 5:00 p.m., LAC, MG18-K8, vol. 7, no. 49, p. 1, reel C-364; Lapause, "Mémoire et observations sur mon voyage en Canada," *RAPQ*, 1931–1932, p. 121; Malartic, *Journal des campagnes*, p. 339.

29 Lévis to Bourlamaque, 12 August 1760, 11:00 p.m., LAC, MG18-K8, vol. 11, f. 420, reel C-365.

30 Lévis to Bourlamaque, 13 August 1760, LAC, MG18-K8, vol. 11, 1756–1760, f. 420, reel C-365.

31 Lévis, "Journal," LAC, MG18-K8, vol. 12, f. 242n, reel C-365.

32 Bourlamaque to Lévis, 12 August 1760, LAC, MG18-K8, vol. 7, no. 49, p. 3, reel C-364.

33 Bourlamaque to Lévis, 14 August 1760, 10:00 a.m., LAC, MG18-K8, vol. 7, no. 49, pp. 2–3, reel C-364.

34 Bourlamaque to Lévis, 15 August 1760, LAC, MG18-K8, vol. 7, no. 53, p. 4, reel C-364.

35 Lévis to Belle-Isle, 7 August 1760, LAC, MG18-K8, vol. 11, 1756–1760, f. 417, reel C-365.

CHAPTER 27

1 Jenks, *Diary of Captain Samuel Jenks*, entry of 15 August 1760, p. 19.

2 Ibid., entry of 17 August 1760, pp. 19–20.

3 Ibid., entry of 21 August 1760, p. 20.

4 Ibid., entries of 28 and 29 August 1760, p. 23.

5 Roquemaure to Lévis, 21 August 1760, LAC, MG18-K8, vol. 9, no. 66, p.1, reel C-364.

6 Bourlamaque, "Suite de la campagne 1760 en Canada. Analyse de la situation militaire après la levée du siège de Québec. Compte rendue des mouvements des troupes françaises et anglaises qui se terminèrent par la capitulation du 8 september," LAC, MG18-K9, vol. 5, f. 365, reel C-363; Roquemaure to Lévis, 21 August 1760, LAC, MG18-K8, vol. 9, no. 66, p. 1, reel C-364.

7 Johnstone, *Mémoires de James Johnstone*, LAC, MG18-J10, f. 385.

8 *État des troupes que se trouvent à l'Île-aux-Noix* [undated], MG18-K8, vol. 9, no. 82, p. 1, reel C-364.

9 Bougainville to Lévis, 2 August 1760, Île-aux-Noix, MG18-K8, vol. 9, "Lettres de differens particuliers à Monsieur de Lévis," no. 78, p. 1, reel C-364.

10 Lapause, "Mémoire et observations sur mon voyage en Canada," *RAPQ*, 1931–1932, p. 121.

11 Johnstone, *Mémoires de James Johnstone*, LAC, MG18-J10, f. 387.

12 Lapause, "Mémoire et observations sur mon voyage en Canada," *RAPQ*, 1931–1932, pp. 121–122.

13 Johnstone, *Mémoires de James Johnstone*, LAC, MG18-J10, f. 387.

14 Ibid., ff. 389–391.

15 Lapause, "Mémoire et observations sur mon voyage en Canada," *RAPQ*, 1931–1932, p. 122.

16 Grant, "Journal," 1741–1763, p. 57, NLNZ, MS-Copy-Micro-0491.

17 Lévis, "Journal," LAC, MG18-K8, vol. 12, f. 243n, reel C-365.

18 Compte rendu des évènements survenus au Canada du 1 décembre au 1 juin 1760, LAC, MG18-K9, vol. 5, f. 365, reel C-362.

19 Malartic, *Journal des campagnes*, pp. 341–342, 345; Lévis, "Journal," LAC, MG18-K8, vol. 12, ff. 242–246, reel C-365; Bourlamaque, "Suite de la campagne 1760 en Canada," LAC, MG18-K9, vol. 5, ff. 368v–369, reel C-363.

20 Pouchot, *Mémoires*, vol. II, pp. 264–265, 270–271, 279–282. See also Vaudreuil to the minister, 24 June 1760 [II], LAC, MG1, AC, C11A, vol. 105, f. 69, reel F-105.

21 Johnson to Pitt, 24 October 1760, *Johnson Papers*, vol. III, ed. Sullivan, p. 273.

22 "Minutes of a Speech Addressed to Sir John Johnson Bart, Superintendent General & Inspector General of Indian Affairs, by the Principal Chiefs of the Village of Lake of Two Mountains, Assembled in Council," Indian Department Office, Montreal, 8 February 1787, LAC, MG11, CO 42, vol. 66, f. 54, reel B-46.

23 "Proceedings at a Treaty with the Six Nations, the Indians of Canada, the Several Dependant Tribes, and the Deputies from the Cherokee Nations, Held at the Upper Settlements, Near the German Flatts in July 1770, by Sir William Johnson Baronet," ed., E.B. O'Callaghan, *Documents Relative to the Colonial History of the State of New York*, vol. VIII (Albany, 1857), pp. 237–238.

24 "Return of Such Indians as Proceeded with the Army under the Command of His Excellency General Amherst, from Fort William Augustus to Montreal, 13 September, 1760," LAC, MG13, WO 34, vol. 39, f. 159v, reel B-2657.

25 Knox, *Historical Journal*, vol. II, p. 376.

26 Master's Log, HMS *Porcupine*, LAC, MG12, ADM 52, vol. 1409, f. 12, reel C-12890.

27 Ibid.; Murray, "Journals," LAC, MG23-GII1, Series 4, vol. 1, f. 161, reel C-2225; "Diary of a Naval Officer," LAC, MG18-N45, f. 30, reel A-652.

28 Master's Log, HMS *Porcupine*, LAC, MG12, ADM 52, vol. 1409, f. 12, reel C-12890.

29 Murray, "Journals," LAC, MG23-GII1, Series 4, vol. 1, f. 158, reel C-2225.

30 "Diary of a Naval Officer," LAC, MG18-N45, f. 32, reel A-652.

CHAPTER 28

1 Knox, *Historical Journal*, vol. II, p. 378.

2 Murray, "Journals," LAC, MG23-GII1, Series 4, vol. 1, f. 159, reel C-2225.

3 Ibid., ff. 159–160, reel C-2225.

4 Knox, *Historical Journal*, vol. II, p. 380, 31 August; Murray, "Journals," LAC, MG23-GII1, Series 4, vol. 1, f. 160, reel C-2225.

5 Murray, "Journals," LAC, MG23-GII1, Series 4, vol. 1, f. 160, reel C-2225.

6 Knox, *Historical Journal*, vol. II, p. 380.

7   Murray, "Journals," LAC, MG23-GIII, Series 4, vol. 1, f. 161, reel C-2225.

8   Knox, *Historical Journal*, vol. II, p. 379.

9   James, "Malachi James Diary," MHS, P-218, entry of 31 August 1760.

10 Murray, "Journals," LAC, MG23-GIII, Series 4, vol. 1, f. 161, reel C-2225.

11 Knox, *Historical Journal*, vol. II, p. 380.

12 James, "Malachi James Diary," MHS, P-218, entry of 31 August 1760.

13 Knox, *Historical Journal*, vol. II, p. 383.

14 "Mémoire du Canada," *RAPQ*, 1924–1925, p. 179.

15 Bigot to the minister, 29 August 1760, postscript of 2 September, LAC, MG1, AC, F3, vol. 16, f. 114, reel F-392.

16 Knox, *Historical Journal*, vol. II, pp. 368–369.

CHAPTER 29

1   Grant, "Journal," NLNZ, MS-Copy-Micro-0491, pp. 60–62.

2   Jenks, *Diary of Captain Samuel Jenks*, pp. 24–26.

3   Ibid., p. 28.

4   Roquemaure to Lévis, 1 September 1760, à la Prairie, LAC, MG18-K8, vol. 9, no. 70, p. 1, reel C-364.

5   Bourlamaque, "Suite de la campagne en Canada," LAC, MG18-K9, vol. 5, 129 bis, f. 368, reel C-363.

6   "Indian Lorette [II]" *The Star and Commercial Advertiser/ L'Étoile et Journal du Commerce*, no. 13, 27 February 1828.

7   "Diary of a Naval Officer," LAC, MG18-N45, f. 38, reel A-652.

8   Knox, *Historical Journal*, vol. II, pp. 382–383.

9   Murray, "Journals," LAC, MG23-GIII, Series 4, vol. 1, f. 162, reel C-2225. See also "Diary of a Naval Officer," LAC, MG18-N45, ff. 40–41, reel A-652.

10 Knox, *Historical Journal*, vol. II, p. 384.

11 "Diary of a Naval Officer," LAC, MG18-N45, ff. 44–45, reel A-652.

12 Grant, "Journal," NLNZ, MS-Copy-Micro-0491, p. 62; R. Paul Goodman, *The General Slept Here: The Amherst British Army Encampment, Île Perrot, 4 & 5 September 1760. A Footnote to the Seven Years' War in North America* (Notre-Dame-de-l'Île-Perrot, 2014), pp. 11–31.

13 Murray, "Journals," LAC, MG23-GIII, Series 4, vol. 1, f. 166, reel C-2225.

14 Knox, *Historical Journal*, vol. II, pp. 388–389.

15 Murray, "Journals," LAC, MG23-GIII, Series 4, vol. 1, ff. 168–169, reel C-2225.

16 Murray to Pitt, 7 October 1760, LAC, MG11, CO 5, vol. 64, f. 126v, reel B-2175.

17 Murray to Amherst, 19 May 1760, LAC, MG23-GIII, James Murray Collection, Series 1, General Murray's Letters 1759–1760, f. 28, reel C-2225; G.P. Browne, "James Murray," *DCB*, vol. IV, p. 569.

18 Jenks, *Diary of Captain Samuel Jenks*, 8 September 1760, pp. 28–29.

19 Lapause, "Mémoire et observations sur mon voyage en Canada," *RAPQ*, 1931–1932, p. 123.

20 Lévis, "Journal," LAC, MG18-K8, vol. 12, f. 247, reel C-365. See also Vaudreuil memoir, 6 September 1760, LAC, MG1, AC, F3, vol. 16, ff. 127–128, reel F-392.

21 "Mémoire à M. le Marquis de Vaudreuil," 8 September 1760, in Lévis, "Journal," LAC, MG18-K8, vol. 12, f. 252, reel C-365.

22 "Réponse de M. le marquis de Vaudreuil," 8 September 1760, in Lévis, "Journal," LAC, MG18-K8, f. 253, reel C-365.

23 "Mémoire du Canada," *RAPQ*, 1924–1925, p. 195.

24 "Journal of the Conquest of Canada," eds. Robert Andrews, Earl John Chapman, Paul Goodman, *Journal of the Society for Army Historical Research*, vol. 90, no. 364 (winter 2012), p. 234.

25 Johnstone, *Mémoires de James Johnstone*, LAC, MG18-J10, ff. 307–311.

26 "Indian Conference, 16 September 1760," *Johnson Papers*, vol. XIII, ed. Hamilton, pp. 163–165; Johnson to Claus, 1 May 1761, LAC, MG19-F1, Claus Papers, vol. 14, f. 43, reel C-1481.

27 Murray to Fraser, 29 July 1760, LAC, MG23-GIII, vol. 1 (3), ff. 32–33, reel C-2225.

28 "Journal of the Proceedings of the 35th Regiment of Foot," entries of 7 and 8 September, 1760, John Carter Brown Library, b6123117; Stephen Brumwell, *Redcoats: The British Soldier and War in the Americas, 1755–1763* (Cambridge, 2002), pp. 69–84, 268–270; Ian Macpherson McCulloch, *Sons of the Mountains: The Highland Regiments in the French and Indian War, vol. II* (Toronto, 2006), pp. 81–82.

29 François-Marie Balthazara d'Albergati-Vezza, "Mémoire des services de M. Albergati," 1764, LAC, MG1, AC, E, vol. 2, "François-Marie Balthazara, Marquis d'Albergati-Vezza," reel F-810.

30 Knox, *Historical Journal*, vol. II, pp. 252, 347, 391.

31 "Journal of the Proceedings of the 35th Regiment of Foot," John Carter Brown Library, b6123117, entries of 7 and 8 September, 1760.

32 F.-X. Gatien, *Histoire de la Paroisse du Cap-Santé par L'Abbé F.-X. Gatien*, ed. Henri-Raymond Casgrain (Quebec: Imprimerie Léger Brousseau, 1884), p. 116.

33 Knox, *Historical Journal*, vol. II, p. 390.

34 "Journal of the Proceedings of the 35th Regiment of Foot," John Carter Brown Library, b6123117, entries of 7 and 8 September, 1760.

35 Certificate of Vaudreuil, 18 September 1763, LAC, MG1, AC, E, vol. 2, reel F-810.

CHAPTER 30

1 Grant, "Journal," NLNZ, MS-Copy-Micro-0491, ff. 63–65.

2 Robert Macpherson to William Macpherson, 24 December 1761, *Letters from North America, 1758–1761*, ed. Chapman, pp. 62–66.

3 Thompson, "Anecdote No. 19," in *A Bard of Wolfe's Army*, eds. Chapman and McCulloch, p. 229.

4 Eudo, Curé de Ste. Famille, Martel, prêtre curé de St. Laurent, Desgly, curé de St. Pierre, le Volles curé de St. Jean, "A son Excellence, Monsieur, Le Gouverneur de Québec, &c.," "Memorial from the Four Parishes of the Isle of Orleans," c. November 1760, LAC, MG13, WO 34, vol. 1, Letters from the Governor of Quebec to the commander-in-chief, July 1760–November 1763, f. 10v, reel B-2637.

5 Letter from the curé of Saint-François to James Murray, c. November 1760, LAC, MG13, WO 34, vol. 1, f. 12, reel B-2637.

6 Eudo, et al., "A son Excellence, Monsieur, Le Gouverneur de Québec, &c.," "Memorial from the Four Parishes of the Isle of Orleans," c. November 1760, LAC, MG13, WO 34, vol. 1, 10v, reel B-2637.

7 Letter from the curé of Saint-François to James Murray, c. November 1760, LAC, MG13, WO 34, vol. 1, f. 12, reel B-2637.

8 Murray to Amherst, 30 November 1760, LAC, MG13, WO 34, vol. 1, f. 8, reel B-2637; Murray to Amherst, 7 January 1761, LAC, MG13, WO 34, vol. 1, ff. 16v–17, reel B-2637.

9 Murray to Amherst, 30 November 1760, LAC, MG13, WO 34, vol. 1, ff. 8–8v, reel B-2637.

CHAPTER 31

1   Marie de la Visitation to the minister, 27 September 1763, in O'Reilly, *Monseigneur de Saint-Vallier et L'Hôpital Général de Québec*, pp. 374–375.

2   Paul-Joseph Le Moyne de Longueuil and François-Marie Picoté de Belestre were former French commanders at Fort Detroit. Major Guillaume Dagneau Douville de Lamothe had served in the Detroit militia during the Seven Years' War. Duruisseau's identity remains unknown. Charles-André Barthe, "Jour Naille Commansé le 29 octobre 1765 pour le voiage que je fais au Mis a Mis," published as *Incursion dans le Détroit*, eds. France Martineau, Marcel Bénéteau (Quebec, 2010), pp. 63–63n.

3   Gaspé, *Mémoires*, p. 82.

BIBLIOGRAPHY

Archival Sources: Library and Archives Canada

MG1 ARCHIVES DES COLONIES
Série B, Lettres envoyées
    vol. 112 [1760], reel F-317
Série C11A, Correspondance générale, Canada
    vol. 104 [1759], reel F-104
    vol. 105 [1760], reel F-105
Série E, Dossiers personnels
    vol. 2, "François-Marie Balthazara, Marquis d'Albergati-Vezza," reel F-810
    vol. 9, "Arnoux, André, Chirurgien-major du Roi à Quebec, sa veuve et ses enfants . . . 1746-an XII [1803]," reel F-811
    vol. 278, "L'Épervanche, Charles-François Mézières de, officier des troupes du Canada," reel F-797
    vol. 39, "de Bonneau, Le Sieur, capitaine au régiment de Guyenne au Canada," reel F-802
    vol. 137, "Doucet, Pierre," reel F-826
Série F3, Collection Moreau de Saint-Méry
    vol. 16, reel F-392

MG2 FONDS DE LA MARINE
Série B4, Campagnes
    vol. 91, reel F-1304
    vol. 98, reel F-1308
Série C7, Dossiers individuels
    vol. 3, "d'Ailleboust de Douglas, Enseigne des troupes de la Marine au Canada," reel F-660

MG4 ARCHIVES DE LA GUERRE
A1, Correspondance générale, opérations militaire
vol. 3540 [Canada, 1759], reel F-724
vol. 3574 [Canada, 1760], reel F-725

MGII GREAT BRITAIN, PUBLIC RECORD OFFICE, COLONIAL OFFICE PAPERS

CO 5 America and West Indies, Original Correspondence, Secretary of State

vol. 57, reel B-2171

vol. 58, reel B-2172

vol. 58 (II), reel B-2172

vol. 59, reel B-2173

vol. 64, reel B-2175

CO 42, Canada, formerly British North America, Original Correspondence

vol. 66, Quebec, October–November 1789, reel B-46

MGI2 GREAT BRITAIN, PUBLIC RECORD OFFICE, ADMIRALTY PAPERS

ADM 1, ADMIRALTY & SECRETARIAT

vol. 482, Admirals' Despatches, North America 1759–1766, Admirals Colvill and Saunders, reel B-1355

ADM 50, ADMIRALS' JOURNALS

vol. 3, Philip Durell, reel B-19

ADM 52, MASTERS' LOGS

vol. 829, HMS *Diana*, reel C-12888

vol. 975, HMS *Penzance*, reel C-12889

vol. 966, HMS *Prince of Orange*, reel C-12889

vol. 1409, HMS *Porcupine*, 12, reel C-12890

MGI3 GREAT BRITAIN, PUBLIC RECORD OFFICE, WAR OFFICE PAPERS

WO 34, Amherst Papers

vol. 1, reel B-2637

vol. 38, reel B-2656

vol. 39, reel B-2657

vol. 51, reel B-2666

vol. 52, reel B-2666

MGI8-JIO MÉMOIRES DE JAMES JOHNSTONE DIT LE CHEVALIER DE JOHNSTONE

James Johnstone, *Mémoires de James Johnstone dit le chevalier de Johnstone*

MGI8-K8 FONDS CHEVALIER DE LÉVIS

vol. 5, Lettres du Marquis de Vaudreuil à Lévis, 1756–1760, reels C-363, C-364

vol. 7, Lettres de M. de Bourlamaque à Monsieur de Lévis, reel C-364

vol. 8, Lettres de Bigot à Lévis, 1756–1760, reel C-364

vol. 9, Lettres adressées à Lévis, 1756–1760, reel C-364

vol. 11, Lettres du Chevalier de Lévis concernant la guerre du Canada, 1756–1760, reels C-364, C-365

vol. 12, Journal des campagnes de Lévis au Canada, 1756–1760, reel C-365

vol. 13, Guerre du Canada—Relations et Journaux de différentes expeditions en 1756–1757–1758–1759–1760, reel C-929

MGI8-K9 FONDS FRANÇOIS-CHARLES DE BOURLAMAQUE

vol. 4, Varium Letters, reel C-362

vol. 5, "Canada—Première Partie," reel C-363

MG18-L1 ALEXANDER COLVILL COLLECTION
"Journal [Memoirs] of Vice Admiral Alex Colvill, 1732–1764"

LAC, MG18-K10 FONDS LOUIS-ANTOINE DE BOUGAINVILLE
vol. 2

MG18-K15 FONDS JEAN-DANIEL DUMAS
Lettres de Vaudreuil, de Lévis, et de Dumas
No. 101, Lettres écrites à Mr. Le Général pendant mon commandement sur la frontière à
    Deschambault

MG18-M NORTHCLIFFE COLLECTION
SERIES 2, GEORGE TOWNSHEND PAPERS
    vol. XII, "Miscellaneous Documents relating to the campaign against Quebec in 1759 and the
        Battle of Sillery on 28 April 1760," reel C-360

MG18-N18 SIEGE OF QUEBEC 1759 COLLECTION
Box 3, Memoirs
John Johnson, *Memoirs of the Siege of Quebec and Total Reduction of Canada in 1759 and 1760*

MG18-N45 FONDS PAULUS AEMILIUS IRVING
Diary of a Naval Officer at the Time of the Quebec Campaign, reel A-652

MG19-F1 CLAUS FAMILY PAPERS
vol. 14, reel C-1481
vol. 23, reel C-1485

MG23-GIII JAMES MURRAY COLLECTION
Series 1 (1), General Murray's Letters 1759–1760, reel C-2225
Series 1 (3), "Letters from and to General Murray, 1759–1789," reel C-2225
Series 4 (1), Murray's Journals, reel C-2225
"Correspondence, n.d. 1765–1766," Letter Bundles #7–8, reel A-1992

MG23-GIIII HENRY HAMILTON PAPERS
Henry Hamilton, "Reminiscences," 1792

NATIONAL MAP COLLECTION
Patrick Mackellar, "Plan of the Battle Fought on the 28th of April 1760 upon the Height of Abraham
    near Quebec, between the British Troops Garrison'd in That Place and the French Army That
    Came to Besiege It," 1760, LAC, NMC 14081

ARCHIVAL SOURCES: OTHER ARCHIVES AND LIBRARIES

BRITISH LIBRARY
Richard Humphreys, "Rich Humphreys, His Journal, Commencing Cork May 1757 with Its Continu-
    ation, Quebec 1766," Blechynden Papers, vol. LXXXV, Add. mss 45662

CENTRE FOR KENTISH STUDIES

James Miller, *Memoirs of an Invalid*, CKS, U1350/Z9A

JOHN CARTER BROWN LIBRARY

"Journal of the Proceedings of the 35th Regiment of Foot," b6123117

MASSACHUSETTS HISTORICAL SOCIETY

James, Malachi, "Malachi James Diary, 1759–1761," P-218

NATIONAL ARCHIVES [UNITED KINGDOM]

War Office, WO 71, Judge Advocate Generals' Office: Courts Martial Proceedings and Board of General Officers' Minutes

vol. 68, Marching regiments, 1760 Oct.–1761 July

NATIONAL LIBRARY OF NEW ZEALAND

John Grant, "Journal," 1741–1763, Alexander Turnbull Library, MS-Copy-Micro-0491

PRINTED SOURCES

An Authentic Register of the British Successes: Being a Collection of All the Extraordinary and Some of the Ordinary Gazettes from the Taking of Louisbourg, July 26, 1758, by the Hon. Adm. Boscawen and Gen. Amherst, to the Defeat of the French Fleet under M. Conflans, Nov. 21, 1759, by Sir Edward Hawke: Also, a Particular Account of M. Thurot's Defeat by Capt. John Elliott. London: Printed for G. Kearsly, 1759.

Andrews, Robert, Earl John Chapman, and Paul Goodman, eds. "Journal of the Conquest of Canada," *Journal of the Society for Army Historical Research*, vol. 90, no. 364 (winter 2012), pp. 225–234. (Journal is from the McCord Museum, Ref. C170, M12314.)

Ayde, Ralph Willett. *The Bombardier and Pocket Gunner*, second edition. London: T. Egerton, 1802.

Barbier, Alfred. "La Baronie de la Touche-D'Avrigny et le Duché de Chatellerault sous François 1ᵉʳ," *Mémoires de la société des antiquaires de l'ouest*, vol. IX, second series (1880).

Barthe, Charles-André. "Jour Naille Commansé le 29 octobre 1765 pour le voiage que je fais au Mis a Mis." Published as *Incursion dans le Détroit*. Edited by France Martineau and Marcel Bénéteau. Quebec: Les Presses de l'Université Laval, 2010.

Bouchette, Joseph, *Description topographique de la province du Bas Canada: Avec des remarques sur le Haut Canada et sur les relations des deux provinces avec les États Unis de l'Amérique*. London: W. Faden, 1815.

Chapman, Earl John, ed., *Letters from North America, 1758–1761: The Private Correspondence of Parson Robert Macpherson 78th Regiment of Foot (Fraser's Highlanders)*. Montreal: 78th Fraser Highlanders (HQ), 2013.

Chapman, Earl John, and Ian Macpherson McCulloch, eds. *A Bard of Wolfe's Army: James Thompson, Gentleman Volunteer, 1733–1830*. Montreal: Robin Brass Studio, 2010.

Cunningham, Anne Rowe, ed. *Letters and Diary of John Rowe, Boston Merchant, 1759–1762, 1764–1779*. Boston: W.B. Clarke Company, 1903.

Dumont, Jean-Baptiste. "To be sold or rented/A vendre ou à louer," *The Quebec Gazette/Le Gazette de Québec*, no. 711 (15 April, 1779), p. 2 (English) p. 3 (French).

Eastburn, Robert. *A Faithful Narrative, of the Many Dangers and Sufferings, as Well as Wonderful Deliverances of Robert Eastburn, during His Late Captivity among the Indians: Together with Some*

Remarks upon the Country of Canada, and the Religion, and Policy of Its Inhabitants; the Whole Intermixed with Devout Reflections. Philadelphia: William Dunlap, 1758. Reprinted in Richard Vanderbeets, ed. *Held Captive by Indians: Selected Narratives, 1642–1836*. Knoxville: University of Tennessee Press, 1973, pp. 151–176.

Equiano, Olaudah. *The Interesting Narrative of the Life of Olaudah Equiano, Or Gustavus Vassa, the African*, 9th edition. London: Printed and sold by the author, 1794.

Fraser, Malcolm. *Extract from a Manuscript Journal, Relating to the Siege of Quebec in 1759, Kept by Colonel Malcolm Fraser, then Lieutenant of the 78th (Fraser's Highlanders) and Serving in That Campaign*. Quebec: Literary and Historical Society, 1866.

Fraser, William. *The Earls of Cromartie: Their Kindred, Country and Correspondence*. Edinburgh, 1876.

Gabriel, Charles Nicolas. *Le maréchal de camp Desandrouins, 1729–1792: guerre du Canada 1756–1760; guerre de l'indépendance américaine 1780–1782*. Verdun, Québec: Renvé-Lallemant, 1887.

Gatien, F.-X. *Histoire de la Paroisse du Cap-Santé par l'Abbé F.-X. Gatien*. Edited by Henri-Raymond Casgrain. Quebec: Imprimerie Léger Brousseau, 1884.

Gosselin, Amédée, ed. "Le journal de M. de Bougainville," *Rapport de l'archiviste de la province de Québec* (1923–24), pp. 202–293.

Hamilton, Wilton W. *The Papers of Sir William Johnson, vol. XIII*. Albany: University of the State of New York, 1962.

Howe, Jemima. "The Captivity and Sufferings of Mrs. Jemima Howe, Taken Prisoner by the Indians at Bridgman's Fort, in the Present Town of Vernon, Vt. Communicated to Dr. Belknap by the Rev. Bunker Gay, 1755." In Colin G. Calloway, ed. *North Country Captives: Selected Narratives of Indian Captivities from Vermont and New Hampshire*. Hanover: University Press of New England, 1992, pp. 89–99.

"Indian Lorette [II]" *The Star and Commercial Advertiser/L'Étoile et journal du commerce*, no. 13, 27 February 1828.

Jenks, Samuel, *Diary of Captain Samuel Jenks during the French and Indian War, 1760*. Cambridge: John Wilson and Son University Press, 1890.

Knox, John. *An Historical Journal of the Campaigns in North America for the Years 1757, 1758, 1759, and 1760: Containing the Most Remarkable Occurrences of That Period, Particularly the Sieges of Quebec, &c. &c., the Orders of the Admirals and General Officers; Descriptions of the Countries Where the Author Has Served, with Their Posts and Garrisons, Their Climes, Soil, Produce; and a Regular Diary of the Weather, and Also Several Manifesto's, a Mandate of the Late Bishop of Canada, the French Orders and Dispositions for the Defence of the Colony, &c. &c. &c*. London: Printed for the author and sold by W. Johnston, in Ludgate-Street; and J. Dodsley, in Pall-Mall, 1769.

Lapause de Margon, Jean-Guillaume Plantavit de. "En 1760," *Rapport de l'archiviste de la province de Québec*, 1933–34, pp. 158–160.

Lapause de Margon, Jean-Guillaume Plantavit de. "Journal de l'entrée de la campagne 1760 [I]," *Rapport de l'archiviste de la province de Québec*, 1932–33, pp. 383–391.

Lapause de Margon, Jean-Guillaume Plantavit de. "Journal de l'entrée de la campagne 1760 [II]," *Rapport de l'archiviste de la province de Québec*, 1933–34, pp. 198–206.

Lapause de Margon, Jean-Guillaume Plantavit de. "Mémoire et observations sur mon voyage en Canada," *Rapport de l'archiviste de la province de Québec*, 1931–32, pp. 3–125.

Lapause de Margon, Jean-Guillaume Plantavit de. "Relation des affaires du Canada depuis le 1er Xbre 1759 au [15 juin 1760]," *Rapport de l'archiviste de la province de Québec*, 1933–34, pp. 140–147.

Legardeur de Repentigny, Marie-Joseph, Soeur Marie de la Visitation, *Relation de ce qui s'est passé au siège de Québec, et de la prise du Canada; par une religieuse de l'Hôpital Général de Québec; adressé à une communauté de son Ordre en France*. Quebec: Bureau du Mercury, 1855.

Little, C.H., ed., *Despatches of Rear-Admiral Philip Durell, 1758–1759, and Rear-Admiral Lord Colville, 1759–1761*. Halifax: Maritime Museum of Canada, 1958.

Malartic, Anne-Joseph-Hippolyte de Maurès de. *Journal des campagnes au Canada de 1755 à 1760*. Paris: Librairie Plon, 1890.

Mante, Thomas. *The History of the Late War in North-America, and the Islands of the West-Indies Including the Campaigns of MDCCLXIII and MDCCLXIV against His Majesty's Indian Enemies by Thomas Mante, Assistant-Engineer during the Siege of the Havanna, and Major of a Brigade in the Campaign of 1764*. London: Printed for W. Strahan and T. Cadell in the Strand, 1772.

"Mémoire du Canada," *Rapport de l'archiviste de la province de Québec*, 1924–25, pp. 96–198.

Muller, William. *The Elements of the Science of War; Containing the Modern, Established, and Approved Principles of the Theory and Practice of the Military Sciences*. London: Longman, Hurst, Rees, Orme and Co., 1811.

Newte, Thomas [William Thomson]. *A Tour in England and Scotland, in 1785. By an English Gentleman*. London: *printed for G.G.J. and J. Robinson*, 1788.

O'Callaghan, E.B., ed. *The Documentary History of the State of New York. Vol. VII*. Albany: Weed, Parsons, and Company, 1857.

Pouchot, Pierre. *Mémoires sur la dernière guerre de l'Amérique septentrionale, entre la France et l'Angleterre. Suivis d'observations, dont plusieurs sont relatives au théâtre actuel de la guerre, & de nouveaux détails sur les moeurs & les usages des sauvages, avec des cartes topographiques*, 3 vols. Yverdon, 1781.

Smith, Philip Chadwick Foster, ed. *The journals of Ashley Bowen (1728–1813) of Marblehead*. Boston: Peabody Museum of Salem in cooperation with the Colonial Society of Massachusetts, 1973.

Sullivan, James, ed. *The Papers of Sir William Johnson, vol. III*. Albany: University of the State of New York, 1921.

Têtu, Henri, ed. "M. Jean-Félix Récher, curé de Québec, et son journal, 1757–1760 (suite)," *Bulletin des recherches historiques*, vol. 9, no. 5 (May 1903), pp. 129–147.

Vézon, Joseph Fournerie de. "Évènements de la guerre en Canada depuis le 13 7bre 1759 jusqu'au 14 juillet 1760," *Rapport de l'archiviste de la province de Québec*, 1938–39, pp. 1–9.

Wilson, Beckles. *The Life and Letters of James Wolfe*. London: W. Heinemann, 1909.

SECONDARY SOURCES

Arthur, Elizabeth. "Henry Hamilton," *Dictionary of Canadian Biography, vol. IV, 1771 to 1800*. Edited by Francess G. Halpenny. Toronto: University of Toronto Press, 1979, pp. 321–325.

Beattie, Judith, and Bernard Pothier. *The Battle of the Restigouche, 22 June–8 July 1760*. Ottawa: Parks Canada, 1977.

Browne, G.P. "James Murray," *Dictionary of Canadian Biography, vol. IV, 1771 to 1800*. Edited by Francess G. Halpenny. Toronto: University of Toronto Press, 1979, pp. 569–578.

Brumwell, Stephen. *Redcoats: The British Soldier and War in the Americas, 1755–1763*. Cambridge: Cambridge University Press, 2002.

Brumwell, Stephen. *White Devil: An Epic Story of Revenge from the Savage War That Inspired* The Last of the Mohicans. London: Weidenfeld & Nicolson, 2004.

Caruana, Adrian B. "Tin Case-Shot in the 18th Century," *Arms Collecting*, vol. 28, no. 1 (February 1990), pp. 11–17.

Casgrain, Henri-Raymond. *Montcalm et Lévis*. Tours, France: Mame, 1898.

Casgrain, Henri-Raymond, *Wolfe and Montcalm*. Toronto: University of Toronto Press, 1964.

Casgrain, Philippe-Baby. "Le moulin du Dumont," *Bulletin des recherches historiques*, vol. 11, no. 3

(March 1905), pp. 65–73.

Chandler, David G. *The Campaigns of Napoleon*. New York: The Macmillan Company, 1966.

Chapman, Earl John, and R. Paul Goodman. "Quebec, 1759: Reconstructing Wolfe's Main Battle Line from Contemporary Evidence," *Journal of the Society for Army Historical Research*, vol. 92, no. 369 (spring 2014), pp. 1–59.

Charters, Erica M. "Disease, Wilderness Warfare, and Imperial Relations: The Battle for Quebec, 1759–1760," *War in History*, vol. 16, no. 1 (January 2009), pp. 1–24.

Claeys, Thierry. *Dictionnaire biographique des financiers en France au XVIIIe siècle*, Troisième edition complete, tome 2, L–Z. Paris: Editions SPM, 2011.

Claeys, Thierry. *Les institutions financières en France au XVIIIe siècle, vol. I*. Paris: Centre Roland Mousnier, 2011.

Depeyre, Michel. *Tactiques et stratégies navales de la France et du Royaume-Uni de 1690 à 1815*. Paris: Institut de stratégie comparée, EPHE IV-Sorbonne: Economica; Saint-Étienne: Centre interdisciplinaire d'études et de recherches sur les structures régionales, Université Jean-Monnet, 1998.

Deschênes, Gilles, and Gérald-M. Deschênes. *Quand le vent faisait tourner les moulins: Trois siècles de meunerie banale et marchande au Québec*. Québec: Septentrion, 2009.

Douville, Raymond. "André Arnoux," *Dictionary of Canadian Biography, vol. III, 1741 to 1770*. Edited by Francess G. Halpenny. Toronto: University of Toronto Press, 1974, pp. 18–20.

Duffy, Christopher. *The Military Experience in the Age of Reason*. New York: Atheneum, 1988.

Dull, Jonathan R. *The French Navy and the Seven Years' War*. Lincoln: University of Nebraska Press, 2005.

Eccles, W.J. *The Canadian Frontier, 1534–1760*, revised edition. Albuquerque: University of New Mexico Press, 1983.

Eccles, W.J. "François (François-Gaston) de Lévis, Duc de Lévis," *Dictionary of Canadian Biography, vol. IV, 1771 to 1800*. Edited by Francess G. Halpenny. Toronto: University of Toronto Press, 1979, pp. 477–482.

Eccles, W.J. "Louis-Joseph de Montcalm, Marquis de Montcalm," *Dictionary of Canadian Biography, vol. III, 1741 to 1770*. Edited by Francess G. Halpenny. Toronto: University of Toronto Press, 1974, pp. 458–469.

Eccles, W.J. "Pierre de Rigaud de Vaudreuil de Cavagnial, Marquis de Vaudreuil," *Dictionary of Canadian Biography, vol. IV, 1771 to 1800*. Edited by Francess G. Halpenny. Toronto: University of Toronto Press, 1979, pp. 660–674.

Gaspé, Philippe Aubert de. *Mémoires*. Montreal: Fides, 1971.

Goodman, R. Paul. *The General Slept Here: The Amherst British Army Encampment, Île Perrot 4 & 5 September 1760. A Footnote to the Seven Years' War in North America*. Notre-Dame-de-l'Île-Perrot: Published for the author, 2014.

Hough, Franklin B. *A History of St. Lawrence and Franklin Counties, New York, from the Earliest Period to the Present Time*. Albany: Little & Co., 1853; reprinted Baltimore: Regional Publishing Company, 1970.

Humphreys, John. "Andrew Rollo, 5th Baron Rollo," *Dictionary of Canadian Biography, vol. III, 1741 to 1770*. Edited by Francess G. Halpenny. Toronto: University of Toronto Press, 1974, p. 565.

Jennings, Francis. *Empire of Fortune: Crowns, Colonies & Tribes in the Seven Years' War in America*. New York: W.W. Norton, 1988.

Igartua, José. "Barthélemy Martin," *Dictionary of Canadian Biography, vol. III, 1741 to 1770*. Edited by Francess G. Halpenny. Toronto: University of Toronto Press, 1974, p. 435.

Lanctôt, Gustave. "Le dernier effort de la France au Canada," *Mémoires de la société royale de Canada*, Series III, vol. 13 (1918), pp. 41–54.

Little, Ann M. *Abraham in Arms: War and Gender in Colonial New England.* Philadelphia: University of Pennsylvania Press, 2007.

MacLeod, D. Peter. *Northern Armageddon: The Battle of the Plains of Abraham.* Vancouver: Douglas & McIntyre, 2008.

MacLeod, D. Peter. *The Canadian Iroquois and the Seven Years' War.* Toronto: Dundurn Press and the Canadian War Museum, 1996.

MacLeod. D. Peter. "The Canadians Against the French: The Struggle for Control of the Expedition to Oswego in 1756," *Ontario History*, vol. LXXX, no. 2 (June 1988), pp. 143–157.

Marcus, Geoffrey. *Quiberon Bay.* Barre, Massachusetts: Barre Publishing, 1963.

Mathieu, Jacques, and Eugen Kedl. *The Plains of Abraham: The Search for the Ideal.* Translated by Käthe Roth. Sillery: Septentrion, 1993.

McConnell, David. *British Smooth-Bore Artillery: A Technological Study to Support Identification, Acquisition, Restoration, Reproduction, and Interpretation of Artillery at National Historic Parks in Canada.* Ottawa: Historic Research Division, National Historic Parks and Sites, Environment Canada–Parks, 1988.

McCulloch, Ian Macpherson. "'From April Battles and Murray Generals, Good Lord Deliver Me!' The Battle of Sillery, 28 April 1760," *More Fighting for Canada: Five Battles 1760–1944.* Edited by Donald E. Graves. Toronto: Robin Brass Studio, 2004, pp. 17–72, 313–317.

McCulloch, Ian Macpherson. *Sons of the Mountains: The Highland Regiments in the French and Indian War, vol. II.* Toronto: Robin Bass Studio, 2006.

McLynn, Frank. *1759: The Year Britain Became Master of the World.* London: Jonathan Cape, 2004.

Moing, Guy Le. *La Bataille navale des "Cardinaux" (20 Novembre 1759)*, Paris: Economica, 2003.

Paradis, Kathy, and Laval Gagnon. *La tournée des vieux moulins à vent du Québec.* Cap-Saint-Ignace, Édition La Plume d'oie, 1999.

Picard, LS-Philippe, and Gaston L'Anglais. *Découvertes archéologiques dans le Parc des braves à Québec.* Quebec: National Battlefields Commission, 2012.

Pritchard, James S. "Jacques Kanon," *Dictionary of Canadian Biography, vol. III, 1741 to 1770.* Edited by Francess G. Halpenny. Toronto: University of Toronto Press, 1974, pp. 321–322.

Proulx, Gilles. "Le dernier effort de la France au Canada: Secours ou Fraude," *Revue d'histoire de l'amérique française*, vol. 36, no. 3 (December 1982), pp. 413–426.

Rioux, Christian. "James Thompson," *Dictionary of Canadian Biography, vol. VI, 1821 to 1835.* Edited by Francess G. Halpenny. Toronto: University of Toronto Press, 1987, pp. 768–770.

Rodger, N.A.M. *The Command of the Ocean, A Naval History of Britain, 1639–1815.* New York: Penguin, 2005.

Rodger, N.A.M. *Wooden World: An Anatomy of the Georgian Navy.* Annapolis: Naval Institute Press, 1986.

Ross, Lester A. *Archaeological Metrology: English, French, American, and Canadian Systems of Weights and Measures for North American Historical Archaeology.* Ottawa: National Historic Parks and Sites Branch, Parks Canada, 1983.

Taillemite, Étienne. "Jean Vauquelin," *Dictionary of Canadian Biography, vol. IV, 1771 to 1800.* Edited by Francess G. Halpenny. Toronto: University of Toronto Press, 1979, pp. 751–752.

Tracy, Nicholas. *The Battle of Quiberon Bay 1759: Hawke and the Defeat of the French Invasion.* Barnsley: Pen & Sword, 2010.

Trudel, Marcel. *Initiation à la Nouvelle-France.* Montreal: Holt, Rinehart and Winston, 1968.

Veyssière, Laurent, and Bertrand Fonck, eds. *La guerre de Sept Ans en Nouvelle-France.* Paris & Quebec City: Presses de l'université Paris-Sorbonne and Septentrion, 2011.

ONLINE SOURCES

Bank of Canada Inflation Calculator. *http://www.bankofcanada.ca/rates/related/inflation-calculator/*. Accessed 17 March 2016.

La Fédération québécoise des sociétés de généalogie. "Chendard/La Giraudais, François-Pierre," Fichier Origine, no. 280119. http://www.fichierorigine.com/detail.php?numero=280119. Accessed 17 March 2016.

Transports Québec. "Outil d'estimation des distances routières." http://www.quebec511.info/fr /distances/index1.asp. Accessed 17 March 2016.

Williams, Glyndwr. "Wallis, Samuel (1728–1795)," *Oxford Dictionary of National Biography*, Oxford University Press, 2004; online edition, Jan 2008. http://www.oxforddnb.com/templates/article .jsp?articleid=28578&back. Accessed 17 March 2016.

ILLUSTRATION CREDITS

1   Richard Short, *A General View of Quebec from Point Lévis*, 1761, LAC C-000355
2   Anonymous, *François-Gaston, Duc de Lévis*, Stewart Museum (1984.8)
3   Anonymous, *James Murray*, c. 1770, LAC C-002834
4   H. Church, *Wolfe Monument, Québec*, LAC C-045480
5   Joseph Légaré, *La bataille de Sainte-Foy*, c. 1854, National Gallery of Canada, no. 18489
6   James Hunter, *A View of Cape Santé in the River St. Lawrence*, 1778, LAC C-01510
7   Thomas Davies, *Passage of Amherst's Army down the Rapids of the St. Lawrence toward Montreal*, 1760, LAC, C-000577
8   Thomas Patten, *An East View of Montreal, in Canada*, 1762, LAC C-002433
9   Richard Henry Sharland Bunnett, *Capitulation Cottage*, c. 1885–1889, McCord Museum, M2000.75.26
10 Francis Hayman, *The Charity of General Amherst*, 1761, CWM 19940037

INDEX